THE LANGUAGE *of* LOVE & RESPECT

CRACKING THE COMMUNICATION
CODE WITH YOUR MATE

DR. EMERSON EGGERICHS

THOMAS NELSON
Since 1798

NASHVILLE   DALLAS   MEXICO CITY   RIO DE JANEIRO

Originally published as *Cracking the Communication Code*, ISBN 978-1-59145-505-9

© 2007 Emerson Eggerichs

Published in Nashville, Tennessee, by Thomas Nelson. Thomas Nelson is a registered trademark of Thomas Nelson, Inc.

Emerson Eggerichs is represented by the literary agency of Alive Communications, Inc., 7680 Goddard Street, Suite 200, Colorado Springs, CO 80920. www.alivecom.com.

Thomas Nelson, Inc., titles may be purchased in bulk for educational, business, fund-raising, or sales promotional use. For information, please e-mail SpecialMarkets@ThomasNelson.com.

From the author: The names of most people have been changed to protect the privacy of these individuals.

Cover Design by: Tim Green / The DesignWorks Group / www.thedesignworksgroup.com
Interior Design by: PerfecType, Nashville, TN

Library of Congress Cataloging-in-Publication Data

Eggerichs, Emerson.
  The language of love & respect : cracking the communication code with your mate / Emerson Eggerichs.
    p. cm.
  Rev. ed. of: Cracking the communication code. c2007.
  Includes bibliographical references.
  ISBN 978-0-8499-4807-7 (pbk.)
  1. Marriage—Religious aspects—Christianity. 2. Communication in marriage. I. Eggerichs, Emerson. Cracking the communication code. II. Title. III. Title: Language of love and respect.
  BV835.E365 2009
  248.8'44—dc22   2009032923

Printed in the United States of America
10 11 12 13 RRD 9 8

I dedicate this book, *The Language of Love & Respect,* to my son Jonathan and daughter-in-law Sarah, and to my son David and daughter Joy. May this message not only affect you personally but may you tell others of this glorious secret hidden in plain sight for 2000 years! Thank you for believing in what mom and I are seeking to say and do.

CONTENTS

PART IV

The Energizing Cycle:
To Better Communicate, Meet Your Spouse's Needs

PART V

The Rewarded Cycle:
The Unconditional Dimension of Communication

ACKNOWLEDGMENTS

I thank those who responded to my request, "How has Love and Respect affected your communication in marriage?" The answers were real and riveting.

I thank all those at Integrity Publishers and Thomas Nelson for their vision to take this Love and Respect message to the nations.

I thank Joann Blunt, Joanne Tims and Ann Starke (my wonderful sister) for their continued support and input during the writing of this book.

I thank Fritz Ridenour, writer and editor of Christian books for over four decades, for serving this message with intensity, industry, insight and intercession.

I thank my godly, wise wife, Sarah, for her prayers, counsel, affirmation, support, patience and respect over the ten months of working night and day on this book.

I thank God the Father, God the Son, and God the Holy Spirit for revealing to the Church the simple but profound truth: husbands must love and wives must respect.

PREFACE

When I wrote the book *Love & Respect*, I was both humbled and astounded at the overwhelming response from couples all over the world. As thousands of e-mails poured in, I rejoiced in the testimonies of husbands and wives who were applying God's wisdom in Ephesians 5:33, which simply says, "Each one of you also must love his wife . . . and the wife must respect her husband" (NIV).

However, I noticed something. While many ably applied the biblical principles of *Love & Respect* to their lives, others struggled. They most often struggled in the area of communication. I heard a repeated appeal.

Because the language of respect is foreign to many women, almost daily a wife would reach out to me for a deeper understanding in how to communicate respect in meaningful ways to her husband. Though an expert at offering words of love, she found the language of respect difficult to grasp, especially when she believed her husband was undeserving of respect and clueless about love!

Because the description of a man's need for respect was so refreshing, repeatedly a husband would e-mail me expressing that he finally felt understood. What I said about respect accurately described his deep-felt need. But his enthusiasm was often short-lived when he attempted to share with his wife what words and actions felt disrespectful. Instead of appreciating his attempt to communicate from his soul, she accused him of being unloving and reacted with more disrespect! Conflict escalated!

This difficulty to communicate between men and women is what I refer to as "Blue vs. Pink." Forgive the stereotype, but it captures in a picturesque manner the wonder of male and female! Neither is wrong for their communication style, just different.

Here's the good news: God intends to use these pink and blue differences in order for us to see His purple perspective. The Bible says that God made us male and female in His image (Genesis 1:27). In other words, as a husband and wife we reflect the image of God. By way of analogy, when blending pink and blue we obtain purple, the color of royalty—the color of God! God is not pink. God is not blue. God is purple. When a wife learns to speak respectfully (blue vocabulary words) about her need for love, and a husband learns to speak lovingly (pink vocabulary words) about his need for respect, they reflect the Jesus Way of Talking (purple) and experience communication as God intended in marriage.

Now, in *The Language of Love & Respect*, I share how to practically apply these principles to communication and conflict resolution. Women, you will learn how to communicate your need for love in a way that sounds respectful to your husband, without losing your identity and influence. Learning the Language of Respect enables your husband to hear you, resulting in deeper connection. Men, you will learn to use the Language of Love in ways you haven't heard before, meeting your wife's deepest need without sacrificing your uniqueness as a man. This will enable her to hear your deepest need for respect.

My wife, Sarah, often says, "These principles take work, but they work!" In the *Language of Love & Respect* you will read practical stories from Sarah and me, as well as numerous testimonies from other couples who have learned how to make these principles work. At the end of the day, I want to do what works in marital communication, don't you? *The Language of Love & Respect* will help you communicate with mutual and godly understanding. Let's learn how to make purple!

With love and respect,

Emerson

TO GET THE MOST
FROM THIS BOOK

Whenever I share the Love and Respect message, I am concerned about how husbands and wives might best use its truths in their marriage. This is especially true when I'm applying Love and Respect principles to a topic like communication. So here are some tips.

First, read to understand how to respond to your spouse's negative behavior. Don't read to find apt descriptions of what your spouse says or does and then put your spouse on a guilt trip by saying, "See? This is you. This is what you do!" As you go through *The Language of Love & Respect,* it may be quite easy to find examples of mistakes your spouse is making, but don't use what you find to attack your spouse. Instead, use what God reveals to you to learn how to respond to your spouse with unconditional Love or Respect.

Second, read to understand your spouse. Learn why your spouse reacts to you the way he or she does. The goal is to have empathy for your spouse so you can respond in a loving or respectful manner.

Third, read to understand yourself, but be careful. Don't seek points that help you understand why you are saying and doing certain things and then use what you learn to justify your own behavior. Also, don't seek to understand yourself so you can blame your spouse by saying, "See? You make me act this way. It's really all your fault!" Your goal is to gain greater self-understanding so you can respond to your spouse more lovingly or respectfully.

Fourth, read to help your spouse understand you, but be cautious here as well. A lot of spouses want to make this goal the first one instead of the last. If you start out by wanting to be understood instead of trying to understand your spouse, you are approaching the entire topic of communication in marriage in a very self-centered way. Self-centeredness does not lead to mutual understanding. So be sure you have tried to understand your spouse as well as yourself. Tell your spouse you are trying to make changes and THEN appeal to your spouse to understand you.

When you read with these points in mind, I believe your personal desires for your marriage will be better served, God will be further honored in your life, and your spouse will be more responsive to you. This is my prayer for you! Let's get started!

Is Communication Really the Key to Marriage?

Ever since *Love & Respect* was published in the fall of 2004, we have received two kinds of responses: (1) *Love & Respect* hit a marital nerve as thousands of couples experienced significant *breakthroughs* in their marriages; (2) others still carry *burdens* as they struggle to get off what I call the Crazy Cycle and have a marriage God blesses.

The breakthrough letters are thrilling to read. Husbands tell us they have learned what can happen when they use loving words to communicate with wives, and wives tell us they have been astounded at the difference it makes when they use respectful words to communicate with their husbands. Here are just two examples from literally thousands of letters and e-mails.

A wife writes to tell us she is amazed at how the Love and Respect message has "healed" her marriage:

> When I converse with my husband, I listen to his heart and filter the words through his "can't survive and thrive without

1

RESPECT" need. No matter what he is saying, I remind myself that he is a good-willed man. . . . If necessary, I start with an apology for my lack of respect, and then we talk through the issues at hand. He does the same thing with me concerning my need to be loved and—Wow!—have we been having fun!

A husband shares that he and his wife have a new perspective on each other:

[The Love and Respect message has] opened our eyes to a new way of thinking about how we are to interact and view each other's roles as designed by God. We understand each other in a new way, and that has led to dramatically improved communi-

> *"The tongue of the wise brings healing"* *(Proverbs 12:18).*

cations! I already see a difference in myself, how I act and react. . . . This has helped me put my feelings into words that [my wife] can understand, and I am beginning to see how what I say and how I say it can feel hurtful to her.

The letters and e-mails keep pouring in. People hear about the Love and Respect Connection through our conferences, DVDs, and books. Love and Respect is being taught in classes of all kinds—in adult Sunday school, in small groups in homes, and in kitchens by wives who want to share with other wives what they have learned that has turned their marriage around.

Love and Respect Is No Magic Formula

Breakthroughs are happening, but Love and Respect is not some kind of magic formula. We get plenty of letters from couples who have read *Love & Respect,* attended a conference, or watched a DVD, and, while they get the point, they still struggle to get off their Crazy Cycle.

One wife admitted that she and her husband had attended a Love and Respect Conference and got some help, but she went on to say, "How faithfully are we implementing the principles? Well, we did at first, but how easily we can go back into old patterns . . . I know we are both growing individually. It is just not showing up too well in our marriage yet."

Another wife confesses:

I wish I could give you great news about understanding the Crazy Cycle and being able to make changes in my marriage. Unfortunately, my husband hasn't been on board even though I have tried giving him compliments and respecting him. He isn't able to receive them because I have criticized him in the past. We are now separated, although living in the same house. I continue to try and pray things will change soon.

> "It's harder to make amends with an offended friend than to capture a fortified city. Arguments separate friends like a gate locked with iron bars" (Proverbs 18:19 NLT).

One husband who attended a Love and Respect Conference with his wife tried to put what he learned into action, but because she was hurting so deeply, she did not respond to his honest attempts to be more loving. He says:

When I asked her about things she wants to change in me, she said I was putting words in her mouth. . . . She is bringing up things I have done in the past, so the wounds are probably the driving force here. If I hear you right, I will need to suffer through a time of showing love, humility, and no defensiveness, or we will probably not get out of this mess.

Communication Is the Biggest Challenge

In a survey conducted by Focus on the Family for the Love and Respect Ministries, respondents were asked, "What was (and possibly still is) the biggest problem affecting your marriage?" For men and women the biggest problem by far was lack of communication.[1] Focus on the Family's findings coincide with our own at Love and Respect Ministries. As we study letters and e-mails from thousands of spouses, the common thread that runs through almost all of them is that, in one way or another, the major challenge for the typical couple is communication.

It would be easy enough, then, to deduce that communication is the key to marriage, but I don't agree. To say that communication is the key to marriage is to assume that both spouses speak the same language.

After more than three decades of pastoring, counseling married couples, and conducting marriage conferences, I have learned that, in fact, the wife speaks a "love language" and the husband speaks a "respect language." They don't realize this, of course, but because he is speaking one kind of language (respect) and she is speaking another (love), there is little or no understanding and little or no communication.

> "If I don't understand what someone is saying, I am a stranger to that person. And that person is a stranger to me" (1 Corinthians 14:11 NIRV).

As I have shared in *Love & Respect*, my wife, Sarah, and I learned that we speak different languages through practical personal experience. While we had a good marriage, we still struggled with irritation, anger, and plenty of hurt feelings. Often we just couldn't communicate, but we didn't know why. A lot of the time it seemed that indeed we were speaking different languages, but we had no idea what to do about it. It was frustrating—and embarrassing. After all, I was a pastor and should have had the answer to something like this! Fortunately, I finally found the answer—or, more correctly, God revealed it to me—in a single passage of Scripture, Ephesians 5:33: "each one of you also must love his wife as he loves himself, and the wife must respect her husband" (NIV).

As I pondered God's clear command (not suggestion) in Ephesians 5:33, I uncovered what I came to call the "Love and Respect Connection." I am commanded to love Sarah because she needs love; in fact, she "speaks love." Love is the language she understands. But when I speak to her in unloving ways, her tendency is to react with disrespectful words. Sarah is commanded to respect me because I need respect; in fact, I "speak respect." Respect is the language I understand. But when she speaks to me in disrespectful ways, my tendency is to react with unloving words. Round and round we would go in a Crazy Cycle, each saying things that were the exact opposite of what was needed!

> *"As far as the Lord is concerned, men and women need each other"*
> *(1 Corinthians 11:11 CEV).*
> *She needs his love; he needs her respect.*

Mutual Understanding Became the Key to Our Marriage

In chapter 2, "In Marriage, the Mouth Matters," I will explain in more detail how Ephesians 5:33 gave Sarah and me what we needed to start speaking each other's language. Basically, I needed to speak more lovingly to her, and she needed to speak more respectfully to me. These changes were not easy or automatic. We took baby steps at first, but soon we were making progress, and eventually we had a major breakthrough.

As I spoke Sarah's mother tongue of love and Sarah spoke my mother tongue of respect, we became friends who shared mutual understanding. For years we had been like a Russian and an Israeli, speaking our different languages. All we did was get louder as we tried to get our respective points across! But as we began to learn each other's vocabulary—as I learned some of her love language, and she learned some of my respect language—amazing things happened. Not only did we start understanding each other (in many ways for the first time), but our communication improved dramatically. This is why I say the key to any marriage is a mutual understanding of each other's language. *It is the mutual understanding that leads to good communication.* (For more on the language barrier between husband and wife, see chapter 3, "Not Wrong, Just Different.")

Does this mean our marriage is completely free of stress, disagreement, and tension? Of course not! Sarah and I still argue over some of the same old things; we still get irritated with each other for certain habits and practices. But now we know how to communicate with each other and deal with our problems. We don't know it all, but we know a great deal more than we did before we started living with Love and Respect.

As Sarah and I have heard and seen the responses to *Love & Respect* and to our Love and Respect Conferences (which we hold twenty weeks a year), we've recognized that there is much more we can share about how husband and wife can communicate with each other and with God, who is the cen-

> *Love and Respect is the way to "use wisdom and understanding to establish your home" (Proverbs 24:3 CEV).*

terpiece of every marriage puzzle. That's why we have crafted this book—to help you apply the principles of Love and Respect so that you will learn to communicate more effectively by gaining mutual understanding. Basic communication principles from *Love & Respect* are expanded, and many new ideas and concepts are added. No matter what your issue is—criticism, constant conflict, sex, money, parenting, etc., etc.—we share how learning the vocabulary of Love and Respect can help you experience a richer communion as you begin to understand each other and communicate in the way that God intended.

A lot, of course, depends on you and how open you are to the simple idea that husbands and wives speak in two languages—hers the language of love, his the language of respect. We know Love and Respect does not click with everyone—at least right away. One wife writes to tell us her husband uses the Love and Respect DVDs for target practice; a husband e-mails us to say he thinks the Love and Respect message is great, but his wife thinks we have no clue about women and, to put it bluntly, I am a chauvinist. But extreme reactions like these only tend to prove our case: a marriage can be fertile ground for disagreement and strong feelings. We know, however, that if you are serious (desperate?) about improving your marriage, Love and Respect can help you succeed or get even better, and that's what *The Language of Love & Respect* is all about.

So, we are ready to begin, but first, a special note about chapter 1, "A Short Course on Love and Respect." In this chapter you will find a condensation of our book *Love & Respect* (Integrity, 2004). If you have read *Love & Respect,* chapter 1 can serve as a review and reminder of Love and Respect principles. Of course, if you feel you need no review, just skip right to chapter 2 to start the discussion of how to improve your mutual understanding and communication through Love and Respect. Some readers, however, may be totally unfamiliar with how Love and Respect works. For you, chapter 1 is an invaluable introduction that will acquaint you with Love and Respect terminology and concepts. This "Short Course on Love and Respect" can help bring you up to speed and make *The Language of Love & Respect* all the more helpful and beneficial.

So, choose where you want to begin: chapter 1 to either review *Love & Respect* or be introduced to the total system; chapter 2 to get started on your journey toward mutual understanding and better communication in your marriage. And may God richly bless that journey.

Emerson Eggerichs
January 2007

PART I

‒‒‒‒⟨⟩‒‒‒‒

A Book Within a Book

‒‒‒‒⟨⟩‒‒‒‒

The chapter to follow is really a book within a book—a summary of the key points I made in *Love & Respect* (Integrity, 2004). This chapter offers an overview of the Love and Respect system, which you may have learned at a Love and Respect Conference, from a Love and Respect DVD, or by reading the earlier book. If you are unfamiliar with the Love and Respect system, this overview will teach you its basic principles and show you how applying them can improve your marriage whether you are currently on the Crazy Cycle, the Energizing Cycle, or the Rewarded Cycle.

CHAPTER ONE

A Short Course on Love and Respect

The Love and Respect approach to marriage is based on the awareness that any couple is always potentially on one of three cycles: the Crazy Cycle, the Energizing Cycle, or the Rewarded Cycle. None of these cycles is a permanent, static situation. A lot of couples, however, seem to spend most of their time on the Crazy Cycle, which is summed up like this:

WITHOUT LOVE, SHE REACTS WITHOUT RESPECT.
WITHOUT RESPECT, HE REACTS WITHOUT LOVE.

Clearly, the Crazy Cycle triggers and fuels itself. When a wife feels unloved, she tends to react in ways that feel disrespectful to her husband. When a husband feels disrespected, he tends to react in ways that feel unloving to his wife. And around and around they go—on the Crazy Cycle.

Love and Respect Must Be Unconditional

Scripture offers the answer to the Crazy Cycle in Ephesians 5:33—"Each one of you also must love his wife as he loves himself, and the wife must respect her husband" (NIV). This verse is the summary statement of the greatest treatise on marriage in the New Testament: Ephesians 5:22–33. In verse 33 Paul pens God's commands (not suggestions) that husbands *must* love their wives and that wives *must* respect their husbands. What is more, the love and respect are to be *unconditional*.

When a husband chooses to come across lovingly even though he feels disrespected, he can prevent the Crazy Cycle from spinning and possibly getting out of control. When a wife chooses to come across respectfully even though she feels unloved, she can stop or slow the Crazy Cycle as well. On the other hand, life gets insane when a husband says to himself, "I'm not going to love that woman *until* she starts showing me some respect! I'll not talk to her!" Likewise, madness reigns when a wife says to herself, "I'm not going to respect that man until he *earns* my respect and starts loving me the way he should. I'll teach him!"

The secret to building a happy relationship is to recognize when you are on the Crazy Cycle—when you are not communicating, when you are in some level of conflict, be it mild or severe, or when life together just isn't going well. The Crazy Cycle can be low-key, with both of you trying to keep the lid on, or it can be intense, with angry remarks, biting sarcasm, shouting, and worse. The point is, whatever the intensity level of your Crazy Cycle, one and often both of you are doing crazy, dumb things that drive the other one nuts. Spouses may be doing these crazy things deliberately or unthinkingly, but always they are reacting to a lack of love (for her) or a lack of respect (for him).

Although the Crazy Cycle is not what God intends for any marriage, all couples get on it at times to one degree or another. In fact, in 1 Corinthians 7:28 Paul flatly states that when two people marry they "will face many troubles in this life" (NIV). Such troubles can come in many ways, but one of the most common is that the best of husbands will say or do things that feel unloving to his wife or the best of wives will say or do things that feel disrespectful to her husband. As any married couple knows, life presents all kinds of opportunities for this to happen.

Sex Tonight? Who Decides?

Earlier in 1 Corinthians 7, Paul addresses a common problem in marriage: sexual relations. He makes it clear that "the wife does not have authority over her own body, but the husband does; and likewise also the husband does not have authority over his own body, but the wife does" (v. 4).

Paul's words seem to describe a standoff. So who decides tonight whether or not there will be sexual intimacy? If he verbally pushes the issue, will she feel used and unloved? If she verbally declines, will he feel disrespected? Most couples know what this situation is like. All too often it turns into a clash. Feeling unloved, she speaks words of contempt: "It's always all about *you*. You never think of how *I* might be feeling." Smarting from what he perceives as disrespect and frigid unconcern for his needs, he speaks harshly and unlovingly: "You *always* have a headache. You care more about the kids than me. I'm just a meal ticket to you."

Obviously, inflammatory remarks like this get the Crazy Cycle shifting into high gear in a hurry. But does either spouse really intend for this to happen? Rarely. Most spouses are full of goodwill: each means the other no harm, but wants only good things to happen between them. Note that Paul says in 1 Corinthians 7:33–34 the "one who is married is concerned about. . . how he may please his wife. . . [or] how she may please her husband." In the normal flow of marriage, neither gets up in the morning thinking, "How can I displease my mate or show I am not concerned about my spouse's needs?" Nonetheless, as the day goes by, things happen. Without realizing it, he may sound harsh and unloving, and she reacts with disrespect. Or she may treat him with disrespect in one of a dozen different little ways, and he reacts by not being loving. Conflict occurs, and that is when spouses can get nasty with each other. Both spouses are goodwilled people, but it sure doesn't seem that way at the moment!

And the problem concerning "sex tonight—yes or no" still remains. How can two goodwilled people deal with this issue so that they both feel loved and respected? Eugene Peterson's paraphrase of 1 Corinthians 7:3–4 offers some excellent clues: "The marriage bed must be a place of mutuality—the husband seeking to satisfy his wife, the wife seeking to satisfy her husband. Marriage is not a place to 'stand up for your rights' " (MSG).

Peterson's phrase "place of mutuality" points to the idea of creating a win-win situation. When the Crazy Cycle is going strong, both spouses are in a win-lose frame of mind. Spouses who seek a Love and Respect kind of marriage have many tools and techniques at their disposal to slow and stop the Crazy Cycle and create a win-win. Couples practicing Love and Respect learn that, because she sees and hears in pink and he sees and hears in blue, they are markedly different. In order to understand these differences, they need to realize that they send each other messages in code and they must learn how to decode each other.

The "Issue" Is Seldom the Real Issue

Just about every couple knows what it is like to get into a conflict that escalates into a full-blown argument and they are not sure why it happened. Spouses tend to write off these kind of arguments, saying, "If only she weren't so sensitive" or "If only he weren't so touchy." But those aren't the real issues at all. For example, when he hasn't called and gets home late for dinner and she erupts in criticism and tears, saying he is an unloving human being, the real issue isn't his lateness or her bitter criticism of his integrity. The real issue is that she feels unloved, and when she angrily attacks his character, he feels disrespected. After all, she knows that he often has to work late. It's part of his job.

The Crazy Cycle happens when spouses focus on their own needs and overlook the needs of the other. That's when the issues arise. The wife needs love; she is not trying to be disrespectful. The husband needs respect; he is not trying to be unloving. And once the Love and Respect couple grasps a basic principle—that the apparent issue is not the real issue at all—they are on their way to cracking the communication code.

Stay Off Each Other's Air Hose

Another key to slowing and stopping the Crazy Cycle is to realize that the wife needs love just as she needs air to breathe. Picture, if you will, that the wife has an air hose leading to a "love tank." When her husband steps on her air hose or pinches it in some way with unloving behavior, he will see her deflate before his eyes. He is stepping on her air hose, and she is crying out, "I feel unloved by you right now. Why are you doing this to me?"

On the wife's side of the Love and Respect equation, she should picture her husband with his own air hose leading to his "respect tank." As long as her respect is flowing through his air hose, he is fine, but if she starts to pinch or cut his air hose with sharp, critical remarks, his supply of respect will leak or be cut off, and he will react negatively because his deepest need is not being met. When either spouse's air hose is cut off in some way, the other will respond in kind. Both air hoses shut down, and the battle—the Crazy Cycle—is on!

Being aware that men see and hear in blue and women see and hear in pink (*very* differently) is extremely important. Working at decoding each other's messages is essential. Being careful not to step on each other's air hose (hers leads to her love tank; his leads to his respect tank) is vital. But all this information will do a marriage little good unless both spouses commit themselves to the tasks of *unconditional* love (by the husband toward the wife) and *unconditional* respect (by the wife toward the husband).

Unconditional Really Means "Unconditional"

Wives have little trouble grasping the meaning of unconditional love. God has wired them to love, but while they tell me they truly do love their husbands, they can't respect their men because of their unloving behavior. They continue to demand that their husbands earn their respect. Love is all that matters. If their husbands would simply love them as they should, all would be well.

For many wives, the concept of *unconditional respect* seems to be an oxymoron (a term created by putting together two words that appear to be incongruous or contradictory). But when a wife insists that her husband earn her respect, she puts him in a lose-lose situation. If he must unconditionally love his wife as she demands *and* he must earn her respect as well, he is likely to just give up, shut down, and say, "I can never be good enough for you."

A major reason why wives have such a hard time with unconditional respect for their husbands is that they see and hear in pink while their husbands see and hear in blue. One wife described the problem perfectly: "We think so differently. I don't even relate to what he considers respect— or the lack of it." I struggled to help marriages for many years before I saw the answer to this problem in Ephesians 5:33. God is saying in so many words, "Yes, the two of you are very different, and I am telling you to love and respect unconditionally anyway."

Since that discovery of what was there all the time in plain sight, I have tried to convince wives that the best way to motivate their husbands to love them is to show them respect whether they deserve it or not. Women need to learn how to understand and use the word *respect* because, in truth, respect is what a man most values. By the same token, his wife's *contempt* is what a man most fears. And no husband will feel love and affection toward his wife if she seems to despise who he is as a human being.

Does unconditional respect mean a wife must respect evil behavior? Let me qualify what I mean by *unconditional respect.* Just as a husband is to come across lovingly even though his wife is not lovable, so a wife is to come across respectfully even though her husband is not respectable. This does not mean a wife must say, "I respect the way you get angry and refuse to talk to me." Such a statement is as silly as a husband saying, "I love the way you nag and criticize me." This is not about loving or respecting sinful behavior. This is about lovingly or respectfully confronting inappropriate behavior.

Unconditional respect, like unconditional love, is all about how one sounds (tone of voice and word choice) and appears (facial expressions and physical actions). A husband may not deserve respect because he has not earned respect, but a wife's disrespect for him is ineffective long-term—and not biblical. No husband responds to disrespectful attitudes any more than a wife responds to unloving attitudes. Yes, if a wife is lovable, it makes it easy for her husband to love her, but the command of God to love one's wife has nothing to do with her being lovable. And if a husband is respectable, it makes it easy for a wife to respect him, but the command of God to respect one's husband has nothing to do with him being respectable. The Love and Respect message is not about a husband earning his wife's respect by being more loving any more than it is about a wife earning her husband's love by being more respectful. Always, Love or Respect is given *unconditionally,* according to God's commands.

On the wife's side, her greatest value is love. One of her greatest fears is that, if she shows her husband respect, he will treat her like a doormat, abuse her, or worse. Feminist voices have trumpeted this idea for years, but I don't buy it. The man with basic goodwill wants to serve his wife, and he would even die for her. When his wife shows him unconditional respect, in most cases he will feel like a prince and be motivated to show her the kind of unconditional love she desires. She is not a doormat or a slave. She is a princess who is loved and, by the way, respected also. Another key passage full of Love and Respect truth is 1 Peter 3:1–7. Peter teaches wives to show "respectful behavior" (v. 2) even when their husbands are being "disobedient to the word" (v. 1), and he goes on to say that husbands are to "show her honor as a fellow heir of the grace of life" (v. 7). To honor a wife is to respect her and treat her as an equal.

To carry further the word picture of the prince and princess, I believe the biblical order sees the husband (the prince) as *first among equals.* This is a responsibility, not a right. The husband and wife are equal in God's sight, but he is called upon to be the first to provide, to protect, to even die for his wife if necessary. The husband instinctively knows this and wants to fulfill his responsibility. On the other hand, the wife (the princess) instinctively thirsts to be valued as *first in importance.* Nothing energizes her more. This is not self-centeredness; it is her God-given nature.

When the wife respects the husband as first among equals and he honors her as first in importance, their marriage is balanced, and the Crazy Cycle will not spin. Granted, achieving this balance is not easy, especially if the Crazy Cycle has been spinning for a long time. A wife can slip back into wanting him to earn her respect; a husband can slip back into getting discouraged, thinking, "What's the use?" Typically, he may go into the familiar male funk known as "stonewalling" (refusing to talk, which drives the typical woman crazy). She may try unconditional respect and then begin to feel like a hypocrite because she really doesn't *feel* respectful, or she may remember all those hurts her husband caused with his lack of love and wonder, "Can I ever forgive him?" Naturally enough, the husband will be tempted to pull away. Since she really can't sustain this respect thing, what's the use? All he hears is how he's blown it again. "How could anyone love that woman!" Such a reaction is all too common. And let it be noted that, in describing these interactions, I am not justifying either's behavior but wishing for each to discover the power of staying the course with their Love and Respect responses.

Love & Respect is full of stories of husbands and wives who struggled to tame the Crazy Cycle yet succeeded. Wives have learned how to respect even when they don't feel like it, even when feeling rejected by their husbands' refusal to talk. Husbands have learned to love even in the face of a wife's criticism and contempt. They have learned to "take" the faultfinding from their wives and rebound in order to prove their unconditional love.

In short, couples can learn that marriage is a two-become-one proposition. Hundreds—and it's going on thousands—of letters prove this to be true. The Love and Respect Connection is stopping the Crazy Cycle in marriages all over the country. If husband and wife can commit to meeting each other's primary needs—unconditional love for her and unconditional respect for him—they will take a giant step toward keeping the Crazy Cycle under control.

Remember, you can never completely get off the Crazy Cycle. She will always see and hear in pink, and he in blue, which means the smallest things can cause the Crazy Cycle to start revving its engines. Does this mean you must always live on edge—walking on eggshells to avoid trouble? Not at all. There is another cycle that will help you build a stronger, happier, more biblical marriage as you energize each other with Love and Respect.

The Energizing Cycle Keeps the Crazy Cycle in Its Cage

While there are ways to slow or stop the Crazy Cycle (remember, you never get completely off), it can always start up again and usually does, even for happy, well-adjusted couples. The way to keep the Crazy Cycle in its cage is to get on the Energizing Cycle, which is summed up like this:

HIS LOVE MOTIVATES HER RESPECT.
HER RESPECT MOTIVATES HIS LOVE.

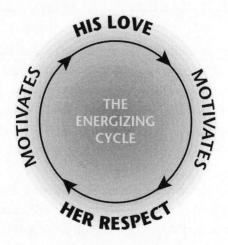

Couples are on the Energizing Cycle when they are practicing Love and Respect principles. To show their love, husbands live out the principles summed up in the acronym C-O-U-P-L-E, which provides six ways to spell love for a wife:

C — Closeness *She wants you to be close—and not just when you want sex.*

O — Openness *She wants you to open up to her, to talk and not be closed off, acting angry or disinterested.*

U — Understanding *Don't try to "fix" her; just listen—and be considerate when she's really upset.*

P — Peacemaking *There is power in saying, "Honey, I'm really sorry."*

L — Loyalty *Always assure her of your love and commitment.*

E — Esteem *Your wife wants you to honor and cherish her.*

To show their respect, wives live out the principles summed up in the acronym C-H-A-I-R-S, which offers six biblical ways to spell respect for a husband's deepest desires:

C — Conquest *Recognize and thank him for his desire to work.*

H — Hierarchy *Thank him for his motivation to protect and provide for you.*

A — Authority *Acknowledge his desire to lead—and don't subvert his leadership.*

I — Insight *Listen appreciatively to his ideas and the advice he wishes to offer.*

R — Relationship *Value his desire for you to be his friend and stand shoulder-to-shoulder with him.*

S — Sexuality *Respond to his need for you sexually; don't deprive him.*

The two acronyms listed above are not just magic words or cure-all formulas. *The Energizing Cycle will work only if you do.* And as you practice C-O-U-P-L-E or C-H-A-I-R-S, your marriage will be happier, stronger, more biblical, and more honoring to God.

C-O-U-P-L-E: A Checkup for Husbands

If a husband applies just one of the C-O-U-P-L-E concepts each day, he takes giant steps toward making his wife feel loved. To check himself on how well he is practicing C-O-U-P-L-E, the husband should ask himself the following biblically based questions on a regular (at least weekly) basis:

Closeness—Because a husband is to "cleave unto his wife" (Genesis 2:24 KJV), my face-to-face time with her causes her to feel emotionally connected and energized.

> Have I been moving toward my wife or away from her? Realizing her deep need to share with me, have I set aside time to talk to her face-to-face? Do I tell her on a regular basis that I love her, admire her, and appreciate her—or do I save those remarks for when I want sex?

Openness—Because a husband is not to be "harsh" (annoyed and resentful) toward his wife (see Colossians 3:19 NIV), I must counter any tendencies to be withdrawn or preoccupied, making her think I have no intentions of being tender and transparent with her.

Do I share my thoughts and problems with her (a big part of *Closeness*), or do I keep things to myself to prove I am strong and capable? Do I come across as irritated or angry when she tries to draw me out, or am I open and transparent when she shows concern or curiosity? Do I turn my spirit more toward TV and the newspaper than toward the heart of my wife?

Understanding—Because a husband is to live with his wife "in an understanding way" (1 Peter 3:7), I need to be attentive to her womanly concerns (even though I may not share her interests) because I want to make her feel understood and cared about.

When she shares her concerns or problems, do I tend to listen and let her talk, or do I try to "fix" her or what is wrong? Do I see my wife as made of porcelain or other fine china, or do I treat her like she is made of cast iron? Do I increasingly see that "just talking" (a big part of *Closeness* and *Openness*) is key to making her feel understood? Do I understand that talking is as important to my wife as sex is to me?

Peacemaking—Because God said, "The two shall become one flesh" (Matthew 19:5), I am always to seek ways to "be at one" with my wife, to always live in peace, which surely includes my apologies for my part in any rift or argument between us.

Do I tend to talk things through and resolve issues, or do I tend to say, "Let's just drop it and move on"? When my wife expresses hurt or anger, do I easily say, "I'm sorry. I was wrong"—or do I tend to get defensive, and express hurt and anger myself? Do I really understand how saying "I'm sorry" touches her deeply and makes her feel connected like few things do?

Loyalty—Because Scripture says, "She is your companion and your wife by covenant" (Malachi 2:14), it is a good idea to let her know repeatedly of my devotion to her and to God.

> Do I look for ways to express my loyalty to her alone, or do I tend to think, "She knows I love her. I don't have to remind her constantly"? In this "swimsuit issue" world, do I openly admire pretty women because I know my wife is secure and can handle it, or do I save my admiration for her alone? My wife is a one-man woman, but is she absolutely sure I am a one-woman man? Do I understand that assurance of my loyalty calms her soul like few things can?

Esteem—Because a husband is to grant his wife "honor as a fellow heir of the grace of life" (1 Peter 3:7), it behooves me to express appreciation for her God-given value as my equal.

> Does my wife feel treasured, like the most loved woman on earth, or is there work for me to do in this area? Do I take my wife's efforts with the family for granted, or do I often let her know "Thanks for everything you do for me and the kids. I could never, ever do your job!" Do I always remember how important birthdays and anniversaries are to my wife, or do I sometimes get busy and forget? Do I remind myself how energizing it is to her to be referred to as my equal?

Husbands, please note: Every one of the letters in the C-O-U-P-L-E acronym is a key to motivating your wife to do the six things listed in the C-H-A-I-R-S acronym, which is discussed below.

C-H-A-I-R-S: A Checkup for Wives

If a wife uses just one C-H-A-I-R-S principle each day, she takes giant steps toward making her husband feel unconditionally respected. Remember that word *unconditional.* Husbands don't need to earn or deserve respect; wives are to extend it graciously and unconditionally.

Simply stated, a wife is to show respect for her husband's *desires* related to C-H-A-I-R-S, not for his poor performance in these areas or, for that matter, not for his outstanding performance in each category. For example, a wife should say, "I respect your desire to provide for me." She should not say, "I respect you for failing to provide all we need this month." The latter comment is preposterous, yet some think this statement is required of wives! Another example is to say, "I respect your desire to offer me counsel." She is not to say, "I respect you for this horrible advice." Again, the latter remark is wacky. On the other side of these harebrained comments, a wife should be cautious about saying, "I respect you for providing everything I want" or "I respect you for your perfect advice." These expressions are okay, but a husband may think, "What if I fail to provide what you want or to give you perfect advice? Will you respect me then?" This is comparable to a husband saying to his wife, "I love you so much for keeping yourself fit and trim for me." Will he stop loving her if she puts on a few pounds? Just as a wife is sensitive to performance comments, so is a husband. Therefore, every wife should think about expressing respect for her husband's desires—not his performance—related to C-H-A-I-R-S.

To check herself on how well she is showing her husband respect for his desires, a wife can ask herself the following questions on a regular (at least weekly) basis:

Conquest—Because "God took the man and put him into the garden of Eden to cultivate it and keep it" (Genesis 2:15), I need to grasp why and how all men feel obligated and drawn to work.

> Does my husband know I am behind his desire to work? Do I support him in his field of endeavor? Do I really understand how important my husband's job is to him—that it is the very warp and woof of his being? Do I realize that my recognition of the significance of my husband's work energizes him and how

fond feelings of affection for me arise in him in response to this recognition?

Hierarchy—Because he is called by God to be "the head of his wife, as Christ also is the head of the church" (Ephesians 5:23), my husband needs to hear my gratitude for his willingness to protect, to provide, and even die for me.

> Do I express my respect and appreciation for his sense of responsibility for me, or do I either openly or subtly resent the biblical concept of the husband's headship, feeling that my husband views headship as a right over me, not a responsibility for me? Am I willing to send my husband a card or note to tell him how much I respect him? What would I say to thank him for his desire to take care of me? Do I fully understand how such a statement of respect for his commitment to protect me can touch him deeply?

Authority—Because Scripture tells wives to "submit to your own husbands, as to the Lord" (Ephesians 5:22), I need to place myself under his protection and provision, and when stalemates arise, I need to let him know I am willing to defer to his decisions, trusting God to guide him.

> Do I let my husband know that, because he has the responsibility to protect and provide for me, I recognize he also has primary authority in our family, or do I insist on an "egalitarian" marriage where we both have equal authority, yet I contradict "egalitarianism" by expecting him to be primarily responsible? Do I recognize my husband's desire to be the leader in relationship to me? Do I allow my husband to be the leader, or do I take the lead because, frankly, I am better at a lot of things than he is? Am I on record with my husband that, because he has 51 percent of the responsibility (to die for me!), he has 51 percent of the authority?

Insight—Because the Bible teaches that it was Eve who was deceived (1 Timothy 2:14; 2 Corinthians 11:3), I should be very aware that there will be moments when I can be misled by my feelings and want to ignore my husband's counsel.

> Do I tend to turn to him for his opinion and analysis, or do I tend to depend more on my intuition? Do I realize that we are a team—that our marriage needs my intuition *and* his insight? Do I regularly ask for my husband's advice? Do I follow it? If my husband offers ideas or opinions that are contrary to mine, am I open to changing, or do I reject out of hand his wish to offer insight? Do I often see my husband as wrong, sinful, and in need of correction and myself as right, good, and correct? Do I sometimes try to be my husband's Holy Spirit?

Relationship—Because the Bible clearly speaks of how a wife should be her husband's friend as well as his lover (see especially Song of Solomon 5:16), I should recognize the value of just being with him.

> How much shoulder-to-shoulder time do I spend with my husband? Do we do things together as friends and companions? Do I ever just sit with him—to watch a ball game or a TV program—because I understand his desire for me to be with him? Do I ever just sit and watch him work on something without having to talk?

Sexuality—Because a husband should have eyes only for his wife (Proverbs 5:19), a wife blesses her husband when she understands his vulnerabilities and meets his sexual needs (1 Corinthians 7:5).

> Do I understand that my husband's need for sex is really an indication of his deeper need for respect? Do I sometimes deprive my husband of sex because I don't feel he meets my need for intimacy and love? Do I think we need to be close before we can share sexually, or do I see having sex with him as a way to feel close? Am I willing to give my husband the sexual release he needs even when I am not in the mood?

Wives, please note: Every one of the letters in the C-H-A-I-R-S acronym is a key to motivating your husband to do the things in the C-O-U-P-L-E acronym, which was discussed above.

So far we have done a quick review of how to slow and even stop the Crazy Cycle, and we've discussed how getting on the Energizing Cycle can keep the Crazy Cycle from starting up again. But there is one more cycle all married couples need to be aware of. It is the most important of all.

The Rewarded Cycle: Reaching Your Ultimate Goal

Knowing how to stop or slow the Crazy Cycle is good. Practicing the Energizing Cycle with C-O-U-P-L-E and C-H-A-I-R-S is better, but there are times when even all of this is not enough. Sometimes a wife will not show unconditional respect for her husband no matter how hard he tries to show her love. Sometimes a husband will not show love for his wife no matter how hard she tries to unconditionally respect him. When this is the case, you are on the Rewarded Cycle, which is summed up like this:

HIS LOVE BLESSES REGARDLESS OF HER RESPECT.
HER RESPECT BLESSES REGARDLESS OF HIS LOVE.

The Rewarded Cycle means that God blesses a husband who loves his wife regardless of her level of respect for him, and God blesses a wife who respects her husband regardless of his level of love for her. These blessings are the rewards God gives to those who love or respect a mate because of their own love and reverence for Christ. Christ is the motivation for such action.

In His parable of the sheep and the goats, Jesus teaches us to do what we do as if we are doing it to Him (see Matthew 25:31–40). Ephesians 5:22 tells wives to submit to their husbands "as to the Lord." Ephesians 5:25 tells husbands to love their wives "just as Christ also loved the church." In these two verses, the apostle Paul teaches husbands and wives that, in marriage, the true believer is always conscious of Christ.

When spouses come to me saying the Love and Respect Connection just isn't working, my advice is always the same: *Don't give up. Keep doing your part because, in God's economy, no effort to obey Him is wasted.* God intends to reward you even if your spouse is unresponsive.

When you love or respect unconditionally regardless of the outcome, you are following God and His will for you. This is the Rewarded Cycle. You aren't *primarily* loving your wife or respecting your husband because of what it can do to improve your marriage. Yes, that may be a wonderful by-product, but your real purpose is to love and reverence God by trusting and obeying His commands to you. In fact, the Rewarded Cycle is as relevant to good marriages as it is to poor ones that seem stuck on the Crazy Cycle. In the long run, husbands and wives should be practicing Love and Respect principles first and foremost out of obedience to God and His command in Ephesians 5:33. No matter how well you think the Energizing Cycle is humming, keep your eyes on Christ. Just when you think you have it all solved, the roof can cave in.

To help you in your practice of the Rewarded Cycle, memorize Ephesians 6:7–8: "Serve wholeheartedly, as if you were serving the Lord, not men, because you know that the Lord will reward everyone for whatever good he does" (NIV). Have you ever thought about what Paul means by "the Lord will reward everyone"? This promise of rewards certainly includes husbands and wives who practice Love and Respect regardless of the outcome here on earth. Whatever happens in your marriage, when you get to heaven, the Lord will reward you in ways beyond anything you can possibly imagine if you faithfully practice Love and Respect out of obedience to Him.

I am not simply making a pie-in-the-sky argument. After more than thirty years of doing marriage counseling and conferences, I have concluded we don't have a marriage crisis in the church; we have a faith crisis. After all, no one can really practice Love and Respect unless he or she does it as unto Jesus Christ. Is this difficult? It can be, and some will fail and feel like bailing out, but—to paraphrase Proverbs 24:16—"a righteous, committed spouse falls seven times, and rises again." Spouses on the Rewarded Cycle know the secret of success—and maturity. They keep getting up and dealing with the issues. They don't demand instant solutions; they are in their marriage for the long haul, and they live in obedience to God in order to someday hear, "Well done, good and faithful servant" (Matthew 25:21 NIV).

The Rewarded Cycle will deepen your love and reverence for Christ as you render Love and Respect to your spouse as unto Him. Remember: *in the ultimate sense, your marriage has nothing to do with your spouse. It has everything to do with your relationship to Jesus Christ.* Whenever you practice Love or Respect, your goal is not simply to slow or halt the Crazy Cycle; nor is it to motivate your spouse to meet your needs. Ultimately, you practice Love or Respect because, beyond your spouse, you picture Jesus Christ, and you envision that time when you will see Him face-to-face and realize your marriage was really His way of testing and growing you to have more love and reverence for Him.

The Rewarded Cycle Can Work Right Now

Above I stress that practicing the Rewarded Cycle guarantees you the greatest of rewards when you meet your Lord face-to-face. But be aware that there are also rewards to help you cope here and now. I hear from many, many spouses who say they have gotten the idea about how to slow or stop the Crazy Cycle, but they stay in a sort of limbo, not quite able to get on the Energizing Cycle and stay there. The Crazy Cycle keeps slipping back into first, second, or even high gear, and it is all they can do to slow it down again. I grieve for husbands and wives who continue to struggle with a spouse's burning rage or withering criticism. But they don't need my sympathy; they need practical help and sound advice, hard as it may be to accept and follow.

A key to benefiting from the Rewarded Cycle here and now is in one word: *unconditional.* I often realize I need to heed my own advice. Happy as Sarah and I are, we still go through Rewarded Cycle moments. At those times I must remember that Sarah doesn't *cause* me to be the way I am; she *reveals* the way I am. When I am unloving toward Sarah, it's because I still have issues; I still have more growing up to do. I have a choice: either admit my failure to be mature or play the victim. As a victim I can blame Sarah, or circumstances, or whatever. But, as a victim, I will not become more mature.

But suppose Sarah is the one at fault. She is being disrespectful, and I have a "right" to feel hurt, angry, depressed. But if I do, I am right back in the victim mind-set again. No matter who is at fault, I can't expect Sarah to heal my hurts or comfort me. My only real comfort will come from my Lord and trusting Him with my situation. Like anyone else, I must grasp a key Love and Respect principle and never let go: *No matter how depressing or irritating my spouse might be, my response is my responsibility.*

You Always Have a Choice

In John 8, Jesus is in the middle of a heated discussion with the Pharisees about who He is and why they should follow Him. Explaining to them the secret of true spiritual freedom, Jesus says, "If you continue in My word, then you are truly disciples of Mine; and you will know the truth, and the truth will make you free . . . if the Son makes you free, you will be free indeed" (vv. 31–32, 36). Jesus' words are just as relevant for us today. No matter how difficult your spouse may be at the moment, your spouse does not have control over your reaction; you do. You may be experiencing disappointment, frustration, or anger, but *you always have a choice*. A wife can choose to be disrespectful *or* respectful. A husband can choose to be unloving *or* loving.

To realize that you are free in Christ and not a slave to the same old negative reactions that lead straight to the Crazy Cycle is a source of real power. No matter how unloving a husband may be at the moment, when a wife unconditionally respects him out of obedience to Christ, she can win him "without a word"(see 1 Peter 3:1–2), that is, influence him to follow Christ, which also results in him treating her better. And the same principle is true for husbands. No matter how disrespectful a wife may be, when a husband unconditionally loves her out of obedience to Christ, he can win her. Hosea the prophet was called by God to unconditionally love his adulterous wife (Hosea 3:1). The Lord knew that unconditional love is the best way to influence a wife to return to Him and to her husband.

Understand, then, that the Rewarded Cycle assures you that when tests come—and come they will—you always have a choice. Conflict is inevitable; it is simply part of living together. The key to keeping conflict from starting up the Crazy Cycle is to choose to practice love or respect. When a husband speaks with a loving tone during a conflict, which may range from a mild argument to a more serious disagreement, his wife will feel one with him. And when a wife softens her facial expressions and comes across more respectfully during those times of friction, the husband will feel one with her. Will the disagreement be solved? Perhaps, but more than likely it will still be there. Yet husband and wife can feel oneness because nobody has to win and nobody has to lose. Winning or losing during conflict is not the goal. Oneness is, and it is gained when the wife feels loved by her husband and the husband feels respected by his wife. They bond with each other; two, indeed, become one.

Practicing a Love and Respect marriage is a lifelong journey, but you don't have to travel it alone. In Christ you are free indeed (John 8:36) to make the mature choice to love or respect no matter how your spouse is acting. *But you must constantly ask Him for help.* Apart from Him, you can do nothing (John 15:5). Asking God for help means prayer, lots of prayer. Not the wish-list kind of prayer that says, "Lord, here is what is on my heart. Please fulfill my desires for me." The Rewarded Cycle kind of prayer says, "Lord, I want to do what is on *Your* heart. Please fulfill Your desires *in me.*"

Pink and Blue Blend into God's Purple

One of the most popular illustrations we use in Love and Respect Conferences compares women and men to pink and blue. The audience responds immediately when I talk about how she sees through pink sunglasses and hears with pink hearing aids, while he sees through blue sunglasses and hears with blue hearing aids. In other words, women and men are *very different.* Yet, when blue blends with pink, it becomes purple, God's color—the color of royalty. The way for pink and blue to blend is spelled out in Ephesians 5:33: "[Every husband] must love his wife as he loves himself, and the wife must respect her husband" (NIV). Living out Ephesians 5:33 is the key to blending together as one to reflect the very image of God.

But to do this on a daily basis, in the here and now, when disagreements and misunderstandings pop up, takes commitment. Following is a prayer of commitment that we invite husbands and wives to say together as we close a Love and Respect Conference. It sums up the Rewarded Cycle, just as it sums up what it means to have a Love and Respect marriage. Living out Ephesians 5:33 is the key to blending together as one in order to reflect the very image of God.

A Prayer of Commitment

Dear Father,

I need You. I cannot love or respect perfectly, but I know You hear me when I ask You for help.

First, please forgive me for the times I've been unloving or disrespectful. And help me to forgive my spouse for being unloving or disrespectful toward me.

I open my heart to You, Father. I will not be fearful or angry at You or my spouse. I'm seeing myself and my spouse in a whole new light, and I will appreciate my spouse as being different, not wrong.

Lord, I also ask You to fill my heart with love and reverence for You. After all, this marriage is ultimately about You and me. It isn't about my spouse. Thank You for helping me both understand this truth and realize that my greatest reward will come from being a spouse as unto You.

Now prepare me this day for those inevitable moments of conflict. I especially ask You to put respect or love in my heart when I feel unloved or disrespected. I know there is no credit for loving or respecting when doing so is easy.

Finally, I believe that You hear my prayer, and I anticipate Your response. I thank You in advance for helping me take the next loving or respectful step in my marriage. I believe You will empower me, bless me, and even reward me for my effort as I approach marriage as unto You.

In the name of Jesus Christ,
Amen.

Reader, please note: In chapter 1 above—"A Short Course on Love and Respect"—you have covered a brief condensation of the book *Love & Respect.* The rest of this book applies the Love and Respect system to the crucial challenge of learning how to gain mutual understanding and start communicating with each other more clearly, more effectively, and, above all, with more Love and Respect!

—◦◦◦—

PART II

Three Vital Truths for Better Communication

—◦◦◦—

The next three chapters address three vital truths that will be invaluable to you and your spouse as you seek the mutual understanding that will lead to better communication. These three truths are:

1. In any marriage, what comes out of the mouth of each spouse matters a great deal. Jesus put it very clearly: out of your mouth comes that which fills your heart (see Luke 6:45). This book is based on the premise that those who read it are practicing—or are at least open to practicing—Love and Respect as it is outlined in chapter 1 and more fully discussed in *Love & Respect* (Integrity, 2004). You will get the most from this book if you make an unconditional commitment to live out Love and Respect and to follow the simple teachings of Scripture.

2. Husbands and wives are very different, as different as the colors pink and blue. It is crucial for husband and wife to see that neither one is wrong, but that both of them are very different—in body function, outlook, and perspective. Research and experience prove that men and women see and hear differently. Recognizing these differences and adjusting to them is absolutely necessary for reaching mutual understanding and better communication.

3. When your spouse has those inevitable moments of pique, anger, or nastiness, you must still see your spouse as a goodwilled person. Your spouse may fail to be loving or respectful, but you still trust your spouse's good intentions. You know that your spouse does not have evil will toward you or ultimately mean to do you any harm. Whatever your spouse's failings might be, you know that deep down your spouse cares for you. And you should feel the same toward your spouse. If you forget that your spouse is basically goodwilled and so are you, it will be hard to practice Love and Respect.

CHAPTER TWO

In Marriage,
the Mouth Matters

Almost everyone has probably heard or read the nursery rhyme that makes the brave but naive claim "Sticks and stones may break my bones, but words will never hurt me." And almost everyone who has outgrown the nursery knows that words can indeed hurt. As I deal with thousands of married couples every year, I see and hear that words cannot only hurt; they can destroy a relationship.

Sarah and I can also testify that words have the power to hurt. Careless words, unloving words, disrespectful words, words spoken in anger or defensiveness—in the early years of our marriage we experienced them all even though we were very much in love and had committed ourselves to a life of Christian ministry together. For example:

We were both in our early twenties, married less than a year, when we visited my parents, who lived in Peoria, Illinois. We arrived and got settled in. That night, as I prepared for bed, I noticed I had forgotten my contact lens case. To improvise some kind of overnight storage for my lenses, I went to the kitchen, got two juice glasses, put water in each, and dropped my contacts into the glasses. Returning to the bathroom, I put the two glasses on top of the toilet tank, side by side.

The next morning when I prepared to put in my contacts, I discovered one of the glasses was empty and the contact was gone! As I tried to figure out what had happened, Sarah became the prime suspect. Anger began surging through my system, and I went to the door and yelled, "Sarah, did you do anything with my contacts in those two juice glasses on the back of the toilet?"

Sarah was out on the patio with my parents, and her first response was no. A few seconds later, however, I heard her say, "Oh, no!" and I had a distinct feeling we had a real problem. I was right. Sarah's next words, in a nervous voice, were "I got up in the middle of the night and used one of those glasses of water to take a pill."

In a nanosecond I was mad as a hornet. "You did WHAT? How COULD you? Sarah, how could anyone do something like this? There were two glasses sitting side by side on the back of the toilet, for heaven's sake! You DRANK my contact!"

> All spouses know that a "harsh word stirs up anger" (Proverbs 15:1).

By now Sarah had joined me in the bathroom, the scene of the crime, but the door was open, and my parents were hearing every word. Sarah was stung by my anger and doubly so because of how I was coming across to my wife with my parents listening. She retorted, "Why would anyone in his right mind not tell everyone he did this and put a sign there 'Do Not Use'?"

"And why would anyone drink out of a glass that looked used and was sitting on the back of a toilet?" I wanted to know.

"Well, why would anyone leave a glass of water there if he didn't want it used?" she responded. Round and round we went, and things got crazy. A big part of what was fueling our mutual frustration and anger was that we had no money to replace the contact, an expensive item at that time. Adding to our anxiety was concern over my ability to read or drive.

Slowly we calmed down, and I started feeling foolish for going off like that on Sarah—and in front of my parents to boot. Within the hour Sarah and I prayed together and invited my parents to join us. I asked for forgiveness for my anger, and so did Sarah. We also claimed the promise in Romans 8:28—that God would cause everything to work together for good for those who love Him. God did just that, but I will save the outcome for the conclusion of this book. Meanwhile, Sarah and I went on with learning to live together and love one another, but there was often tension that left us wondering when the next clash would come.

Our Happy Journey Would Turn into a Demolition Derby

We didn't have a rotten relationship. Far from it! But we did have our moments, and those moments twirled us around like a spinning top, making us dizzy with confusion and consternation. We felt like two moonstruck lovers zooming down the wonderful track called marriage, but every so often one little word, or maybe a few little words, turned our happy journey into a figure-eight demolition derby, causing us to collide in ways that jarred and bruised us, leaving us a bit frightened by the verbal whiplashes we gave one another.

Ironically, my ministry took me into the area of marriage counseling.

As I received—and handed out—hurtful words at home, I also heard about much more of the same from married people who came to my office for help. Usually it was a wife who came alone because her husband did not want to join her. The pain and confusion in these women were intense, and their tears flowed. These women longed to improve their marriages and wanted to do what they could to increase the feelings of love between their husbands and them.

I would strategize with them on ways to motivate their husbands to be more loving, and they would leave with new resolve to turn their marriages around. Almost inevitably, however, they would return with reports of more hurt and rejection: "He doesn't want to talk to me," "He just gets angry with me," or "He uses words that hurt me deeply."

> *Your spouse won't hear your heart when your "sharp words cut like a sword" (Proverbs 12:18 CEV).*

What struck me, however, was that these same women would often confess, "I know I get nasty with him," "I realize I should be more positive," or "I know my words can shut him down." And then they would almost always add, "But he should *know* that I really don't mean these things. He should know I am hurting. Pastor, *why* doesn't he understand me—and my heart? Why won't he *love* me?"

How I Discovered the Three Cycles of Marriage

These stories were repeated over and over. I would despair as I tried to help wives who felt so unloved. I could see why they criticized, but the more they did, the less love their husbands showed them. Then, one day as I worked in my office at home, it dawned on me to ask "What does the Bible say about how to motivate a husband to be more loving?" Here I was, a pastor and Bible teacher, but I had never asked myself this obvious question!

> *In your marriage, remember that "all his guiding principles are trustworthy" (Psalm 111:7 GW).*

And as I sought the answer, I studied Ephesians, especially 5:22–33, a passage that contains the New Testament's best teaching on marriage, which concludes: "However each one of you also must love his wife as he loves himself, and the wife must respect her husband" (v. 33 NIV).

There it was, a command from God, because obviously He knows a wife needs love and a husband needs respect. As I meditated on verse 33, I began to see a connection between love and respect. I asked myself, "What happens to a husband when his wife meets his need for respect?" The answer came to me: "He is energized." But energized to do *what*? It seemed to me that he would be motivated to meet his wife's need for love.

Next I asked myself, "What happens when a husband meets his wife's need for love?" And again came the answer: "She is energized." Energized to do what? Of course! She is motivated to meet his need for respect!

As I completed this line of reasoning, it became clear that I had the answer to my earlier question "What does the Bible say about how to motivate a husband to be more loving?" The more I thought about how wives and husbands can motivate and energize each other, the more I recognized that I was onto something unconventional, extraordinary, and electrifying that could help many marriages. I soon came up with a concise way to describe the sequence in terms of a cycle:

The Energizing Cycle
His love motivates her respect.
Her respect motivates his love.

Ideas were flooding my mind. Along with the positive, energizing cycle in Ephesians 5:33, I also recognized a negative, "de-energizing" cycle. I asked myself, "What happens to a husband when a wife does *not* meet his need for respect?" The answer seemed plain: he is not energized in the marriage, and he loses his motivation to meet her need for love. In fact, it seemed to me that, if a husband is disrespected by his wife, he loses his feelings of love and affection for her and is prone to react in ways that feel unloving to her just to "teach" her to be more respectful! (This, of course, is ineffective!)

"And what about the wife?" I asked myself. "What happens when her husband does not meet her need for love?" Again, the answer was plain enough: an unloved wife is not energized in the marriage, and she loses her motivation to meet her husband's need for respect. She is prone to react in ways that are critical and disrespectful when she feels unloved! (This, too, is ineffective!)

At this point I knew I was onto something really huge that went a long way toward explaining why husbands and wives go back and forth with the crazy behavior I heard about in my counseling office—and also engage in from time to time with Sarah! A concise way to put this negative connection between Love and Respect came to me as follows:

The Crazy Cycle
Without his love, she reacts without respect.
Without her respect, he reacts without love.

I had worked out the Energizing Cycle and its counterpart the Crazy Cycle, but there was still one more crucial question to deal with: "Can either a husband or a wife justify treating each other unlovingly or disrespectfully?" My mind shifted into overdrive as I went back to study Ephesians 5:33 to see what the verse was *not* saying. What I realized is that the passage does not say, "Each husband must love his wife *if and only if* his wife first respects him." Nor does the verse say, "Every wife must respect her husband *if and only if* her husband first loves her in ways she deems meaningful."

The answer to my question was quite clear: both the husband's love for his wife and the wife's respect for her husband must be *unconditional*, an act of grace, of unmerited favor. This idea was so important that I searched for a concise way to put it in "cycle" language and came up with this:

The Rewarded Cycle
His love blesses regardless of her respect.
Her respect blesses regardless of his love.

In other words, as a husband or wife unconditionally loves or respects, God blesses or rewards this person's faithfulness. Regardless of how

your mate may act, your respect for your husband must be unconditional; your love for your wife must be unconditional. There is no justifying anything else. This is God's command to the husband and wife
independent of a spouse deserving love or respect. One cannot argue
with God, "My spouse must first earn my love or respect before I will
obey Your command!" And this is, without question, a tough assignment. The husband is commanded to love his wife even when she is disrespectful, critical, and full of contempt.

A husband must go the extra mile and
meet his wife's deepest need for love
while his own need for respect goes
unmet and is even denounced because he
"hasn't earned it" in her opinion. Even
tougher, however, due to cultural condi-
tioning, is that the wife must respect her
husband even when he is unloving, cold,
and inconsiderate.

> *Unconditional respect means showing "complete respect, not only to those who are kind and considerate, but also to those who are harsh"*
> *(1 Peter 2:18 GNB).*

Let me highlight the novel aspect of
this message in our current culture:
unconditional respect toward a husband.
This concept is laughable to many wives
because of what they think *unconditional
respect* means. Some ask, "So am I to give
my husband license to do whatever he wants? Am I to say, 'I respect the
way you rarely talk to me. Sure, spend more time with your buddies than
with me'?" That is absurd to any woman. What most women fail to
understand initially is that unconditional respect isn't about giving a husband carte blanche. Instead, it means confronting his hurtful behavior
respectfully—confronting him without the rolling of the eyes, heavy
sighs, hands on the hips, pointing fingers, sour looks, and over-the-top
comments like "You have no love in your heart for me!" This isn't easy,
but contemptuous corrections are ineffective long-term.

Unconditional Respect for Husbands? No Way!

The idea that she must show him unconditional respect because he has a deep need for it is simply counterintuitive for a woman. She thinks, "He is supposed to love me. *Then* he will have my respect." Even more daunting is the fact that unconditional respect for a husband is countercultural. When I made my Ephesians 5:33 discoveries in the late 1990s, feminism had been holding sway for many years and had leveled the playing field in the minds of many women. If any man hoped to receive any respect at all from a woman, he'd better earn it!

I began to think, "This idea of unconditional respect for husbands sure won't play in Peoria!" Wondering if I was incorrect in my thinking, I decided to search elsewhere in the Bible for confirmation of Paul's words in Ephesians 5:33 that the wife must respect her husband unconditionally. That confirmation came through with deafening force when I came upon 1 Peter 3:1–2. Here Peter is talking to wives who are married to "disobedient husbands" who are either unbelievers or carnal believers not following Christ as they should, and he makes the bold claim that "even if any of them are disobedient to the word, they may be won without a word by the behavior of their wives, as they observe your chaste and respectful behavior."

I believe that when Peter mentions "disobedient husbands," he is thinking of everything from husbands who were not believers to Christians who were harsh, gruff, and not treating their families very well. Nonetheless, Peter tells the wives that their unconditional respect is foundational to winning these men. The unbelieving husband can be won to Christ, and the carnal Christian can be won back from a life of disobedience. In fact, unconditional respect motivates any husband to change poor behavior. A wife's respectful words, tone of voice, and look on her face convict him. Over time, she can win his heart. When she meets his need to feel respected, she impacts his heart in the same way a husband touches his wife's heart when he meets her need to feel loved. In marriage, this isn't about people deserving love or respect but needing love or respect. Peter says nothing about these husbands earning or deserving their wives' respect. The truth is the guy is disobedient to Jesus Christ and very undeserving! Let me repeat: he does not deserve respect! Peter simply says, in effect, "No matter how he acts, come across respectfully toward the big oaf anyhow." In other plain and simple words, "Show him *unconditional* respect."

The Three Cycles Happen in Everybody's Marriage

As these ideas from God, by way of Paul and Peter, flooded my soul, I was awestruck at first and then overjoyed. I literally stood up and shouted, "Glory! Glory to God!" Then I called, "Sarah, come here!" (Actually, she was halfway there already. Her husband does not often shout "Glory!" when he's studying.) As she came hurrying in, I said, "I think I have just had an illumination. Look at these connections I found between love and respect."

As I explained my rough diagrams of the Energizing Cycle, the Crazy Cycle, and the Rewarded Cycle, she got the point almost instantly: "These cycles are what happen in our marriage—and everybody else's marriage too!" she exclaimed. "It's so simple, but it still captures what we all experience."

"What do you think about the Rewarded Cycle and the unconditional part?" I wanted to know.

"The Rewarded Cycle is what touches me most," she replied. "This is it! Someone in the worst of marriages can listen to this teaching, and God can do a mighty work in that person's soul even if their spouse isn't at the conference!"

Sarah and I continued to talk about the three cycles, especially the Rewarded Cycle because it seemed so freeing to her. She, too, thought God had put me onto something really huge, and she was eager to share these ideas with everyone she could. She had always been burdened by much of the teaching on marriage that said, in so many words, "If you do this and this, everything will be hunky-dory—and if it isn't working, there is something wrong with you." As she put it, "The Rewarded Cycle isn't saying there is a magic formula for marriages. Sometimes we must do what we do out of love and reverence for God. We must obey God *regardless.*" When we do love or respect, God rewards us. This is the greatest of all motivations to act on this. A person can do this even if a spouse doesn't respond."

I give a much shorter version of how I discovered the Love and Respect Connection and the Crazy Cycle in *Love & Respect,* but I believe it is helpful to explain what happened in more detail in this book that will focus on finding mutual understanding and better communication in your marriage. For you and your spouse to get the most from this second book, it is critical to see the importance of how Love and Respect interplay in the three cycles. In our Love and Respect Conferences, we always start with the Crazy Cycle because that is where so many couples find themselves to some degree at least some of the time. They struggle with communicating, and the things that trigger a lot of the craziness often begin with what comes out of the mouth.

Even after husbands and wives get the idea of how Love and Respect can change their relationship for the better, the battle has just begun, as Sarah and I well know. Discovering the Love and Respect Connection is one thing; living it out is another. Practicing Love and Respect takes work, lots of work. And much of that work has to do with how we use our mouths. In marriage, the mouth matters a great deal. But even more important is the heart because what is in my heart will come out of my mouth. As Jesus said, your mouth speaks from that which fills your heart (see Luke 6:45).

Paul Had a Lot to Say about How to Use the Mouth

Paul knew the teachings of Jesus, and I am sure he was thinking of Jesus' words when he wrote his letter to the Ephesian church (Ephesians 4:20, 21). Look especially at what Paul says in Ephesians 4 and 5 where he makes several points about how Christians are to use their mouths:

We are to stop falsehood and speak truth (4:25).
We are to stop unwholesome words and speak words that edify (4:29).

We are to stop the clamor and the slander and be kind and forgiving (4:31–32).

We are to stop silly talk and coarse jesting and be thankful (5:4).

We are not to get drunk with wine but be filled with the Spirit, speaking to one another in psalms, hymns, and spiritual songs (5:18–19).

All of what Paul writes in Ephesians 4 and the first part of Ephesians 5 applies to all Christians, but note that he goes on to talk specifically to husbands and wives in Ephesians 5:22–33. I am sure Paul knew that if anyone needed to apply what he had just said about how to use the mouth, it was married couples.

In later chapters we will look more closely at some of the passages cited above, but for now we can ask ourselves this question: "Can I expect my spouse to have confidence that I have love or respect in my heart if I speak untruthful, unwholesome, unforgiving, unthankful, or unscriptural words?" Obviously, the answer is no, but by the same token we can ask another question: "What might happen in my marriage if my words *are* truthful, wholesome, forgiving, thankful, and scriptural?"

Your Words Reveal What Is in Your Heart

Be aware that your words are a very good indication of what is going on in your heart—and your spouse knows it. If a husband pledges Love and a wife pledges Respect, but they speak words that feel unloving and disrespectful, they simply plant seeds of doubt about what is really in their hearts. For example, if Sarah is talking with me about something and I reply with an absentminded "Uh-huh" as my attention wanders to the television screen or the newspaper, she might easily start to feel unloved.

Or imagine if we get into a discussion where we disagree and I finally become exasperated and say, "You just don't seem to get it, and I am baffled by the dozen or so unconnected things you just said that had no bottom line. I don't think I will ever understand you," she would feel more than just a bit unloved. She would start questioning if I really do love her in my heart because my words are telling a different story. She might try to laugh it off, saying men could never understand women anyway, but while she might be laughing on the outside, something else could be going on within. As Scripture observes, "Even in laughter the heart may be in pain" (Proverbs 14:13).

It is not hard to see why a wife can feel insecure. She feels strongly that if her husband loves her in his heart, he will communicate that love. This does not necessarily mean that a husband must shower his wife with romantic poetry daily. But she expects him to somehow, sometime tell her of his love if it is in his heart.

Men also need assurance. If I try to share how satisfying it was to have helped someone who came to me with a problem and Sarah answers with a mere "Um-hmmmmmm. That's great, honey. What do you want for dinner tonight?" I could begin thinking she does not value my work all that much.

Or if I invite Sarah to just sit and relax with me for a while to watch the pair of Canadian geese that come every year to take possession of the small marsh behind our home, but she says, "You *know* I have things to do right now, and I really don't have time to watch some geese," I could easily deduce that being with me is not a big value for her and that what energizes me does not show up on her radar screen as very important.

And if Sarah kept saying things like "You go ahead and watch the evening news. I need to call some friends," it would be a small jump for me to wonder if she really wanted to be with me because I am her good friend, and from there it would be just another small jump to wondering if she really respected me in her heart.

The point is that husbands can also feel insecure if they do not hear words coming from their wives that say in many subtle or not-so-subtle ways "I respect you." Any man knows that if his wife respects him in her heart, she will communicate that respect. This does not mean that a wife must compose songs of admiration and sing them to him at sunrise and sunset. But at some time, in some simple way, the message will come through if respect is truly in her heart.

Right about here you may be saying, "Wait a minute, Emerson. Just because I slip up and use careless words doesn't necessarily mean that I don't have love or respect in my heart. Give me a break. I can't speak *perfectly* all the time. I can't always say just the right thing every moment of the day." That's a good point, and Sarah and I would both agree that neither of us speaks perfectly all of the time. As James says, "If anyone does not stumble in what he says, he is a perfect man" (James 3:2). James was well aware that we do stumble, and he warns, "The tongue is a small thing, but what enormous damage it can do" (James 3:5 NLT). For this very reason, Sarah and I realize that if we are interested in living out Love and Respect, we must do all we can to measure our words more carefully. We cannot talk perfectly, *but we can ask God to help us talk less imperfectly!* Scripture clearly advises us to use our mouths to speak more wisely. Just two examples:

- "The heart of the wise instructs his mouth and adds persuasiveness to his lips" (Proverbs 16:23).
- "The heart of the righteous ponders how to answer, but the mouth of the wicked pours out evil things" (Proverbs 15:28).

Those Hot-Button Words Can Cause Trouble

After living and teaching Love and Respect for over eight years, Sarah and I are constantly amazed at the power of words and how they are spoken. And it's my educated guess that almost every couple has certain hot-button words or phrases that can cause trouble between them. For example, when Sarah is quite concerned (irritated) about something I have done or said (again), she uses the expression "You always . . ." Whenever I hear "You always . . . ," I immediately lock up inside and think, "That's not true. I don't *always* [do or say whatever Sarah is accusing me of]." I am tempted to launch a counterattack on how wacky her claim that "I always . . ." sounds and avoid listening to what she is really trying to say.

> *"Losing your temper causes a lot of trouble, but staying calm settles arguments"*
> *(Proverbs 15:18 CEV).*

Fortunately, over the years I have learned to tune in to what Sarah is trying to communicate when she accuses me of "You always . . ." These words, which once were a real hot button for me, do not mean "You do this 100 percent of the time." She assumes that I know she is not making a statistical judgment of my behavior. What Sarah is trying to do is get my attention concerning her feelings and help me understand her annoyance. She uses "You always . . ." to capture the intensity of her disgruntlement. She is saying, in effect, "You really frustrate me right now!"

For the most part, I have accepted Sarah's use of "You always . . ." for what it is, and I try not to let this hot-button expression distract me from her real point. I realize that Sarah doesn't use these words to disrespect me. Ultimately she speaks this way to increase the understanding and love between us. She wants me to grasp the hurt in her heart; she does not want to create hurt in my heart.

For example, I sometimes find the back door has been left unlocked all night. When I ask Sarah if she had used the door and forgotten to lock it on the way to bed, she defensively replies, "You always blame me for the door being unlocked. It's always my fault." Since I know I don't always blame her, the temptation for me is to get irritated and reply, "I do not ALWAYS blame you." So instead of getting into a "No, I don't"/ "Yes, you do" exchange, I try to recognize that Sarah feels attacked—and all the more so if she had nothing to do with the door being unlocked. I am learning to get the facts straight rather than jump to conclusions and make accusations.

In fact, lately when finding the door unlocked, I ask Sarah about it in a much gentler way, and she is less likely to say, "You always blame me." When spoken to gently, Sarah is much more likely to respond in the tone she used just this morning: "No, I'm pretty sure I didn't leave the door unlocked. I had gone to bed, and you went out to the garage for something, remember?" And then, as usual, I recall that I am indeed the culprit, and I sheepishly apologize for even thinking she might have left the back door unlocked.

On my side of the ledger, words I use that can set Sarah off are "Honey, may I make a suggestion?" When I say these words, Sarah often hears a message of genuine disapproval. Why is this so? Because the thing about hot-button words is that, when they are spoken, the listener tends to expect the worst possible meaning. For example, suppose I say, "Sarah, may I make a suggestion to you concerning your role as vice president of Love and Respect Ministries?" Immediately, Sarah is tempted to think, "I am failing in my role as VP, and it is so serious I am jeopardizing the entire Love and Respect operation." In her mind Sarah knows this is not so, but emotionally she experiences an impulsive surge that tells her she has done something that deserves a pink slip.

Over the years Sarah has learned not to allow that impulsive surge to cause her to react defensively. She realizes that when I say, "May I make a suggestion?" I am seeking to approach her in a sensitive manner. My comments are truly suggestions for her to receive and use as she sees fit.

At this point in our marriage, because of her natural impulses, Sarah does not shout for joy when I infrequently say, "May I make a suggestion?" Instead she engages me with maturity and a willingness to listen and, after the conversation, expresses appreciation for my input. The hot button is a warm button now. Using and reacting to hot-button words is just one way Sarah and I can start spinning on the Crazy Cycle like everyone else, but we can find ways to slow and stop the craziness. As Sarah puts it, "We go there, but we don't stay there."

I will come back to hot-button words in another chapter and talk about how to rephrase certain expressions to make them less hot for your spouse to hear. For now I simply wanted to share that Sarah and I are very aware of how powerful our words can be as we try to practice

Love and Respect. I get many letters from spouses who also know the power of words, especially once they have been introduced to Love and Respect.

His Hockey Theory Put Them on the Crazy Cycle

One husband wrote to tell me of what can happen even when sitting in a Love and Respect Conference listening to me teach. I had just finished making a point about how women grow up socializing and loving to talk things out face-to-face, while men grow up learning they should provide, protect, and even die for their wives. As I expounded from the platform on these concepts, it caused the husband to recall a personal theory—speculation about male and female behavior—that he had worked out: "In Minnesota, guys grow up playing hockey, and girls grow up watching guys play hockey."

At that moment the hockey-theory husband heard me start to talk about how men can be goaded into physically wanting to fight if they're not shown respect. For reasons known only to him, the husband leaned over and whispered his hockey theory to his wife. Her only comment was "That irritates me."

"Starting a quarrel is like opening a floodgate, so stop before the argument gets out of control" (Proverbs 17:14 GW).

When his wife used the word *irritates*, what he heard her saying was that she did not respect him or his theories. "I totally shut down," he writes. "I turned my back on her and moved to the other side of my seat."

As I went on to talk about how easy it is for husbands and wives to become trapped in the Crazy Cycle, he realized that this was exactly what had happened! His letter continues:

I began talking to myself, saying, "Hello! You are in a marriage conference, and the man on stage is actually talking about what you are doing right now. He is saying how easy it is to get into the Crazy Cycle and how difficult it is to break out of it. WAKE UP!"

The husband went on to relate that he couldn't snap out of his funk. The session soon ended, and during the break he avoided his wife and would not speak to her. Fortunately, she realized they had been trapped in a Crazy Cycle, and when she finally caught up to him, she immediately apologized for what she had said. The burden was lifted, and the two of them were soon laughing about the irony of attending a marriage conference to make their marriage stronger and falling into the very trap the conference was designed to help them avoid!

The husband who chose an unfortunate time to share his hockey theory with his wife concluded his letter by observing that they had both learned a valuable lesson from what happened: spouses really need to be aware of what they are saying to each other and how they are reacting to what is said. He adds that he and his wife do not ride the Crazy Cycle too often, but their experience at the conference where they first learned about the Crazy Cycle proves that it can happen anywhere and at any moment "because of how we are naturally wired."

This husband has good insight. He realizes that husbands and wives are wired differently and, when those wires get crossed, the communication sparks can fly! Why did God create husband and wife to be so different? How important are these differences to learning how to communicate—and how can we identify them? We'll answer these questions in the next chapter.

CHAPTER THREE

Not Wrong, Just Different

One of the most popular analogies we use at our Love and Respect Conferences describes the differences between men and women in terms of pink and blue. Women look at the world through pink sunglasses, while men look at that same world through blue sunglasses—and, believe me, they do not necessarily see the same thing!

For example, I have often heard the generalization that women go to movies to excite their emotions and men go to movies to escape their emotions. In other words, even though they may have careers, because most women are relationally oriented, they enjoy chick flicks that appeal to their love of romance or their heart for families. Women can be scientists or engineers, but they still have this bent toward the family due to their nurturing nature.

And because most men are career- and achievement-oriented, they enjoy action movies that enable them to block out what happened today at work. Men can be great husbands and fathers who are quite capable of loving and nurturing, but they still have their "guy" side that likes watching the honorable gladiator defeat his despicable enemy.

Not too many years ago, these same men were little boys building their forts to protect the innocent and conquer their evil foes. And these same women were little girls furnishing their playhouses and caring for those dolls they loved. These differences between little boys and girls are obvious and intriguing, and they continue into adulthood and show up in movie preferences. In general, men are inspired by movies dealing with honor, and women are inspired by movies dealing with love.[1]

Men and Women Hear the Same Words Differently

Pink and blue perceptions not only affect seeing; they affect hearing as well. My work with husbands and wives tells me that women hear with pink hearing aids and men hear with blue hearing aids. And perhaps even more important to understand as you and your spouse seek to gain better communication is that you two can hear the very same words, but each of you will hear different messages.

My favorite illustration of this is when a wife says, "I have nothing to wear." She means she has nothing *new* to wear. When her husband says, "I have nothing to wear," he means he has nothing *clean* to wear (*Love & Respect*, p. 30). Each uses the same words but means something different based on pink and blue views! Or consider the words *excess oil*. Two women discussing excess oil are concerned about their skin. Two men discussing excess oil are concerned with machinery or perhaps a slippery garage floor.

Pink and blue have different worlds which impact what words mean. When a wife hears the words, "Let's go shopping," she thinks, "How wonderful!" (Sarah, my wife, is an exception to this!) When a husband hears the words, "Let's go shopping," he thinks, "How can I get out of this?" (I, Emerson, am not an exception to this!) Each hears a different message based on what each likes or dislikes as male or female!

But the difference between male and female goes far beyond pink and blue sunglasses and hearing aids. As the husband with a hockey theory pointed out in chapter 2, he and his wife are "wired differently." That different wiring usually causes husband and wife to be interested in different things. And these different interests can sometimes lead to miscommunication that results in tension (i.e., the Crazy Cycle).

A wife wants to talk and connect emotionally, but her husband says, "I'm tired." Is he reporting the facts, or is he rejecting her? Because a wife usually requests to talk more than her husband requests to talk (she feels this need in her femaleness), his words are interpreted as rejection. Yet, to him the day has been exhausting, and he wants to disengage by watching TV. On the other side of the equation, is a wife reporting the facts or rejecting her husband when a husband wants to be sexually intimate but his wife says, "I'm tired"? Because a husband usually pushes for sexual intimacy more than his wife pushes for sexual intimacy (he feels this need in his maleness), her words are interpreted as rejection. Yet, to her the day has been very tiring, and she wants to bathe, wash her hair, and go to bed early. Not wrong; just different! Yet, these differences between Pink and Blue negatively affect communication and sometimes cause one spouse to accuse the other of being wrong when he or she is just different.

"Next Time Ask about the Really Important Stuff!"

For example, I recently had a nice, long chat with our good friend Ray, who has been on the Highway Patrol for a number of years. After I hung up, Sarah asked, "How was your conversation with Ray?" I explained in typically sparse blue terms that "It was good," but Sarah then asked, "What did you talk about?" To this I responded, "Nothing much."

Sarah was just getting started: "Did you ask Ray how Connie and the family are doing?" To this I responded, "Not really," and Sarah quickly asked, "Why not?" Beginning to feel a bit interrogated, I replied, "It didn't surface, but we did talk about his new responsibilities on the Highway Patrol. He is now in charge of a special unit that assists the Secret

Service and the State Department with protecting the President whenever he visits Los Angeles and uses the freeway system."

Sarah was incredulous: "And you never talked about Connie and the kids? I can't believe it. Next time be sure to ask Ray about his family."

By now I was a little irritated, enough so to say sarcastically, "Well, next time you talk to Ray, ask him about the trust the Highway Patrol has put in him to help the Secret Service protect the President of the United States."

Sarah looked stung. "Why are you saying this? Your comments hurt me. I was just trying to be helpful because sometimes you overlook what is really important."

"That's exactly my point," I snapped. "I talk with Ray about his important new responsibilities, and you seem to think our discussion is second-rate because I didn't ask him about his family. That makes me feel judged, as though I'm not a good person, because the nature of my conversations is not like yours."

Taken aback, Sarah said apologetically, "I was not trying to judge you. I was just trying to be helpful and offer a reminder . . ."

Feeling a little guilty, I said a little more softly, "I am not trying to hurt you, but what you said angers me. I was simply trying to explain how passionate Ray is about how God is using him, and he wanted to tell me about it. He believes he is on a significant mission."

> *Pink and Blue are different in many ways so "accept one another, just as Christ also accepted us" (Romans 15:7).*

Seeking reassurance, Sarah replied, "I am truly sorry for coming across as though I was saying your conversation was unimportant. Will you forgive me? I *am* excited for Ray. I only was curious about the family."

"I know that, and I'm sorry I reacted the way I did. I will make it a point to ask Ray about the family the next time we talk. But, so you know,

Ray and I have chatted about his family in other conversations, and I know if anything serious comes up, he will let me know."

"Okay, I appreciate knowing that," she said as she headed back to what she had been doing, and I turned back to my computer.

What happened to Sarah and me is not that unusual. What husband has not taken a phone call from friends while his wife was out and, when she learned later about the call, found himself barraged with a dozen questions he "forgot" to ask? Following my phone call with Ray, Pink (Sarah) and Blue (Emerson) got through a tense conversation that could have landed them right on the Crazy Cycle, but my wonderful pink wife saved the day by maturely asking forgiveness for anything she had said that contributed to the tension, while in typically slow blue fashion I finally got around to admitting I had reacted poorly.

Just a Few Words Can Make All the Difference

In so many dialogues between Pink and Blue, the Crazy Cycle may threaten to start up, but it can be stopped with just a few words that make all the difference. Sarah and I have observed that our conversations are like a dance. We wish to waltz effortlessly, but too often we step on each other's toes. Fortunately, a humble "I'm sorry" can keep the Crazy Cycle from spinning.[2]

As we worked on this chapter, Sarah reminded me of other "blue" conversations I have had when I "forgot what is really important." I have a friend who has a son serving in Iraq, and we talk on the phone quite often about business matters. When Sarah hears I have talked to Kevin, she always asks, "Did you ask Kevin how Jacob is doing?" Somehow my answer is always the same: "No."

Just tonight we went through the same routine, and Sarah added, "I will bet Kevin doesn't bring it up either, does he?" I sort of grinned sheepishly and replied, "No, I guess he doesn't."

I could relate many other examples of how Pink has one thing on her mind and Blue has another. The following story is representative of the kind I hear all the time. Michael and Tom, who work together as mechanical engineers and are the best of friends, went on a three-day hunting trip. When they returned to their homes, Tom's conversation with his wife, Dawn, went something like this:

"How was your time with Michael?"

"Good."

"What did you talk about?"

"Well, we mostly hunted. . . . We did talk some about the infant incubator we're designing. It could save the lives of hundreds of kids each year."

"You mean you were out there for three days together and you never once talked about how Katelyn is feeling since becoming pregnant? It's her first child. I can't believe at least one of you didn't bring it up."

To which Tom responded blankly, "Is Katelyn pregnant?"

I will spare you details about what Dawn said next, but it had to do with how uncaring, insensitive, and unloving Tom was for not once asking Michael how his pregnant wife was doing. Nor will I share how Tom came back at Dawn, wondering how she could be so judgmental because his conversations with his hunting buddy did not touch on pregnancies. Husbands like Tom write to tell me of such incidents—how it puts them on the Crazy Cycle for a couple of days—and ask me, "What is the best way to avoid similar situations?" When I write back, the first thing I point out is that a major reason for conversations like these is because of the way God made male and female. The Lord made Pink and Blue with differences, and He expects us to recognize and deal with those differences in a loving and respectful way.

> *Warning to married couples: "If you keep on biting and devouring each other, watch out or you will be destroyed by each other" (Galatians 5:15 NIV).*

In the Beginning, God Created Them Pink and Blue

References to the differences between men and women are found throughout Scripture. In an encounter with the Pharisees, Jesus reminded them of the first major difference: "Have you not read that He who created them from the beginning made them male and female?" (Matthew 19:4). Jesus was quoting Genesis 1:27—"And God created man in His own image . . . male and female He created them." It is no coincidence that the first chapter of the Bible quickly establishes that God created male and female or that the second chapter of Genesis elaborates on His creation as He places Adam in the Garden, with orders to "cultivate and keep it." Then, noting it is not good for Adam to be alone, God creates a woman to join him and be his helper.

All goes well in Paradise until sin enters, and then everything is changed. Adam is "cursed in the field," as are all men who follow. He is destined to work, sweat, and struggle, and the field will never be what he hopes (see Genesis 3:17–19). Nonetheless, just as God made Adam to work, most men identify themselves in relationship to their "field," their occupation. Tom and Michael, the two hunters, readily talked about what they were doing to save the lives of tiny babies, but they did not discuss Michael's wife and her pregnancy. In fact, Tom didn't even know about it!

On the other hand, God creates Eve to give birth, but after the Fall, she is "cursed in the family." She and all women to follow will have pain in childbirth and tension with her husband. The family will never be what she hopes. Even so, most women identify themselves in relationship to their families. World-renowned radio talk-show hostess Dr. Laura Schlessinger identifies herself daily on the air with "I am my kid's mom," and she sells thousands of T-shirts with this slogan.

So the differences between men and women were established from the beginning. Women tend to be relationship oriented, and the family is their primary place for relationships. The deepest question you can ask a woman—a question she asks herself quite often—is "Are you loved?"

Men, however, tend to be achievement-oriented, and their "field" is the primary place for achievement. The deepest question you can ask a man—a question that he asks himself quite often—is "Are you respected?" No wonder, then, that in a marriage Pink wants Blue to be more loving, and Blue wants Pink to be more respectful.

Again, these generalizations help us understand each other. I do not want to box someone in or shame anyone. After all, my whole life is focused on helping improve relationships. I lean toward the family side of things—and my mother worked full-time! Yet I can hear Mom say, "I agree with what you are saying about us as women." I am trying to create mutual understanding between the sexes, not further a battle between us!

With these fundamental foundational differences established in the early chapters of Genesis, Scripture records many other examples of how Pink and Blue are different and even how they should be treated differently. For instance 1 Peter 3:7 says, "You husbands, in the same way live with your wives in an understanding way, as with someone weaker, *since she is a woman*" (italics mine). That phrase *someone weaker* is translated "weaker vessel" in the King James, but Peter is not saying a woman is inferior or unequal to a man in God's sight. In fact, the rest of 1 Peter 3:7 clearly says she is to be granted honor "as a fellow heir of the grace of life."

As I explained in *Love & Respect*,[3] Peter is speaking of a woman's vulnerability to her husband in marriage. She is like a delicate porcelain bowl, not a cast-iron pot, and I believe God has placed a sign on that porcelain bowl for all husbands to read: "Handle with Care."

And then there is the matter of childbearing. As Jeremiah points out, seemingly tongue in cheek: "Ask now, and see if a male can give birth" (Jeremiah 30:6). And when Paul wants to remind the church at Thessalonica of how compassionately he, Silas, and Timothy cared for new converts, he compares their efforts to the nurture of a mother when he says,

"We proved to be gentle among you, as a nursing mother tenderly cares for her own children" (1 Thessalonians 2:7). In females we see the nature to nurture: it is instinctive, created by God.

Male traits are also described in many places in Scripture. For example, while Paul could say he tried to imitate the nurturing nature of a mother to make one point, he could also switch gears and use a male analogy to make another. As Paul closes his first letter to the Corinthians, for instance, he urges them to "stand firm in the faith, act like men, be strong" (16:13). (By the way, women are called to emulate certain male virtues, but women can never be men any more than men can be women. Women do not have a "masculine side" any more than men have a "feminine side." We are created male and female. However, we can appreciate each other's virtues and mirror the finer qualities.)

When Nehemiah sought to rally the troops to defend the wall they were rebuilding, he gave a speech that included the line "fight for your brothers, your sons, your daughters, your wives and your houses" (4:14). Nowhere in Scripture does anyone command wives to fight for their husbands.

I do not cite the above verses to suggest that men cannot nurture. Obviously, Paul did nurture the new churches he started throughout Asia and Europe. Nor am I saying women can't be combative defenders of their homes. A good biblical illustration of this is Jael, the wife of Heber the Kenite, who did in Sisera, general of the Canaanite army, with a tent peg (Judges 5:24–27). And we should not forget Deborah, a female judge of Israel who was instrumental in helping defeat Sisera's army (see Judges 4–5).[4]

However, simple observation tells us a woman has a body that can nurture a child. Her nature equips her to nurture. A husband doesn't dream about nursing a baby. His nature equips him to dream of doing other things. For example, squeeze the typical man's arm, and he will flex. Something inside of him compels him to want to demonstrate that he is strong. And that same nature compels him to want to protect his wife. Squeeze the typical woman's arm, however, and she will not flex. She might say, "Ouch," but she has no built-in need to show you how hard she is.

Vive La Différence!

Truly, husbands and wives are as different as pink and blue; nonetheless, especially in our present-day culture, it is easy to overlook or discount these differences. In recent years, the feminist movement has emphasized the equality of the sexes—and rightly so—but, in so doing, often tried to claim that because we are equal, we are the same. Obviously, I disagree. Sarah and I are equal in value, but Sarah and I are *not* identical—and vive la différence!

Scripture is very clear that God views us as equal: "there is neither male or female; for you are all one in Christ Jesus" (Galatians 3:28). But this verse does not do away with gender differences. Anatomy alone proves that. But what this verse does say is that, in the eyes of God, *we are equal in value.*

> *Not wrong, just different because "He created them male and female" (Genesis 5:2).*

Have you ever thought about how basic biology and anatomy affect the mind, will, and emotions? These three components combine to become what is called a person's "soul." We can quibble over what exactly is the soul, but in my opinion, mind, will, and emotions certainly have plenty to do with it. The question before us, then, is "Because of different biology and anatomy, do men and women think differently, prefer differently, and feel differently in their very souls?" Research and experience tell me the answer is a resounding "Yes!" The male's body affects his soul; the female's body affects hers. Two graphic, if possibly a bit disturbing, examples that keep popping up in the e-mail and other correspondence that pours into my office daily are the male's visual attraction to the female, which often results in sexual temptation, and the female's natural menstrual cycle, which often results in PMS (premenstrual syndrome). I am not equating these two examples but offering them as illustrations of how gender issues affect the soul.

Pornography Is Basically a Male Problem

Men are sexually stimulated by what they see, and there is no disputing the fact that the male's visual orientation impacts his thoughts, preferences, and feelings. Anyone who has been part of a candid discussion in a men's group knows this to be true. For further proof, consider the pornography industry. Males view pornography disproportionately more often than do females. In fact, females involved in the porn industry are there for the money, not the sex. I have received hundreds of e-mails and letters from wives who have husbands struggling with pornography.

A female therapist writes:

> My ex-husband basically was living a double life: the one I saw (good Christian man) and the other that surfaced during our marriage, revealing a secret life steeped in Internet pornography . . . There came a point where his choices were so hurtful and destructive to me that I filed for divorce. He chose his "right" to view and masturbate to pornography (which by the way became the only "sex life" going on in our marriage) over working on our relationship. . . . Unfortunately, Internet pornography becomes more prevalent with men (and therefore for women) every day. I see it in my practice on a daily basis with men in all walks of life, from pastors to truck drivers.

> *To steer clear of mental adultery, "don't lustfully fantasize on her beauty, nor be taken by her bedroom eyes" (Proverbs 6:25 MSG).*

A husband's e-mail said:

> I have not committed adultery in the physical sense, but I have in the spiritual and emotional sense. I have viewed pornography on the Internet for most of the last six years. More destructively, I have spent time on a free dating site, advertising for a mis-

tress, and while borrowing my computer to do a paper, my college freshman step-daughter discovered it.

This man's sexual vulnerability tempted him into pornography, which has further resulted in a breakdown in his family, and his wife no longer trusts him.[5] Viewing pornography not only destroys marriage, but these "fleshly lusts [that] wage war against the soul" of the husband also render him ineffective for Christ (1 Peter 2:11).

How the Pain of PMS Affects Her Soul

Premenstrual syndrome is a well-documented reality for many women. If ever a woman's physiology can affect her soul (mind, will, and emotions), it is during those days just before her monthly period. As many a husband knows, during PMS a woman can have extremely negative thoughts and feelings (i.e., outbursts of anger that seem to come from nowhere) as well as strong preferences that certain things be done right now. For some people, Christian as well as non-Christian, PMS is a touchy subject, due mostly to residual feminist thinking from the seventies and eighties, which is quick to condemn any mention of a difference between men and women that might make a female look weaker and thus inferior to a male.

But when viewed through the lens of Love and Respect, PMS is only a God-given difference between male and female that is to be understood and treated with understanding. Granted, as many husbands have shared with me, this is not always a piece of cake. When in the throes of PMS, a wife can explode in raging anger at her husband. He *never* does anything right and is *always* doing everything wrong! Most of the husbands I have talked with tell me that, during these times, the best approach is just be quiet and wait out the storm. They have learned the hard way *not* to say, "Just relax. You are having a PMS moment." This kind of remark does little or no good. Because she is so upset about the injustice she is suffering, she will quite probably deny that PMS is the cause of her irritations and frustrations. She knows what she knows, and she just knows that if *he* would just change his behavior, their marriage would be far better—and furthermore she is *sick and tired of him putting the blame on her!* The following letter vividly portrays how PMS can put a couple on the Crazy Cycle:

> I have the most wonderful, loving, and respectful wife that God could ever give a man, but . . . during those one or two days a month when the blackness was upon her, she would become a completely different person. I almost wondered whether she might literally be possessed by a demon. At those times, she'd become absolutely enraged and would spew out verbal venom or bitter contempt upon me. In my head, I knew this was simply a hormonal imbalance causing this, and that this was not really my loving wife. But by this time she knew the right buttons to push . . . and she could succeed in making me utterly miserable. Sometimes I couldn't keep from lashing out in return, which I realized was *really* counterproductive.

My heart goes out to the many wives who suffer PMS and write me e-mails like this: "I feel the worst when I am PMSing, but also struggle at other times. I HATE it because it only serves to put distance between us, rather than drawing us together. I need HELP with this."

> *Never justify sin, saying, "It's just the way I am." Acts of the sinful nature include "enmities, strife . . . outbursts of anger . . . and things like these" (Galatians 5:19–21).*

As women age, they can look back and see the PMS pattern for themselves, particularly if they have recorded their monthly cycle on a calendar. It is doubtful that Paul had PMS in mind when he advised younger women to get together with older women to receive advice and encouragement (see Titus 2:3–5), but it is not a bad idea. Older women have come to realize that their hormone-induced negativity and lack of friendliness in the home do not get through to a male—or anyone else for that matter.

Letters from Pink and Blue Confirm the Difference

I have referred to pornography and PMS not to demean either sex, nor to suggest PMS is equal to pornographic addiction, but to only point out that, while we are equally valuable in God's sight, we are not the same. We are not identical. The bodies, thinking, preferences, and feelings of males and females can be vastly different. The struggles of the soul and the things that affect our souls vary. But that does not mean husbands and wives cannot live in harmony. We get a continual flow of mail that confirms male and female differences and how things improve when Pink and Blue recognize these differences and handle them with Love and Respect.

The following excerpts are just a few examples from the hundreds of letters we receive from men and women who have learned that they can extend empathy and understanding to their spouses even though the challenges are real. Husbands can understand that their wives are not wrong for being women; they're just different when it comes to the trials that impact their female souls. Wives can understand that their husbands are not wrong for being men; they're just different in the temptations that affect their male souls.

A *wife*: "Your seminar increased my husband's understanding of me and acceptance of me. (I knew I was a typical woman because I talk to my friends, and they are just like me; however, women don't act like me at his work, so he thought I was different in a bad way.) Likewise, your principles about men increased my understanding of my husband and his needs, making me more appreciative and empathic rather than judgmental. These attitude changers affected our communication . . . I have learned to 'go silent' in respect when my husband hurts my feelings, understanding that most of the time it is unintentional. Likewise, he has increased his effort to talk through issues with me, rather than 'go silent' to avoid conflict. Our relationship is much more peaceful and slowly moving toward intimacy again."

A husband: "While reading your book, I took every opportunity to have face-to-face conversation with her. I am learning to be a better listener, giving her attention and sympathy rather than 'fixing' her problem. I went out to eat with her last night willingly and then helped shop for groceries. It makes a difference when I do these things cheerfully. I intend to do all the little things that will express love by actions rather than just words."

A wife: "We have been married for almost twenty-one years and have drifted apart. All that you have to say about the different ways that men and women hear and see things is SO right. A lot of the statements that he has made to me over the years that didn't make any sense are starting to make sense now. And of course I am now seeing why he didn't understand all the times I have tried to reach out to him."

A husband: "For years I carried frustration over an inability to 'touch' what I was feeling. I would invariably come across to my wife as insensitive in some areas, when quite honestly I wasn't trying to be . . . I just didn't think of things the same way and quite naturally put a different priority on things. It's liberating to understand I'm simply being blue, not bad. But it's also empowering to know how to bless my pink wife in my quest to live as a man of honor."

As we get feedback from couples who have attended a conference or who have read *Love & Respect,* one of the concepts that is often considered more important than anything else we say is that men and women are:

NOT WRONG, JUST DIFFERENT[6]

As obvious as this is to most of us, there is always someone who misses the point. One wife wrote to relate how her husband told her, "Well, I am blue and you are pink, so get over it. I am not supposed to understand you." Obviously, he hadn't "gotten it," but fortunately his wife had, and although she was hurt by his ultrablue comment, she replied: "Well, honey, what I got out of Emerson's teaching was that, yes, you are blue and I am pink, but that means that I need to work real hard to think outside my pink box and try to understand blue, not that I should just discount you because you are blue."

To this wife I say, "Great answer!" She shared the truth of the Pink and Blue analogy by applying it to her own need to look outside her pink box, but she showed him respect by letting him draw his own application concerning his need to look outside his blue box.

In Part III, we will be looking more closely at how being aware of Pink and Blue perspectives can be invaluable to husbands and wives who are seeking mutual understanding and the ability to communicate better. For now, however, use the key point from this chapter to look at your mate with new eyes. If you want to understand your spouse better; if you want to communicate more effectively, hold firm to this fact: neither of you is wrong. You are just very different—as different as Pink and Blue.

CHAPTER FOUR

Can You Trust Your Spouse's Goodwill?

(Can Your Spouse Trust Yours?)

So far we have covered two vital truths that can help the Love and Respect couple develop mutual understanding and good communication:

1. *The mouth matters.* What comes out of the mouth depends on what is in the heart. Unconditional commitment to living out Love and Respect—through your words as well as your actions—is vital.

2. *Husbands and wives are not wrong, just very different*—as different as pink and blue, as different as her need for love and his need for respect.

The third vital truth focuses on another simple but crucial concept: both of you must see each other as goodwilled persons. When one or both of you see the other as goodwilled, good things are in store for your marriage!

What Does It Mean to Have Goodwill?

"But what," I am often asked, "is goodwill? And how do I know I am showing goodwill toward my spouse? How can I be sure my spouse has goodwill toward me?"

A simple definition of goodwill is "the intention to do good toward the other person." But there is much more to it than that. A spouse may *intend* to do good, but fail to deliver. Good intentions do not necessarily guarantee good results.

As Jesus said to His disciples when they went to sleep on the job in the Garden of Gethsemane, "the spirit is willing, but the flesh is weak" (Matthew 26:41). Jesus knew His disciples had goodwill toward Him even though their follow-through didn't match their good intentions.

The apostle Paul captured the reality of good intentions but poor follow-through when he wrote about his own struggles with the flesh in Romans 7:19: "I don't do the good things I want to do. I keep on doing the evil things I don't want to do" (NIRV).

We all know what Paul is talking about. You or your spouse may want to do the right thing, but you don't; or you or your spouse may want to stop doing the wrong things, but you don't. When your spouse fails to follow through on good intentions, your definition of goodwill must also include the idea that goodwilled people do not mean any harm; they do not intend real evil toward one another. Your spouse may be neglectful, forgetful, or make a careless, even thoughtless remark. As a result, you may be hurt or angry and may lash out in some way to retaliate. But despite all these failings, deep down you both care for each other. Beneath the turmoil on the surface of what is going on, your goodwill remains intact.

How Does Goodwill Square with Total Depravity?

Wherever I teach about goodwill, I am asked, "How do you reconcile the concept of goodwill with the total depravity of the human heart?" Some people go so far as to say, "We can't really have goodwill because we are so sinful," and they usually quote Jeremiah 17:9 to prove their point: "The heart is deceitful and desperately wicked. Who can know it?" (KJV). I believe what Jeremiah teaches, but I also believe what Jesus teaches: "The seed in the good soil, these are the ones who have heard the word in an honest and *good heart*, and hold it fast, and bear fruit with perseverance" (Luke 8:15, italics mine).

The obvious question, then, is "If the heart is 'deceitful and desperately wicked,' how can a person have an 'honest and good heart' at the same time?" The answer is that we have two dimensions: the side created in the image of God and the fallen side corrupted by sin. As I just mentioned, when Jesus said, "The spirit is willing but the flesh is weak," I understand this to mean we have a spiritual side that longs to do what is good, based on the moral law implanted in us by God, but we have a carnal side that pulls us into sin. This is precisely Paul's point in Romans 7, which I cited above. Paul knew he had been freed from the penalty of sin and had the promise of eternal life (see Romans 6:22–23). As a Christian he did many good works and served Christ tirelessly, but he wrestled with his inability to obey all of God's law and live a completely sanctified life (see Romans 7:1–21).[1]

All of us recognize Paul's plight, for it is ours as well. We are goodwilled people—or at least want to be—but sin still holds us in its grip. This is why, even though we have goodwill toward our mate, we can still sin against our mate in all kinds of ways. So, my counsel to married couples who are serious about practicing Love and Respect is always the same: whenever your spouse's good intentions fail to produce loving or respectful actions toward you, you have only one good option, and that is to make a deliberate choice to trust your spouse's goodwill. For example:

> When there are slipups and conflicts, trust each other's goodwill because "you don't always do what you intend to do" (Galatians 5:17 GW).

You have to leave very early in the

morning, and you haven't had time to fill the car with gas. Your spouse promises to go out and take care of it while you do some last-minute packing and reports. The next day, as you are rushing to leave, you find the gauge on "Empty," and you feel a surge of anger. In the next few moments, you can choose to believe your spouse "just doesn't care" and has ill will toward you, or you can choose to believe your spouse made an honest mistake because you know she (or he) does not normally neglect a known need.

Choices to believe in your spouse's goodwill when he or she forgets or gets distracted are relatively easy to make. But what about those times when your spouse does something that is consciously nasty or maybe even a little hateful (perhaps to "teach you a lesson")? To stay with the didn't-fill-the-tank example, suppose you had come home late for dinner, hadn't called, and then forgot to pick up what he or she wanted at the store? Perhaps your spouse is so angry they decide to let your gas tank go unfilled as payback for your careless behavior.

I have heard of all kinds of payback couples pull on each other, particularly if they are on the Crazy Cycle to any degree. One couple had a spat, and both were so angry they hadn't spoken to each other all day or evening. Before going to bed he wrote her a note and left it on her pillow: "If I don't hear the alarm, please wake me up at 5:30 a.m. since you get up at 5:00. I have an important breakfast meeting." At 7:00 the next morning, he finally woke up and was in disbelief. His wife had not awakened him! As he angrily rolled out of bed, he noticed her note on the nightstand: "Wake up! It's 5:30 a.m."

Almost all married couples have encounters that lead to reactions designed to send the message "You hurt me, so I am going to hurt you so you will stop hurting me!" Does this sort of encounter mean that one or both of you lack basic goodwill toward the other? Of course not. Your angry spouse might temporarily not wish you well, but these exceptions don't do away with the rule, and the rule says, "I will choose to believe in my spouse's goodwill when he or she does me wrong, whether it is unintentional or intentional."

Along with his Romans 7 confession of not being able to always do what he wants and not do what he doesn't want, Paul also teaches that, despite our weaknesses, goodwill is a reality. Following through on our good intentions is possible when we seek to do God's will from our hearts and "with good will render service, as to the Lord, and not to men" (Ephesians 6:7).[2]

Can Goodwill Be Overlooked?

As I got more involved in doing marriage counseling, I was amazed at how even Christian couples would rail and scream at one another. It appeared they were not at all interested in serving each other with goodwill. I would sometimes despair, wondering, "Don't these people care about each other *at all*?" But I kept at it, searching the Bible for something that could help husbands and wives, and then I came across 1 Corinthians 7:32–34:

> One who is unmarried is concerned about the things of the Lord . . . but one who is married is concerned about . . . how he may please his wife . . . And the woman who is unmarried . . . is concerned about the things of the Lord . . . but one who is married is concerned about . . . how she may please her husband.

I had read this passage any number of times before, but now I saw something that encouraged me. Even though Paul had the gift of celibacy[3] and preferred that believers stay unmarried so they could concentrate on serving the Lord, I noted that 1 Corinthians 7:32–34 plainly says that husbands and wives are concerned about how to please each other. Certainly, I reasoned, this suggests they have goodwill toward one another—or should have.

I began questioning the couples I was trying to help with their marriage problems. "Does your spouse have basic goodwill?" I asked. "That is, although your spouse fails you at times, does your spouse, generally speaking, intend to do you good?"

I was not just surprised, but I was a bit awed when most answered yes almost immediately.

I thought to myself, "Emerson, you are onto something significant." And then I followed up with the couples who had seemed hesitant to answer when I asked if their spouses had basic goodwill. Rephrasing my question, I said, "Let me put it this way: In general, is your spouse getting up in the morning with the purpose of trying to displease you or show you a lack of concern? Is your spouse intending to be unloving or disrespectful?"

Most of those who initially hesitated at my original question volunteered, "No, I don't think my spouse plots to do evil, but I wish my spouse *would* plan on being more loving or respectful."

"I agree with you," I would respond, "but that's another matter. I just want to be sure you don't believe your spouse is premeditating evil or ill will?"

For the most part, the hesitant couples answered, "No, I wouldn't be so strong as to say my spouse is premeditating evil."

"So," I pressed, "even though on occasion your spouse can be nasty or selfish, you are married to a person who has basic goodwill toward you?" Almost all the couples answered the same: "Yes."

> *Even in the bad moments, trust your spouse's goodwill because love and respect "keep no record of wrongs" (1 Corinthians 13:5 NIV).*

Can a Mate Choose the Dark Side?

While I was greatly encouraged by most of my counselees saying their spouses had basic goodwill, I also had to recognize that a small percentage were saying that their spouses were acting so badly on a consistent basis that they did indeed believe their spouses held evil will toward them. Even more to the point, Scripture clearly attests that we live in a fallen world in which some people choose the dark side. There are evil-willed people, yes, even toward God. In Psalm 21:11, for instance, David exults in how God's strength will overcome the enemy: "Though they intended evil against You and devised a plot, they will not succeed" (Psalm 21:11). In Psalm 36:4, David describes the wicked person like this: "Even as he lies in bed he makes evil plans. He commits himself to a sinful way of life. He never says no to what is wrong" (NIRV). Proverbs also speaks of evil people and their premeditations: "One who plans to do evil, men will call a schemer" (24:8), and, still worse, "Evil plans are an abomination to the Lord" (15:26).

Scripture also points to how evil can destroy a marriage. A husband can love his mate, but deep within her soul she turns her heart against what is good. She becomes an adulterous, wayward wife with seductive words "who has left the partner of her youth and ignored the covenant she made before God" (see Proverbs 2:16–17). And in Malachi 2:13–14, the prophet tells wayward men that God no longer honors their offerings and instead is "acting as the witness between you and the wife of your youth, because you have broken faith with her, though she is your partner, the wife of your marriage covenant" (NIV).

I get a lot of mail from spouses who have been the victims of evil treatment by their partners. These partners made a decision to no longer act in goodwill. Following are some representative samples:

One husband I knew committed adultery twice in one year and then divorced his wife, saying to me, "She gave 110 percent to this marriage, but I want out." This man set his heart on his own course and was very candid with me about realizing he was the culprit. He knew he was not doing good toward his wife; he was well aware that he was deliberately crushing her.

—————

A wife I knew would go out at night, leaving the children in her husband's care. She did this for years, being vague about where she went and whom she was with. She wanted no close relationship with her husband, a goodwilled servant of Christ and others, an outstanding provider, and an all-around nice guy. The marriage finally ended.

Another wife would fabricate story after story, lying about her husband even in court. Her goal was to ruin her husband. Fortunately a female judge discerned this woman's evil intentions, reversed all of her rulings, and ruled in favor of the husband.

I could go on and on. The point is, there do seem to be spouses who do evil-willed things to their mates on a continuing basis. As you read these lines, you may be a victim of your spouse's evil will. I do not know your situation, so I have no way of knowing if you are totally accurate in your assessment and if your spouse does indeed have an evil will toward you. What I do know, however, is that it is a serious thing to make the severe judgment that someone is completely evil willed. (For help with what to do when your spouse seems almost totally lacking in goodwill, see Part V—"The Rewarded Cycle: The Unconditional Dimension of Communication.")

> *Sadly, not all spouses have goodwill. Jesus said, "A man's enemies will be the members of his household" (Matthew 10:36).*

Let me ask two sobering questions: 1. If a wife, looking for love in all the wrong places, commits adultery, is she evil willed? I go on record to say she has committed an evil act but is not necessarily evil willed. 2. If a husband, feeling verbally assaulted and abused by his wife, shoves her up against the wall, is he evil willed? Again, I say he has committed an evil act, but he is not necessarily evil willed.

My Own Father Appeared to Have Evil Will

I would like to tell you a very personal story. I can recall instances from my early childhood when my dad would go into a rage. On one occasion my mother had purchased several pieces of new furniture and had it delivered to the house. Dad was furious over how she had spent the money, and he threw out all the furniture. I can still see in my mind one of the pieces tumbling down the stairs to the sidewalk. I was petrified by my dad's temper, and there were other explosions that were even worse.

After Dad died, I shared with my mother another memory of something that happened when I was around three years old. It comes to me in scenes, and in the first scene my mom and dad are having some kind of argument. In the next scene my father is strangling my mother! He has her up against the refrigerator with his hands around her throat, and he is choking her. I run to help and hit my dad with my little fists, trying to make him stop. He just slaps the top of my head and pushes me out of the way. In the final scene, my mother is sitting on a brick wall somewhere outside, and she is crying. A neighbor lady is talking to my mom through her window, asking, "Jay, are you all right?" Then the horrific episode fades from my mind.

When I told my mother my recollection of what happened, she was in shock. Her face displayed utter dismay: "You remember this? You were *too young* to remember this. I can't believe you remember this!" But I did.

My father's violent fits of temper finally became too much, and he and Mom separated and later divorced. Mom, my sister, and I moved to a different address, and for the next three years, my father would come over practically every day for lunch to see us. As I shared in *Love & Respect,* my parents finally did get back together, and Mom was instrumental in Dad coming to Christ.

I feel free to share their story now that they are both with the Lord in heaven, but I do not do so to shame my father. My mother never minimized his actions. She never went into denial, saying he didn't know what he was doing. At the same time—despite the painful, unnerving episodes that stick in my mind—neither my mother nor I, young as I was, ever concluded that Dad was evil willed. We chose to believe that, while Dad had committed evil acts, he was not evil willed.

Look at Your Spouse as Jesus Would

I don't know your situation or the right decisions for you to make in your marriage. But I urge everyone I counsel to take the same view of their spouse that Jesus would. In a vast majority of cases, I predict that the Lord would say about your spouse, "The spirit is willing, but the flesh is weak." Always try to look at your spouse the way the Lord does. That begins by making sure you are fairly representing your spouse's spirit. If at all possible, put it in Paul's terms from Romans 7: "My spouse wants to do good, but often ends up doing the very thing he/she does not want to do." In a word, give your spouse some grace.

One way to look at your spouse as the Lord does is to distinguish between snapshots of your spouse and a video of your spouse's entire life. Perhaps you are fixated on isolated moments (snapshots) and conclude that these represent the true spirit of your spouse. If so, you need to take a step back and ask, "Are these snapshots a fair representation of my spouse's heart? Is this how the Lord sees my mate?" My point is this: suppose I were to live with you for a week and take several unobserved snapshots of you during moments of frustration or anger. And suppose I then put these pictures on the front page of the newspaper, claiming that they are a true representation of the kind of person you really are. Obviously, I could be sued for libel or slander.

Nonetheless I constantly receive mail from frustrated and angry spouses who condemn their mates because of snapshots taken in their minds that "prove" their case. They call them everything from "demon possessed" to "a tool of the devil." Whenever I get a chance to interact with someone who is in this state of mind, I often remind this person that there are two sides to the story. "Your spouse has indeed erred, but this does not represent your mate's deepest soul."

As Sarah and I conduct Love and Respect Conferences and counsel couples across America, we often see that people can pass too severe a judgment on their spouses, convincing themselves they are married to Hitler's distant cousin. But we must never label a Peter as a Judas even though on a certain occasion Peter did act like Judas. As you recall, Judas betrayed Jesus into the hands of His enemies. Since that fateful act, Judas has been seen as one of the most sinister traitors in all history. But Peter was also a traitor, denying three times that he knew his Lord, just as Jesus said he would. (For an account of both acts of treachery, see Matthew 26.) Everyone knows, however, there is a 180-degree difference between the spirit of Peter and the spirit of Judas. Full of remorse but not repentance, Judas committed suicide (see Matthew 27:1–5). Peter matched his remorse with repentance and was restored to fellowship with his Lord (John 21).

> "Don't get ahead of the Master and jump to conclusions with your judgments before all the evidence is in. When he comes, he will bring out in the open and place in evidence all kinds of things we never even dreamed of—inner motives and purposes and prayers. Only then will any one of us get to hear the 'Well done!' of God" (1 Corinthians 4:5 MSG).

Evil Acts Do Not Always Equal Evil Will

To repeat, when a spouse fails to do good and instead does bad, this act—or even series of actions—does not necessarily mean the spouse lacks goodwill. A spouse's evil act (anything from thoughtless, harsh, or cruel words to committing adultery) can put a couple on the Crazy Cycle. When your spouse gets mean or nasty, it is easy to label him or her evil willed. Granted, you may not use the term *evil will,* but at the moment you are certainly not experiencing your spouse's goodwill, and your natural inclination is to react unlovingly or disrespectfully. But if you are trying to live out Love and Respect, your spouse's temporary feistiness, nastiness, or selfishness must be distinguished from evil character.

All of us get crabby, snappy, or needy. Sarah and I do, but when Sarah is hurt by something I have done or said and she reacts in a disrespectful way that offends me, should I conclude that Sarah lacks goodwill? Or when Sarah angers or irritates me and I react in an unloving manner, should she conclude that I have ill will? The right answer is "No, of course not." But it is not always easy to come up with this right answer when we're stung or irritated, tired or impatient. After all, I have certain expectations of how Sarah should treat me, and she has expectations of how I am to treat her. When either of us fails to meet those expectations in the daily flow of life, it is tempting to play the character assassination game with each other.

> *As you make judgments about your mate, can you honestly say, "Everything I say is fair, and there is nothing twisted or crooked in it" (Proverbs 8:8 GW)?*

Suppose the irony of ironies might happen and I, "Mr. Love and Respect," forgot to show my love for Sarah by failing to give her a card on Valentine's Day. She might have a momentary thought that I am an unloving hypocrite, but that would be overkill. Or, to reverse the irony, suppose that Sarah, who teaches her own session at our Love and Respect Conferences, forgot to show me respect and made a negative remark about me in front of our children that left me feeling totally let down. I could easily conclude she is a disrespectful phony, but that, too, would be overkill. In either case we would both be like the farmer who saw a fly on his kitchen wall and killed it with his shotgun. He took care of the fly, but he was left with a huge hole in his wall. In much the same way, we could put holes in our relationship by overreacting when we fail to meet each other's expectations.

Sarah and I are like every other married couple. When the tension rises, when the Crazy Cycle threatens to cough into life, we need to remember when we first met and fell in love. We did not say, "I hate you and you hate me, so let's get married." The same person each of us met and married is still there, even though, *at the moment*, it doesn't seem that way.

How Being on the Crazy Cycle Can Be Your Opportunity

If you are trying to live with Love and Respect, being on the Crazy Cycle to any degree gives you a great opportunity to try to see the goodwill in each other. For a husband, being on the Crazy Cycle reminds him that when his wife feels unloved, she reacts in ways that he feels are disrespectful. He could conclude she has ill will toward him, but he would do much better to realize that the Crazy Cycle has started to turn and that she does not intend to be disrespectful; what she is really doing is crying out for love. As one husband put it:

> I used to just get mad when I felt that Yvonne was criticizing me, but now I might ask her what did I do that was so unloving to provoke such a reaction on her part . . . We have been married for almost twenty-eight years, and things do get better. I try to always think that she is goodwilled and only trying to help me with her "suggestions."

For a wife who is coping with the Crazy Cycle, trusting in her husband's goodwill can help her be slow to feel offended. Although her husband might say something that feels unloving to her, that may not be his intent at all; he may simply be reacting to something in his typically blue fashion. One wife explains:

> One day he said one of those things that cause women to say, "I can't believe he said *that!*" But instead of being instantly offended

and stewing over it for days, I thought of our friendship, which is tried and true, and I remembered your words, "Trust his goodwill." So rather than seething over it, I calmly asked him what he was thinking when he said it. I let him know that I wanted to understand. I let him know how I heard it as well. He clarified and, sure enough, I had heard his blue thoughts through my pink hearing aids. I was thrilled to see how this practice opened communication between us. It deepened my belief that I can talk about my feelings and get clarification without being afraid of the other person's response.

Choosing to believe in your spouse's goodwill can and does work! Successful marriages experience those Crazy Cycle moments that feel offensive, but one spouse or both can choose to trust that the other has goodwill. One husband put it succinctly: "We still have issues where we get on the Crazy Cycle, but then I stop and realize how petty we're being. We're both goodwilled. I think I forget that too often."

A wife reports:

> My husband and I have learned to communicate more effectively. Thinking about the pink and blue hearing aids helps me not to get my feelings hurt so readily by something Mark says. As you say, most men are coming at whatever situation we are in with the intention of goodwill, so trying to understand what he is truly trying to say can eliminate a lot of unnecessary hurt.

You are not foolish to trust your spouse's goodwill because love "always trusts, always hopes, always perseveres" (1 Corinthians 13:7 NIV).

These folks "get it." They epitomize the wisdom in Proverbs 14:9—"Fools mock at making amends for sin, but good will is found among the upright" (NIV). So often, when communication misfires, someone must step up and try to make amends—to listen, try to understand, and reach out. Either spouse can step up when both trust each other's goodwill. It is foolish not to; it is "upright" to do so.

I could quote many more testimonies on how the goodwill principle works wonders in a marriage. Ever since I began teaching the importance of believing in the goodwill of your mate, even when unloving or disrespectful things happen, I have been overjoyed at the responses that keep coming in. One man wrote to say *Love & Respect* solved the root problem in his marriage:

> The foundational truth that each of us does not mean ill will toward each other, but rather goodwill was HUGE. We have nipped many a miscommunication in the bud before it got a chance to go into the "bank of unresolved resentful issues" that can later try to rear its ugly head to bite one of us in the fanny. We have had a richness and freshness added back to our marriage.

Building Mutual Understanding

As we close this section on vital truths for better communication, be aware of how these three truths we have discussed work together to help you and your spouse build mutual understanding.

First, your mouth matters, and what comes out of your mouth depends on a heart committed to living out Love and Respect in your marriage. Second, neither of you is wrong. You are just different from each other. Your pink and blue perspectives shade and influence every communication that passes between you. And, third, each of you must see the other as a goodwilled person even when—*especially* when—the Crazy Cycle starts to spin.

I often hear from a wife who feels her marriage is utterly hopeless and that her husband lacks goodwill. She draws this conclusion because he reacts in ways that she would not—and if she reacted in such a fashion, it would mean that she lacks goodwill and is cruel. One woman wrote:

I felt so hopeless as a couple—especially a Christian, born-again couple. He was frozen, and it had always been that way. I would either get a stonewall or intense anger and threats. Our relationship felt abusive—and we were Christian leaders! In despair I asked him if I could read part of *Love & Respect* to him. He agreed and lights have been going on ever since! My husband kept saying, "That's me!" He even wanted to kiss the author of the book. This, from an Asian man, is almost unheard of. We are just beginning our journey of vulnerability and intimacy. We have so far to go, but I feel hope now! This is an incredible miracle!

I replied to this woman along these lines:

God made us male and female, not wrong, just different. Scripture tells us we have basic goodwill because neither of us intends to displease the other (1 Corinthians 7:3—34). We simply have different needs, and this is where the challenge arises! Once we break through to the truth—that she isn't trying to be disrespectful and he isn't trying to be unloving—bingo!

I realize that some couples will shout "Bingo!" sooner than others. Unfortunately, many couples struggle on the Crazy Cycle because they have labeled each other as being without goodwill. She sees him as unloving, and he sees her as disrespectful. She feels he just doesn't care about her need for love; he feels she could care less or is just plain clueless about his need for respect.

More often than not, these conclusions are the result of a gigantic misunderstanding. In Part III we will look at how to stop the Crazy Cycle by using skills to gain mutual understanding and the first skill is vital. As we send pink and blue messages back and forth, we must learn to decode those messages and really *hear* each other—perhaps for the first time ever. We'll learn about decoding in the next chapter.

--~ᴍᴜᴜ~--

The Crazy Cycle: A Relentless Enemy of Marital Communication

--~ᴍᴜᴜ~--

If you have read chapters 2, 3, and 4, you are now armed with wisdom based on Love and Respect principles.

First, you know that what comes out of your mouth matters a great deal because the words you speak are an overflow of what is in your heart.

Second, you are now well aware of how different you and your spouse are. You know about the pink and blue sunglasses and hearing aids, and you are anxious to see if you can adjust your perspective to your mate's.

Third, you know how important it is to see your spouse as a person of goodwill even when things get tense, maybe a little crazy, and the Crazy Cycle starts to spin. You are committed to the idea that, deep down, your spouse wants a relationship with you and has goodwill toward you even if it is not discernible at the moment!

Yes, you have these key Love and Respect principles firmly in mind, but beware! The Crazy Cycle is a clever, relentless enemy. Even "experts" like Emerson and Sarah have to be on constant alert lest they fall victim to the Crazy Cycle.

Remember, no married couple is ever off the Crazy Cycle for good. It is always there, ready for you to take a spin, but you can avoid it by using the basic skills and techniques described in the following chapters: decoding each other's words, being careful about each other's air hose, and forgiving each other. Practice these procedures prayerfully and consistently, and the Crazy Cycle won't have a chance.

Are you ready? Adjust your sunglasses and hearing aids—and let's get started!

CHAPTER FIVE

Decode—and Stop the Crazy Cycle

Despite how long Sarah and I have worked at learning to communicate, we still have our moments when we misunderstand each other, and the Crazy Cycle starts to spin. It seems almost inevitable as we go through the ebb and flow of daily life. For example, recently we were catching a plane on our way to conduct another Love and Respect Conference. As we entered the terminal, I checked my watch and saw we had about forty-five minutes to get to the boarding gate. Just then Sarah turned and said, "I am really hungry. I was thinking about getting something to eat. Is that okay?"

Thinking she wanted to grab some fast food at a counter a few steps away, I replied, "Fine. I'll wait here for you." Sarah gave me that look that says, "You have completely missed my meaning." Then, almost demurely, she said, "Well, I was thinking about both of us getting something to eat."

Perhaps I was distracted or worried about missing the plane. Still not picking up on what she had on her mind, I said, "Well, I'm not that hungry."

With disbelief in her eyes, Sarah spelled it out for me: "Well, I thought the two of us could sit down and be together for a nice meal. Okay, then, I'm going to go get something to eat." Before I could reply, she steamed off, less than happy and clearly upset with me.

"Sarah, wait!" I called after her, but she just kept going, leaving me standing there, holding all the bags—in more ways than one. Were we on the Crazy Cycle? Not exactly, but I could hear it revving its engines.

Whoops! I thought to myself. *Here is another illustration of a husband-wife misunderstanding.* I sat down and waited, hoping we wouldn't miss our plane. When Sarah came back (with only a few minutes to spare before boarding), I could tell she was still unhappy, but there was no time to talk because we had to dash to our gate. Once in our seats, however, we quickly got into a discussion about our little episode in the terminal. I could see that Sarah was still feeling provoked; for that matter, so was I. "This whole scene frustrates me," I said. "I truly misunderstood what you were trying to convey. I didn't mean to ignore your invitation."

"Well, I'm frustrated too," Sarah replied. "I know you don't intend to do anything unloving. But you are so preoccupied. You are always thinking of other things. I thought we had a chance to spend a few quiet minutes together before roaring off on another plane ride . . ."

We sit there in silence, neither wanting to budge any further. We both know we will apologize to each other, but we both have to be stubborn for a few more moments. Neither of us wants to make the first move. Both of us are expecting the other to be mature, to be first to say, "I'm sorry." Both of us are also hoping no one comes down the aisle wanting me to sign their copy of *Love & Respect*.

A few more minutes pass, and our tension drains away. Sarah grins at me. We are both thinking about how petty we can be. I then apologize for not being sensitive to her invitation, and I vow—again—to be less preoccupied. She tells me she is sorry for losing her patience and trotting off the way she did and asks if I will forgive her. I do, and then I ask her if she will forgive me, which she does. Episode over.

Over the Years We Have Learned the Hard Way

Fortunately, over the years we have learned how to stop the Crazy Cycle before it can really get going. When we do or say something that bruises or cuts, we know how to put salve on the wound almost immediately. But early on in our marriage, before Love and Respect, we tended to watch each other bleed for a while, not knowing how or why to put down our sharp knives.

Actually, what happened to us back there in the terminal on the way to our gate was caused by our individual needs for Love and Respect. Sarah was expecting Love—my willingness to grab a bite to eat with her—and didn't get it because I was too preoccupied to decode her invitation properly. As our interaction proceeded, I was expecting Respect—a positive response to my calling out to her!—and didn't get it because Sarah was so exasperated that all she could do was walk away in a huff and refuse to even look back when I called to her.

Tension and anger in marriage commonly happen due to what I call the "Love and Respect conflict." As Sarah stalked away to find a restaurant and eat alone, she was quite probably thinking, *If he loved me, he would be more sensitive and read between the lines.* As I sat there waiting for her to come back, I found myself thinking, *If she respected me, she would stop condemning me every time I am slow to figure out what she wants and seem insensitive.*

In a very real sense, our airport scene aptly illustrates the fundamental and ageless battle of the sexes. In a marriage, as the skirmishes mount up over the years, each side accumulates evidence. Pink knows her posi-

> *"Avoiding a quarrel is honorable. After all, any stubborn fool can start a fight" (Proverbs 20:3 GW).*

tion is more correct; Blue knows precisely the opposite. And this war will continue unless Pink and Blue can take a step back and see what they are doing to each other. The war can be over quickly if they will both just realize they are not wrong, just different.

Avoiding the Battle of the Sexes

One big reason Sarah and I are now able to apologize to each other more quickly is because we have simply called a truce in the so-called battle of the sexes. Obviously, we have our lapses, but we are usually quick to stop passing judgment on each other for being pink and blue. We are ready to accept our gender differences and work with them instead of blasting away at each other for saying or doing "unacceptable" things. Our tiff in the terminal proves we are still a work in progress, but we have made— for us—a *lot* of progress. Although I still frustrate her, Sarah refuses to call me an unloving blue dummy. And although she frustrates me, I refrain from calling her a disrespectful pink basket case.

Actually, I thank God that Sarah is "so sensitive" because her emotional responses enable her to feel for me when I need empathy. And Sarah thanks God that I am "so insensitive" because my less emotional responses enable me to act matter-of-factly, protect during crises, and lead in moments that are emotionally overwhelming. As someone said, "Your strength can be your weakness, and your weakness can be your strength."

Can you decode your mate's negative comments? "A person's thoughts are like water in a deep well, but someone with insight can draw them out" (Proverbs 20:5 GNB).

Our "can we get something to eat?" story nicely illustrates the key truth of this chapter: *to communicate, you must learn to decode.* From my own experience married to Sarah and from working with thousands of other couples, I am convinced that men and women actually speak to each other in code. Until they learn how to crack each other's code, they are bound to have difficulties and misunderstandings that can cause the Crazy Cycle to spin.

Even an "Expert" Can Fail to Crack the Code

Later, as I relaxed during the flight and Sarah caught a nap, I thought about what had happened in the space of just a few seconds when she said, "I am really hungry. I was thinking about getting something to eat. Is that okay?" Hidden in those words was her *real* message: she was letting me know she wanted me to be with her. She was hungry, yes, and could use some food, but to Sarah, as with many women, a meal is much more than food. It is fellowship. I had not been quick enough to decode that message—and I'm the one who teaches this Love and Respect stuff!

As embarrassing as this story is for me, it clearly shows why husbands and wives need to constantly work at decoding each other's messages. As chapter 3 emphasized, husbands and wives are as different as pink and blue. We often send each other messages that have different meanings because we have different expectations based on our maleness and femaleness. The important thing is to remember that being pink and blue is okay. You and your spouse are not wrong, just different.

Sarah had not been wrong for her pink expectations of me. To her, the message was clear. She was paying me a compliment because she wanted to be close to me for a few minutes before the flight. From my blue perspective, I was not wrong for misunderstanding her expectation. My message to her had been "I am speaking truthfully based on the information I am receiving." In her original invitation ("I am really hungry. I was thinking about getting something to eat. Is that okay?"), she had not really included me by saying something like "I was thinking we could get something to eat." When she added, "Is that okay?" I took it as asking for my approval, which I didn't feel she needed, but it was kind of her to ask.

At that moment, however, Sarah was thinking more relationally, as most wives do; I was more matter-of-fact, as many husbands are. Sarah

had said she was hungry and wanted some food. On many other jour-
neys through an airport terminal (we travel a lot), Sarah would occasion-
ally say something like "I didn't take time to eat breakfast. Now I'm really
hungry. Honey, can we stop for a minute while I grab a bagel?"

Her fast-food forays had programmed me to think this was what she
wanted to do again when she said, "I am really hungry. I was thinking
about getting something to eat. Is that okay?" And when she had followed
up by saying, "Well, I was thinking about both of us getting something
to eat," I was still looking at things on a face-value basis and didn't hear
what she thought was a clear invitation. Since I wasn't hungry, I felt the
freedom to relay this and actually thought she did not know I was feeling full. At that point, however, Sarah had had it with my blue denseness.
By the time she said straight out, "Well, I thought the two of us could sit
down and be together for a nice meal," she was turning on her heel to
leave in a huff. At about that moment the light finally started to go on in
my mind, and I tried to call after her: "Hey, wait! I finally get what you
are saying. Let's get something to eat. That will be great." But by then it
was too late.

Pinks Tend to Decode One Another Naturally

From the pink point of view, womanly intuition is a wonderful gift.
Many Pinks decode naturally when it comes to intimate relationships or
close friendships with other Pinks. Consider this snapshot from Sarah's
world. She's at a committee meeting at church, and her friend Sheila will
say, "I was thinking of stopping for a cappuccino after the meeting.
Would you like to join me?"

Sarah replies, "Really? Do you think the meeting will end early
enough?"

Sheila answers, "I think so, but we don't have to stop if this won't
work for you."

Sarah comes back with, "No, Emerson is at his own meeting, and I
have time. It would be fun!"

Sheila says, "Okay, if you are sure there is no time crunch, there is this new café called Perky's. Would you like to stop there?"

Sarah is pleased. "You know, I just drove by there the other day, and it is so quaint. I said to myself, 'I need to try that place.'"

Sheila is equally pleased: "Oh, this will be perfect. Maybe we can leave the meeting early."

Women are very sensitive about an invitation, whether they extend it or receive it. They will negotiate, volleying back and forth, looking for hidden feelings, and seeking to draw out what may be unspoken. They naturally seek to reassure and to be reassured themselves. There is a great deal of mutual affirmation. This capacity for sensitivity is God-given—to Pink, but not necessarily to Blue. That day at the airport, Sarah expected me to be sensitive, pick up on her cues, and negotiate with her in a conversation something like the following:

> "I am really hungry. I was thinking about getting something to eat. Is that okay?"
>
> "Oh, that would be great. Where do you want to stop?"
>
> "Well, I want to sit down someplace nice, just the two of us. Would you like to?"
>
> "Of course, but do we have time?"
>
> "I think so. Boarding isn't for another forty-five minutes. Do you think we might not have enough time?"
>
> "I'm not worried. Forty-five minutes is enough. Where do you want to go?"
>
> "We just passed a place with booths. I was wanting to be cozy. Does that place sound good?"
>
> "Honey, being with you is *always* good!"

In reality, most husbands and wives do not have conversations like this, even on their honeymoon, because this just isn't how most men talk. For a male, I am fairly intuitive about communication issues, and that is what helped me develop the material we teach on decoding at our Love and Respect Conferences. Still, I basically approach life with quite a bit more of the male's "here are the facts of the situation" approach.

If my best buddy said, "Do you want to grab a cup of coffee after the meeting?" my response might be, "Sorry. I really need to get home tonight, but if you have some issues to discuss, call me tomorrow. I'll be able to focus better then." My friend might be a bit disappointed, but he would accept my refusal at face value, and take no offense at my short, slightly terse male response. I am not saying that Sarah would never say no to a friend's invitation to have a cappuccino. If she had been short of time when Sheila invited her, she would have felt free to decline, but there would have been more conversation, expressions of regret, concern about feelings, and "we must do it as soon as we can" kind of talk. Females are usually tuned in to being sensitive; males are typically matter-of-fact and even rather blunt.

> *As you gain understanding to God's design for Pink and Blue, each day is full of wonderful discoveries. "A wise person will listen and continue to learn, and an understanding person will gain direction" (Proverbs 1:5 GW).*

My inherent maleness caught up with me that day at the airport. Preoccupied (as I often am) and in a hurry, I misread Sarah's message and my very blue male response hurt and exasperated my very pink and sensitive wife. Fortunately, we both had sense enough to realize what had happened and to apologize and ask forgiveness, which stopped the Crazy Cycle in its first revolution. (Because asking for and receiving forgiveness is such an important communication tool, we will be examining it more closely in chapter 7.)

By telling my airport story, I am not contending that women personalize everything and only men are up-front and to the point. I have known women who were quite matter-of-fact, and I have male friends who are more sensitive than the average woman and who freely communicate their feelings. But I am saying that, in the typical marriage, the woman will be the sensitive, intuitive one while the man will be more matter-of-fact and, at times, insensitive without meaning to be. This is why every husband should know how to decode his wife—and vice versa. Because of those pink and blue hearing aids, women are geared to hear a certain way, and men are geared to hear in a much different way, as the following story illustrates.

"Where Did You Get These Hamburgers?"

When Sarah and I got married, I was in graduate school working on a master's degree in communication. My studies often had me thinking about male and female differences. Because Sarah and I were experiencing plenty of our own tensions with being male and female, I was constantly intrigued by examples of how men and women see and hear so differently.

On one occasion we were at a friend's house, and he was cooking hamburgers on his backyard barbecue. I asked him, "Where did you get these hamburgers?" He replied, "At the meat market that just opened downtown." My male friend heard my question as a simple request for information. Nothing more.

Not too long afterward, Sarah and I were sitting down to dinner in our apartment, and she served hamburgers. I decided to conduct a little experiment, so I asked her, "Where did you get these hamburgers?" Sarah shot back, "Why? What's wrong with them?"

Because of Sarah's sensitivity as a woman and a new wife who wanted to serve good meals, she was immediately concerned. In classic female style, Sarah read between the lines and received an entirely different message in my question than my male friend had heard. I assured her the hamburgers were great and explained I was just conducting a little experiment to see if her response to my question would be different from my male friend's response. Obviously relieved to hear nothing was wrong with her hamburgers, Sarah just smiled and said, "Of course. How else would you expect me to respond?"

"Can We Talk?" Would Put Me on Red Alert

Despite my airport lapse, I am better at decoding than I used to be, but in the earlier years of our marriage, the Crazy Cycle would often threaten to spin because I wasn't sure what was really on Sarah's mind. Of particular concern to me was the way Sarah would ask me the same question over and over: "Can we talk?" Or she might vary it and say, "When can we talk?" Most of the time I wanted to ask, "Now what did I do?" I was thinking, *She wants to talk because things are not going well in our marriage, and I am the reason.*

> "Through presumption comes nothing but strife" (Proverbs 13:10 NASB 1977).

Instead of asking, "Now what did I do?" I would try to be a little more casual: "Okay, what do you want to talk about?" Sarah's answer didn't give me much comfort: "I don't know. I just need to talk." I took this to mean that whatever she had on her mind, it must be about me and something I was doing or maybe not doing, but she was hesitant to tell me right up front.

When we had our talks, as often as not, what she had on her mind did *not* involve any problems with me. She did, indeed, just want to talk. It took me years, however, to be fully convinced that Sarah's invitation to talk did not mean I was in trouble.

Sarah still asks me, "Can we talk?" but now I decode her message much more quickly. She isn't lying in wait, ready to pounce and tell me what I have done wrong. She simply needs to talk about her feelings. This may include something about me, positive, negative, or neutral, but usually I am not what she has on her mind. The bottom line is that talking is cathartic for Sarah (and most women). Now I listen to her reports and share ideas and feelings on many subjects. Over the years, though, while

I was still trying to master this skill, she sometimes detected that I was not as energized as she was by all of our talk (especially when I glanced periodically at my watch). She would say, "You don't want to talk to me. I can tell."

I would try to assure Sarah that I did want to talk to her, and I'd ask her to be patient with me. But on many occasions I was left looking a lot like one husband I heard about. His wife accused him: "You aren't interested in talking to me. It's obvious." The startled husband replied, "What are you saying? I have said no such thing. In fact, I am working hard on listening to what you have to say." To which the wife replied, "Perhaps, but you are listening in an unpleasant manner."

These days when Sarah says, "Can we talk?" I usually succeed in listening well rather than unpleasantly. "Can we talk?" is her signal that she seeks rapport with me. She enjoys being with me and talking about people and relationships. Sarah tends to focus on feelings. Whenever there is tension between us, she wants to move toward me in a cooperative spirit. She wants us to be flexible, enjoy the moment, and laugh together.

Sarah is a typical female, tuned in and sensitive to people due to her nurturing nature. Women can think, plan, and reason as well as men, but when it comes to the intimate relationship of marriage, they let themselves follow their hearts—and they want men to do the same. Males are typically matter-of-fact due to their analytical bent. Although men can be emotional and trusting, when it comes to decisions in their marriage, they let themselves follow their heads—and they want women to do the same. This is why a typical man's first line of thought focuses on what is being said rather than on what *isn't* being said.

Are there exceptions? Of course, but as I said in an earlier chapter, exceptions don't invalidate generalizations that prove generally true about a large number of people. Throughout my many years of counseling couples, I have learned that it is typical for a wife to complain that her husband is insensitive (too much head and not enough heart) and for a husband to complain that his wife is overly sensitive (too much heart and not enough head). My advice is always the same: instead of judging each other for your God-given differences, put your heads and hearts together as best you can. Choose to see your differences as essential to being a great team. And let your differences result in decisions motivated and determined by the best of goodwilled feelings!

To be a team is always my goal with Sarah, and I usually succeed. But if I let myself get preoccupied with the myriad concerns that flood my mind due to our Love and Respect ministry, I will not really hear her, much less be able to decode her words. When that happens, our team does not function well, as our airport terminal tiff so clearly demonstrates.

Listening and Decoding: Twin Tools for Better Communication

From personal experience as a husband plus hours of listening to thousands of spouses share their hearts during counseling, I have concluded that listening and decoding go hand in hand as twin tools for better communication. Opportunities to decode arise constantly, and if a spouse is not listening, they will be missed.

Sarah and I often hear from married couples who have seen the benefits of learning to listen and decode. One wife's e-mail related how our Love and Respect teaching on decoding had really helped them. In fact, as she related in her humorous tongue-in-cheek way, it "saved her husband's life." She writes:

> *To decode what your mate is saying, "be quick to listen, but slow to speak and slow to become angry" (James 1:19 GNB).*

While going through your video series in our small group, I encountered the opportunity to decode something my husband had said. We were traveling in the car on our way to a movie. He was quiet and smiling smugly. I said, "What are you thinking?" He replied,

"I was just thinking how critical you are." My natural instinct was . . . well, you know. But I thought, *This is a goodwilled man. Maybe he means something else.* So I asked, "What does that mean, that I'm critical?" He replied, "I mean our family couldn't exist without you. You are so critical to us."

As she closed her letter, she added, "Thank you, Emerson, for saving us from a fiery crash!"

This "critical" wife's story is a perfect example of what might happen when one spouse sends a message that could be taken wrong. In this case, she almost took offense at his use of the word *critical.* She decoded him enough, however, to ask for an explanation and learned that he was paying her a compliment; he meant she was invaluable in his eyes.

But what would have happened if she had not decoded and the temperature in the car suddenly dropped near freezing? At moments like that every spouse needs another skill equally as important as decoding. In our Love and Respect Conferences, we call it "Beware of stepping on your spouse's air hose!" We will look more closely at this important part of communicating Love and Respect style in the next chapter.

CHAPTER SIX

—•—

"Ouch! You're Stepping on My Air Hose!"

In all marriages, there are times when one spouse fails to decode the other, or perhaps somebody just says something harsh, critical, or sarcastic that angers or hurts the other person. At that kind of moment, your mate's face may fall, or perhaps the eyes grow dark and the tone of voice grows icy. In other people, the body stiffens, the eyes flash and the tone of voice goes up a few octaves. When you see any of these telltale signs, be aware that you have probably stepped on your mate's air hose, deflating the inner spirit (see chapter 1, p. 15).

We All Have an Air Hose

When I introduce the air hose analogy at a conference, I ask the audience to picture a wife's air hose leading to a big tank labeled "Love" because she needs love just as she needs air to breathe. When, through her pink hearing aids, she hears an unfortunate message in her husband's words, that air hose can get pinched and her love supply cut off. That's when she will find it very easy to come back with unfortunate words of her own, often angry words that are trying to tell her husband "I don't feel loved right now." But she doesn't say it just like that. Instead she might say, "That was stupid! You always foul things up, and here we are again."

Her husband, of course, has his own air hose leading to a big tank labeled "Respect." And he needs respect just as he needs air to breathe. He probably meant nothing by his unfortunate remark, but when his pink wife heard it through her pink hearing aids, she was stung, irritated, or perhaps deeply hurt. Naturally enough, she lashed back, and when her husband heard her disrespectful words through his blue hearing aids, those words stung him, and his air hose got pinched as well. And from there the whole thing can escalate in a hurry. A cardinal rule for learning to communicate the Love and Respect way is to always remember:

WHEN YOUR WORDS STING YOUR SPOUSE AND CAUSE AN ISSUE, THAT ISSUE IS SELDOM THE REAL ISSUE.

The real issue is that words heard by a wife can sound unloving and words heard by a husband can sound disrespectful. And each can respond defensively with more words that sound unloving or disrespectful. And back and forth they go—right onto the Crazy Cycle.

When you and your spouse are on the Crazy Cycle, what you say and how you say it sounds unloving or disrespectful even when you don't intend to sound that way. To get on the Crazy Cycle, you had to give a certain look, say some unfortunate word (like *jerk* or *witch),* or perhaps scream a little. Once you two are on the

> *When your spouse steps on your air hose, remember "a man's discretion makes him slow to anger, and it is his glory to overlook a transgression" (Proverbs 19:11).*

Crazy Cycle, whatever you say is bound to grieve or provoke the spirit of your spouse. But whatever your issue might be, it is no longer the real issue because you have reduced the importance of your partner. *That* is the real issue, and that is why all your spouse will hear at the moment is "You don't matter to me. I don't love you." Or "You don't matter to me. I don't respect you."

How King David and His Wife Got on the Crazy Cycle

Couples in Bible times didn't use terms like *Crazy Cycle, decoding,* and *air hose,* but they still faced the same kind of communication problems people face today. And these women and men had the same basic needs for Love and Respect. One incident from the life of King David is a classic illustration of how a wife can stomp on her husband's air hose.

When King Saul gave David his daughter Michal to be his wife, the marriage appeared to start out well. First Samuel 18:20 tells us, "Now Michal, Saul's daughter, loved David." But did Michal *respect* David? See what happened over in 2 Samuel 6 when David brings the ark of the covenant back to Jerusalem. It's an occasion of joy beyond description. The tablets containing the Ten Commandments are in the ark, which will eventually be placed in the Holy of Holies in the temple, the design of which God will reveal to David, but it will be built many years later by David's son Solomon (1 Chronicles 28:11–19).

There is shouting and the sound of trumpets, and as the procession with the Ark enters the city, David dances "with all his might" in joyous worship of the Lord. As he leaps and whirls about in wild celebration, he is not wearing his royal robes. Instead he has chosen to garb himself as a Levite high priest, in a linen ephod, or tunic, because, as the king of Israel, he wishes to transport the ark of the covenant in priestly fashion (see 2 Samuel 6:1–15). But dressed as he was, David did not look kingly, nor was he in full Levite dress either, which would have included a blue robe under the ephod.

Gazing down on David from her window, Michal sees David looking like anything but a king and dancing in a fashion which, to her, is shameless, and she is "filled with contempt for him" (2 Samuel 6:16 NLT). David continues on to a special tent set up just for the celebration. There the ark is placed, and he proceeds to offer burnt offerings and peace offerings. Then he blesses the people in the name of the Lord of hosts and distributes to all those present cakes made of dates and raisins (see 2 Samuel 6:17–19).

His responsibilities as leader of the nation completed, David returns home to "bless his own household." But, sadly, his wife has missed the holiness of an event that has glorified God. She says nothing about the return of the ark, nothing about David's desire to praise God with all his might, nothing about how carefully the ark had been transported according to God's law, nothing about thanksgiving to God, and no affirmation that Yahweh, the Lord, was glorified.

In 2 Samuel 6:20–23, the New Living Translation clearly catches the spirit of a conversation that quickly starts Michal and David spinning on the Crazy Cycle. With sarcasm and contempt dripping from her every word, Michal says, "How glorious the king of Israel looked today! He exposed himself to the servant girls like any indecent person might do!"[1]

Stung but not at all cowed, David retorts defensively, "I was dancing before the LORD, who chose me above your father and his family! He appointed me as the leader of Israel, the people of the LORD. Yes, and I am willing to look even more foolish than this, but I will be held in honor by the girls of whom you have spoken!" And then the final verse of the passage brings down the curtain on this Crazy Cycle scene and adds a postscript: "So Michal, the daughter of Saul, remained childless throughout her life" (2 Samuel 6:23). For her disdain of both the king of Israel and the holy event over which he had presided, God sentenced Michal to the disgrace of childlessness.

In violating her husband's basic need for respect, Michal had stepped much too far over the line. We may wish to pass judgment on David's angry reaction, but the facts are that he came home from leading an incredible worship experience to bestow a blessing on his own household and was met by his wife's contempt. The entire incident illustrates how Blue needs and wants appropriate respect and can lose fond feelings of affection when Pink shows him such obvious contempt.

Rachel and Jacob Also Rode the Crazy Cycle

In another Bible story where air hoses are pinched, we find Rachel commenting that she has borne no children for Jacob, and she becomes jealous of her sister, Leah, who has already borne him four sons. She goes to Jacob and says, "Give me children, or else I die"(Genesis 30:1). Put on the spot by an unreasonable wife, Jacob becomes angry with Rachel and replies, "Am I in place of God, who has kept you from having children?" (Genesis 30:2). Instead of having compassion, Jacob overreacts to his hurting wife, who is desperate to have a baby.

Rachel is being very pink at this point: not rational but very emotional. The longing in her soul was for a precious baby. Then as now, giving birth to a baby was the heartfelt dream of most wives. Women have love to give and love to spare, and they yearn to shower that love on a priceless little human being. In making her request of Jacob, does Rachel actually expect him to act in God's place? Of course not. But Jacob's answer to her request is facetious and unkind. Rachel is sharing a heavy burden, and Jacob should decode her message. She is not suicidal, but she is expressing her disinterest in living if she cannot have and hold a child. Jacob is being blue to the core, answering his wife logically and rather impatiently. He chooses to be angry with Rachel rather than understanding and loving.

Whether he is a husband from the days of the patriarchs or a husband who lives down the street, a man can fail to read between the lines and decode his wife's cry for love. If only Jacob had asked himself, "Is Rachel feeling insecure and in need of reassurance from me? Can I say something that feels loving in order to help offset her discouragement?" Rachel desperately needed her husband's assurance that, even if she did not have a baby, he would always love her.

From Issues to Air Hoses

Jacob, Rachel's husband, and Michal, David's wife, are examples from the Bible of how one mate can step on the other mate's air hose and keep the Crazy Cycle spinning. And whether they occur in Bible times or in marriages today, issues between husband and wife can pop up anywhere over just about anything. For example, a couple gets in a discussion over their son's poor grades. The wife wants the husband to spend more time with the boy and help him with his homework; the husband is under tremendous pressure at his job and is having to work a lot of overtime. He says there is no time to help. The discussion quickly becomes a real issue. They go back and forth, getting louder and louder, stepping on each other's air hose as they make their points to win the argument. Finally they go to bed angry, not speaking to each other, and definitely on the Crazy Cycle.

Examples like the one above are legion among married couples. Questions, problems, and decisions come up daily (sometimes it seems hourly), but if they grow into arguments, they become issues that sometimes lead to all-out battles. At this point, air hoses are almost always being pinched to some degree, but the issue being addressed is not the real issue at all. At the bottom of any issue that is causing conflict is the deeper issue of a lack of Love and Respect.

The key to cracking the communication code is realizing your mate always hears with different hearing aids and sees with different sunglasses. When your spouse deflates before your eyes, instead of just defending yourself by saying, "That's your problem," admit that it's *always* also *your* problem. What you have said has either sounded unloving to your wife or

> *Stop saying, "That's your issue." Jesus said you and your spouse are "no longer two, but one" (Matthew 19:6), which means it's always our issue.*

disrespectful to your husband. Instead of helplessly or unwisely allowing the Crazy Cycle to spin, you must seek to stop it.

Practical Steps to Stopping the Crazy Cycle in Mid-Spin

"Okay, Emerson," you ask. "How do we keep the Crazy Cycle from spinning after one or both of us has said things that are getting it started?" Here are some basic steps:

1. Remember that your spouse is a goodwilled person. Even if your spouse has done or said something that causes you to doubt this at the moment, proceed with a positive attitude. Anything else will only get the Crazy Cycle spinning faster.

2. Thinking about what you might have done to step on your spouse's air hose, take your time answering any heated remarks. Think to yourself, *Something is bothering him/her. Instead of getting defensive, I need to go slow, giving him/her the benefit of the doubt. I must not jump to a conclusion. I need to be patient.*

3. At this point you can take the standard approach that we teach in Love and Respect Conferences. To try to find out what is wrong, *never* say, "You are unloving" or "You are disrespectful," accusations that only pinch the other person's air hose all the more.

Instead, the wife can say, "That felt unloving. Did I just come across as disrespectful?" If he says yes, the wife can say, "I'm sorry for being disrespectful. Will you forgive me? How can I come across more respectfully?"

Or the husband can say, "That felt disrespectful. Did I just come across as unloving?" If she says yes, the husband can reply, "I'm sorry for being unloving. How can I come across more lovingly?"[2]

Use Terminology That Feels Comfortable to You

Many couples use this simple exchange successfully when there is a sharp disagreement, and one spouse has stepped on the other spouse's air hose. They have bought into the need for unconditional Love and Respect to the point where they are comfortable with this terminology. Here are two typical reports:

Before Love and Respect, we were more prone to use "fighting" words like "you always" and "you never" or "I can't believe you did/said that" After Love and Respect, we are more prone to use healing words (loving for Catherine, respectful for Charles) such as "Was I disrespectful? That felt unloving" and "Was I unloving? That felt disrespectful." Catherine and I were reflecting during one of our weekly dates not too long ago on how we rarely get into the nit-picky "discussions" that plagued us for so many years.

⸺⁙⦿⁙⸻

Jim and I are doing AWESOME. [This approach to communication] has changed our marriage. We now listen and stop and say, "Have I done something to disrespect you? Because I am feeling unloved" or "I'm feeling disrespected. Did I do something unloving? " It has changed how we treat each other. Since the conference we have not had even one cold silent war.

⸺⁙⦿⁙⸻

Other couples are not as comfortable with our standard approach—at least not at first. Saying "That felt unloving" or "That felt disrespectful" might seem a bit stilted or awkward, especially for husbands who have not even realized that what has been bothering them is a lack of respect by their wives. We constantly hear from husbands who knew something was missing, but they dismissed it as all their fault because they were failing to be loving enough. One husband had attended many marriage groups and conferences that focused on how the husband can love his wife. His response to Love and Respect teaching was this:

> *"The wise of heart is called discerning, and sweetness of speech increases persuasiveness" (Proverbs 16:21 ESV).*

When you discussed the man's need for respect from his wife, you pierced a desire that I long buried. I did not even realize or know what I was lacking. My focus was my wife and her needs. My wife was blown away with the concept of unconditional respect and is working to understand respect in the same way I continue to work to understand love. She has quickly picked up on different ways of communicating her thoughts, ideas, corrections, etc., without stepping on my air hose. These principles have put a spark back into our marriage and a greater enjoyment and anticipation of spending time together.

As helpful as the "That felt unloving" or "That felt disrespectful" approach can be, it needs to be used with care in certain situations. For example, suppose a husband steps on his wife's air hose by saying or doing something really blue that makes her angry, and she lashes out at him in hurt and frustration. She is still smarting from his remark or whatever he did, such as saying to the children, "Don't ask me. Your mother overrides anything I say to you. She's the boss around here." Yes, it would be ideal if she would say, "That felt unloving. Have I prompted this by coming across as disrespectful?" But perhaps she is too hurt or angry and verbally blasts away, "You are insulting. On top of that you are cruel. How could you say that to the kids?"

To be told at that moment by her husband that her angry remark felt disrespectful (when he has clearly been at fault for using the children to make a point to her) would simply put her on the defensive because he would be misapplying the expression *that felt disrespectful.* If a husband verbally slaps his wife and she verbally slaps back, the husband has no right to claim she is disrespectful. He needs to confess he was unloving!

Suppose, however, the husband is a man of honor and realizes he has stepped way over the line with his crack about his wife "being the boss around here." Then he could say instead, "Honey, I think I might have stepped on your air hose. I am really sorry. I apologize to you and the kids as well."

Obviously, there are situations where the roles would be reversed. The wife has clearly been at fault, and the husband makes the angry remark or perhaps he does the typical blue thing and stonewalls her. Instead of telling him, "That felt unloving," she might do better to just say, "Honey, I think I might have stepped on your air hose. Tell me what I said that was disrespectful."

The point is, there is no standard set speech you have to make. It is okay to use different ways to stop the Crazy Cycle from really getting started. Use the terms and phrases that both of you understand and that feel the most comfortable. One husband reported:

I now pay a whole lot more attention to her expressions and body language when I talk, to verify that I'm not wounding her spirit, particularly when we're discussing difficult (for us, at least) topics. We have agreed to give each other the freedom to say, in effect: "You're crossing the line and squashing my spirit with how you're saying what you're saying." Neither of us actually uses that line as a quote. Instead, I grab my throat and act like I'm choking, and my wife tells me I'm stomping on her air hose.

> *To keep the Crazy Cycle in its cage, remember that there is "a right time to laugh" (Ecclesiastes 3:4 MSG).*

This couple prefers a lighter tone that relaxes tension. Here are some other ideas along those lines:

- "Whoa, are we trying to take a spin on the Crazy Cycle?"
- "Help me out here. I think my pink/blue sunglasses are fogging over."
- "Honey, could you borrow my pink/blue hearing aids to hear what I'm trying to say?"

(For more ideas on how to lighten up your dialogue, see Appendix A in *Love & Respect*.) Remember, use the "light" approach only when you are fairly sure your spouse will take it well and see the humor in the situation. If your spouse thinks your "light" remark is making light of the problem, it will probably mean more spins on the Crazy Cycle.

How Well Does All This Work in Real Life?

How do the strategies outlined above work in an actual conversation? Before I give some examples, I want to share a letter from Roy, who read some of our materials and decided he would do "whatever it took" to persuade his wife, Nancy, to attend a Love and Respect Conference. He succeeded, and the conference did wonders for their marriage, which had been on shaky ground because of constant underlying tension. He wrote to tell me that practicing Love and Respect had changed the language in their home. They had never been hateful toward each other, but now they viewed each other not as enemies but as allies with different perspectives. His letter continued:

> I have begun assuming that whatever my wife says, I do not really understand. That has become a good thing. It has made me listen not to the words, but to whatever may be underneath them. Since I assume I am not getting her true meaning the first time, I ask more questions, I dig for more feelings, and I get more thoughtful responses from her. Then I can FINALLY figure out what she MEANT, because most of the time, it is not what she said! As a result, we are starting to share more effectively. She is trusting that I know her heart better, and she is not making as many assumptions about my intent. It is bringing more respect for me from her since she feels heard.

Now that they are aware of the need to decode and not step on each other's air hose, Roy and Nancy have been finding many opportunities to apply Love and Respect principles. Below are suggestions for having a husband-wife discussion, suggestions that are based in part on their efforts to practice Love and Respect.

One evening after the kids are in bed, Holly says to John, "I have decided that I should be the one who takes the kids to school instead of you."

As John tries to decode this message, he realizes it could mean anything from "I know you have to fight the freeways in the morning and need all the time possible to get to work" to "The kids have been late to school several times lately, and I am taking over because you are so incompetent."

Truth be told, John has gotten the kids to school late at least four times in the last month, but in all but one instance he had to wait for one of them to get ready to leave; the other time he was the victim of an unavoidable traffic jam. John and Holly have attended a Love and Respect Conference and are reading a copy of *Love & Respect* together. Before hearing Love and Respect teaching, John might have responded to his wife's announcement in a defensive manner: "That is *so* much like you—just taking over and making me feel like I can't do anything right!"

In this answer to Holly's announcement, John has made accusations, impugned Holly's motives, and also used the overkill word *never*. All or even any of this is guaranteed to step on her air hose and leave her feeling quite unloved. On the other hand, if Holly had remembered to avoid stepping on John's air hose and to practice respecting him, she could have brought up her idea like this: "John, what would you think of me taking over on driving the kids to school? That would give you more time to get on the freeway and get to work." This opening remark leaves room for a discussion, does not make John feel like his wife makes all the decisions, and gives him a chance to express what could be on his mind. Perhaps he, too, has been thinking it would be nice if Holly started driving the kids to school, or he may even be ready to admit that he has gotten the kids to school late a few times recently and give his side of why it happened.

In many conversations, especially those that contain possibly sensitive matters, both spouses should be aware of the need to decode what the other is saying. Do not jump to conclusions. With your spouse's air hose in mind, make replies that assume your spouse's goodwill and that give him or her room to share opinions. For example, instead of coming back with accusations and impugning Holly's motives when she announces that she has decided to start driving the kids to school, John could ignore his own slightly pinched air hose and say, "Honey, this sounds like a pretty big change to me. It would be nice for me to have more time to get to work. The freeways have been a bear lately. But tell me a little more about why you think this would be a good idea."

Holly could make several possible responses to John's invitation to tell him more. She might be rather blunt, continuing to be unconcerned about his air hose, and say, "You've been consistently getting the kids to school late. Jimmy complained about it to me yesterday." If John is interested in keeping the Crazy Cycle from spinning, he could reply, "Yes, it's true we've gotten there late sometimes." From there he might give his side of how often the kids were late and why, or he might let it go, choosing not to get in an argument about how many times and who is correct—Jimmy or his father.

Instead, John could say, "You know, this is a problem we need to work on. Are you sure you want to take over driving the kids? You have your own job to get to. Maybe we can work out a better system for leaving a little sooner." From there the discussion can continue as John tries to assure Holly he cares about her and the children and they make a decision together about what to do.

Another possible response by Holly, who has a part-time job, could be, "Well, I go that way to get to work anyway, and it would give me a chance to connect more with the kids at the beginning of the day." To this John could respond with appreciation and, if he is not too proud, admit that he has gotten the kids to school late on occasion and that this would free him up to get to work on time himself.

Or, in perhaps a best-case scenario, Holly might say, "I know you have been working hard lately, and this is just another thing on your plate. I'd like to help." To this respect-laden statement John could reply, "Honey, you are the best. I just want to be sure that this is going to work okay for you. You have things on your plate too." And from there they can work out who will finally drive the kids to school.[3]

Obviously all of the above ideas are only possibilities. If you and your spouse were having a similar conversation, it might take an entirely different turn. The point is, however, that Love and Respect couples always try to decode what the other one might be saying and try not to step on each other's air hose.

For some couples it often appears there is little to decode; for other couples, such as Roy and Nancy, they might be at a place where one or both of them are sending a lot of messages that need decoding. Remember what Roy wrote to me? He said: "I have begun assuming that whatever my wife says, I do not really understand." This has helped him listen better and draw her out. As a result, they have better discussions, she trusts him more, and he feels more respected.

Does All This Sound Like a Lot of Work?

About now it's possible that some spouses may be thinking, *This decoding and avoiding air hoses is an awful lot of work.* You're right. There is work involved, and every couple who wants to succeed in their marriage must go through exchanges just like the ones illustrated above. But it is actually less work than you might think. You can decide not to bother decoding your spouse's words, and you can forget to worry about your spouse's air hose. But realize you are *already* in a pattern of some kind, responding to your spouse in some fashion, quite possibly jumping to conclusions and sidestepping deeper issues. Guess what? You end up spending just as much—if not more!—time and energy getting angry, withdrawing, pouting, accusing, defending, worrying—and losing sleep.

> *Spare your spouse's air hose and think before you speak. "The heart of the wise instructs his mouth" (Proverbs 16:23).*

If we were all perfect, we would not have to do decoding or think about avoiding air hoses. But because these processes are necessary, do not somehow conclude that you have a bad marriage. I wish I could tell you, "Hey, Sarah and I never have misunderstandings. We just cruise through a wonderful life." The truth is Sarah and I decode each other and step gingerly around each other's air hose practically on a daily basis. You will have to do the same if you want to keep the Crazy Cycle from turning.

The challenge is there: whether or not you are willing to make the mature decision and take a few minutes now and then to go back and forth asking questions to decipher what each of you mean. And are you willing to tune in and notice when you are stepping on your mate's air hose—and then apologize on the spot? These steps aren't particularly convenient or always enjoyable, but it is the process for the best of marriages, which explains why they are the best of marriages!

Two Questions Well Worth Asking

Along with the skills of decoding and avoiding air hoses are two helpful questions spouses can ask themselves as they go through their day. One is for him; the other is for her.

- "Is what I am about to do or say going to feel unloving to her?"
- "Is what I am about to do or say going to feel disrespectful to him?"

This may sound easy, almost a no-brainer, but I assure you it is not. In the hurry, pressures, and stress of everyday life it is all too easy to forget, and without meaning to, we treat each other unlovingly or disrespectfully. Sarah and I still struggle at times, and the Crazy Cycle starts to growl. As I mentioned earlier in this chapter, we still need to apologize to each other on occasion, and that means both of us have to:

BE WILLING TO MAKE THE FIRST MOVE.

If you both know the other is goodwilled and if you both know about each other's air hose, then all you really need is the willingness to share your feelings honestly, humbly, and nondefensively. I cannot emphasize too strongly that, in a marriage, *a willing attitude is everything*. For example, in almost any instance, you can stop the Crazy Cycle in its tracks if one or preferably both of you are willing to simply say, "Hey, we're acting crazy here. It is probably me. I am sorry. Please forgive me."

Forgiveness is a lost art in society, in church, and, sadly enough, in marriage. Because forgiveness is so important, we will devote chapter 7 to learning how to forgive as Jesus did.

CHAPTER SEVEN

---∞∞---

Forgiveness: The Ultimate Strategy for Halting the Crazy Cycle

We have looked at two important communication strategies for stopping the Crazy Cycle:

1. *Learn to decode each other's messages.* Husbands and wives speak to each other in code, not all the time, but often enough to be a continuing factor in the quality of their communication. Unless they learn to decode the real needs being expressed in each other's spoken messages, they will ride the Crazy Cycle a lot more often than necessary. A major challenge in learning to decode is to realize you and your spouse are very different, as different as pink and blue. Typically, women are sensitive and men are matter-of-fact. They hear with different hearing aids—pink for her, blue for him. A key to decoding your spouse is to adjust your hearing aid and really listen to what he or she is saying.

2. *Don't step on each other's air hose.* Her air hose leads to a big tank labeled "Love"; his leads to a big tank labeled "Respect." With just a few words, sometimes one word and a certain look, you can trample your mate's air hose and shut off what he or she needs to survive in your marriage. Remember the Crazy Cycle principle? If her tank isn't regularly filled with love, she reacts without respect; if his tank isn't regularly filled with respect, he reacts without love, and the Crazy Cycle spins unmerrily along for both of you. This is not to defend the disrespectful or unloving reaction but to describe what tends to be the first impulse when you're feeling unloved or disrespected.

It would be ideal if simply knowing these two basic strategies meant an end to all communication problems. Unfortunately, it is not that simple. Sometimes, as hard as we may try, we don't decode properly or in time. Far more often than we intend, we do step on each other's air hose. What then? The third and, really, the most important strategy for stopping the Crazy Cycle is the easiest and sometimes the most difficult of all: *Forgive each other as Christ forgave you.*

There Are Plenty of "Reasons" Not to Forgive

Have you ever been offended by your spouse? Have you ever struggled with forgiving your spouse? Perhaps it was a decoding issue. Whatever it was, undoubtedly somebody's air hose was pinched, and the Crazy Cycle started to turn. Perhaps the struggle went on for a few minutes or hours, or it might have lasted for several days, weeks, or even longer. What goes on in our minds when we struggle to forgive each other? From personal experience, I believe the following thoughts possess us. We tell ourselves "I won't forgive" for all kinds of reasons, including these:

- "I don't deserve to be treated this way!" (Translated: "I am a good person and this is unfair.")
- "I refuse to be treated this way anymore!" (Translated: "I must protect myself from being the fool and victim again.")

- "My spouse must pay. He or she will not get off the hook!" (Translated: "I will punish my spouse for how I have been treated.")
- "I have a right to feel this way." (Translated: "I can justify myself and prove that I am right and my spouse is wrong. Even Jesus was righteously indignant at times.")
- "My friends will back me up." (Translated: "They listen and understand because they have been there too.")
- "God has let me down. Part of this is His fault." (Translated: "I have a right to be mad at God for allowing this. He needs to make amends by doing something good.")
- "Forgiveness is a nice ideal, but I have to survive." (Translated: "I live in the real world where it's an eye for an eye or you always lose.")

Most of us can see through any of the above excuses for not forgiving even though we may have used some of them in a pique of anger from time to time. Besides, we know that Jesus taught His followers to "forgive seventy times seven" (Matthew 18:22). And many of us squirm a bit when we read our Lord's words: "If you forgive those who sin against you, your heavenly Father will forgive you. But if you refuse to forgive others, your Father will not forgive your sins" (Matthew 6:14–15 NLT).

Over the years I have had many people ask me exactly what these words mean. They wonder, "Is Jesus saying that if I don't forgive, God won't forgive me and I'll lose my salvation?" It helps to remember that because Jesus went to the cross and died for our sins, the forgiveness that provides our salvation is a "done deal," so to speak. After Christ was resurrected, believers were primarily exhorted to forgive because they *have been forgiven* rather than exhorted to forgive in order to be forgiven (see Ephesians 4:32; Colossians 3:13).

Not Loss of Salvation, but Loss of Fellowship

Refusing to forgive someone will not cost you your salvation, but it will disrupt your fellowship with the Lord. In effect, the Lord is saying, "You cannot fellowship with Me and experience My cleansing power until you forgive the person who has wronged you." God will not damn you for your unforgiveness, but He will enact discipline, which He lovingly does for all waywardness (see Hebrews 12:5–11). This is why people who are bitter and unforgiving do not experience the presence, peace, and power of God. The heavens seem as brass, and God seems far away.

It doesn't take much to find yourself in the "heavens as brass" mode. Just a little spat will do it, as Sarah and I have discovered. During our first years of marriage, a typical scene would find Sarah angry with me and I with her, and neither of us would forgive or ask forgiveness. Still smoldering with anger I would leave the house and head down to my office at the church to prepare a sermon for the following Sunday. But after I closed my office door and sat down to pray and read the Scriptures, I found that the heavens would not open. God seemed to have something against me. He wasn't mean about it. In fact, I felt He was just being matter-of-fact.

I heard no audible voice, but He spoke quite clearly nonetheless: "If you do not forgive Sarah and seek her forgiveness, I am not allowing My Spirit to touch your spirit. Things will not be right between us until you call Sarah and reconcile with her." I would reach for the phone to make that call, and more often than not the phone would ring before I could pick up the receiver. It would be Sarah calling me to reconcile because she had been getting exactly the same kind of message from the Lord.

Our spats were never much more than that—just two married people butting heads over little or nothing. We still have one on rare occasions, as our tiff in the airport terminal shows (see chapter 5). Our conflicts have been quite tame compared

> *God doesn't want us to carry grudges. "Forgive . . . so that your Father . . . will also forgive you" (Matthew 11:25).*

to what some people go through due to adultery, physical abuse, or desertion, to name just a few. But whether the conflict is minor or major, the principle is the same. If a small conflict can result in an unforgiving spirit toward a spouse and the heavens become as brass, consider how much more serious it is when there is a major trespass and the person who was wronged chooses to be bitter and vindictive for years, perhaps for life.

Whether a matter is weighty or light, the path to forgiveness is to realize that this issue that prompted your need to forgive isn't primarily about your spouse. First and foremost, your communion with God must be the real focus. Suppose Sarah might be 100 percent guilty of wronging me. Her guilt cannot justify my unforgiving heart. I can remain unforgiving toward Sarah as long as I wish, but as long as I do so, I forfeit my enjoyment of God's tender fellowship. While I lick my wounds, I can argue with God or anyone else all day long and explain that I have a right to be unforgiving. But God's spiritual law does not change. If I don't forgive, I remain unforgiven by God in the sense that my unforgiving spirit is sinful, and this sin blocks my fellowship with Him. My issue with Sarah is secondary to my relationship to God.

Jesus Is a Model of How to Forgive

Through the years I have read and listened to many excellent thinkers discuss the question "How does one forgive? What is the process and how can you do it especially when you don't feel all that forgiving?" For me, the best of insights continue to reinforce what I have learned from the Person and teachings of Jesus. Jesus was wronged more than anyone. Finally, all the sins of the world were placed unjustly on Him! What did He, the Perfect One, demonstrate about how to forgive? Jesus' words and ways reveal the secret, which includes three steps:

Jesus **sympathized** with the offender.
He **relinquished** the offense to His heavenly Father.
He **anticipated** the Father's help.

These three steps may sound unfamiliar, even impossible. You're thinking, *Yes, but you don't know what my spouse is like!* But stay with me. These three steps are a pathway out of bitterness and a way to avoid becoming bitter in the first place. Have you ever thought about sympathizing with your spouse, relinquishing your offended feelings to your heavenly Father, and anticipating God's help?

"Sounds great if you're Jesus," you might reply. "You just said He was the Perfect One. That puts Him out of my league. I can't do what Jesus did."

On the contrary, Peter indicates that Jesus is the example for husbands and wives. In 1 Peter 2, the apostle continues to explain the meaning of grace in a believer's life, a discussion he began in chapter one. He spells out how Christians are to be holy,

> *Finding it hard to forgive? Jesus said, "Learn from Me . . . and you will find rest for your souls" (Matthew 11:29).*

God-fearing, loving, honoring, mature, and submissive to authorities even when subjected to unfair treatment. And why should Christians do all this? "For you have been called for this purpose, since Christ also suffered for you, leaving you an example for you to follow in His steps" (1 Peter 2:21).

After taking several more verses to describe how Jesus responded when He was mistreated, Peter goes on to say, "In the same way, you wives . . . You husbands likewise . . ." (1 Peter 3:1, 7). In the same way as what? Like what? You are to respond to your spouse and to any mistreatment or misunderstandings in your marriage *in the same way* that Jesus responded to the mistreatment He received. Peter is saying Jesus is not out of our league at all. By becoming a man and dwelling among us, He put on our uniform, so to speak. He is not a model "who cannot sympathize with our weaknesses." Instead He "has been tempted in all things as we are, yet without sin" (Hebrews 4:15).

If you are tired of being angry with your spouse all too often or if you are growing weary carrying the burden of an unforgiving spirit, you can learn Jesus' process for forgiving. It won't be automatic; you will have to work at it. But if you don't work at it, it will burn you with a fire that sears but does not consume. You will be like a pig on a spit, slowly roasting over flames hour after hour, day after day. The pig, of course, doesn't mind because it is dead. You, however, are very much alive, and your unforgiving spirit puts you close enough to the flames to be in excruciating pain, but far enough away to never die. (See Appendix A, "How to Get Off a Chronic Crazy Cycle Caused by Low-Grade Resentment," p. 327.)

It may be true that in your marriage you have encountered far more pain and mistreatment than I have. But even though I have not had to forgive Sarah for much of anything, I still know a little about family-of-origin forgiveness issues due to the hurt I suffered at the hands of my father. I know from experience that the insights of Jesus regarding forgiveness are invaluable. It is worth your time and effort to follow His approach to forgiving. The whole basis of His approach is different, and this difference is exactly what can help you.

1. When Offended by Your Spouse, SYMPATHIZE.

When you sympathize, you try to look beyond the offense to other factors that help explain why your spouse offended you. The better you understand your spouse, the more easily you can forgive. How does Jesus model this step? While He is suffering in horrible agony on the cross, He prays, "Father, forgive them, for they do not know what they are doing" (Luke 23:34). Jesus prays for forgiveness of the Jews and the Roman soldiers who are taking part in crucifying Him. He forgives by looking beyond their heinous crime to see the ignorance, mindless fear, and blind hatred

> *Paul and Peter urge "sympathy" (Philippians 2:1; 1 Peter 3:8 ESV). Sympathy makes forgiveness easier.*

that have driven them to do this. On the cross, in terrible pain, Jesus sees the true condition of His enemies and feels compassion for them.

The apostle Paul echoes Jesus' teachings on forgiveness. For example, before he addresses the topic of marriage in Ephesians 5, Paul speaks about forgiveness in chapter 4, so husband and wife can extend it to one another: "Let all bitterness and wrath and anger and clamor and slander be put away from you, along with all malice. Be kind to one another, tenderhearted, forgiving each other, just as God in Christ has forgiven you" (Ephesians 4:31–32). Because we are Christ followers and forgiven by God, we can and should forgive one another. Because we need His forgiveness, we can and should understand someone else's need for forgiveness from us. Because we are all in the same boat, we can and should sympathize with one another.

I am often asked, "What if my spouse has hurt me far more than I have hurt my spouse? How can I forgive when I have been treated so unfairly?" Suppose, for example, your husband hurts you with rage and angry harshness. But suppose you learn that, while he was growing up, your husband was wounded and, to a certain extent, shaped by his father's anger and harshness. Consequently, your husband struggles with a volatile temper and doesn't even realize how harsh he sounds most of the time. As you look beyond how he is treating you to his upbringing, it helps explain why he is so harsh and angry. This does not minimize your husband's sin, nor does this "looking beyond" suggest you never confront his anger and harshness.[1] But because you know his background, you see a bigger picture. You are more able to understand his heart and struggle.

My own mother was an incredible example of one who could look beyond the offense and see other factors. When I was around ten years old, I told my mother how hurt and angry I was because of my father's neglect and cursing at me. She explained, "Well, your dad did not have a dad. His dad died when he was three months old. He doesn't know how to be a daddy."

At first I didn't understand, but later I realized my mother was sympathizing with my father even though she hurt far worse for me. Mom was wise, and her attitude enabled her—and me—not to become bitter. Eventually I was able to see my father not as my enemy, but as the victim of an enemy—the death of his own father and the suffering he went through growing up without a dad to love and guide him. I was also able to accept certain things about my father that otherwise would have embarrassed and infuriated me. Yes, his name-calling and outbursts of anger wounded me, but with my mother's guidance I was able to look beyond the offenses to see other factors that explained why he hurt me. Because I was able to understand my father, I was able to forgive him.

Looking beyond my father's offenses prevented me from reducing him to a one-sentence description such as "He was a miserable excuse for a father." Years later, when I was in college, my father placed his faith in Jesus Christ. How sad it would have been for me if I had passed judgment on my father in a way the Lord Himself did not. Because the Lord called my dad to Himself, He clearly had not given up on my dad. Because my dad responded, his own heart was obviously tender and open to the Lord. So, what if I had refused to see the painful backdrop of my dad's life? What if I had judged my father as despicable and hopeless, refusing to ever talk to him again? My lack of sympathy and forgiveness would have deprived me of many years of an enjoyable friendship with my dad before he died.

What about seeing your own spouse in light of certain factors that might help explain his or her behavior? Repeating his advice in Ephesians 4:32, Paul writes in Colossians 3:13 to "forgive as the Lord forgave you" (NIV). In the final analysis, your spouse is like you and you are like your spouse when it comes to forgiveness. You both have done and said things that need forgiving. So, why not start by sympathizing with each other?

As I have counseled people, I notice something about those who can forgive. They understand the well-known saying "There but for the grace of God go I." One husband told me:

Even though I feel betrayed by her adultery, I understand in part why my spouse did what she did. I won't justify her actions, but I clearly see she was seeking to meet a need. She should not have done this, and there are consequences, but if I had been more sensitive in meeting her needs, perhaps she would not have been as vulnerable. I'm confident we can turn the corner on this. As she has sought my forgiveness, so I've sought hers. This will be a tough time for us, but I already see a greater openness and honesty between us, and we are both making changes that we should have made many years ago.

A wife wrote to tell of her husband's adultery with a co-worker. She was devastated but decided to fight for her marriage by looking at her own behavior and praying that God would show her what she needed to know about her husband in order to rebuild their relationship. She heard our radio program on Love and Respect. What she heard about her husband's need for respect was totally new. His adultery was not excusable, but the Love and Respect message helped her understand—and sympathize:

I see now how my attempts to get him to love me were just the opposite of what I should have done . . . The Love and Respect message has had a profound effect on me and in me, as it has allowed me to open my heart again to my husband and see many of his actions in a different light.

For many people in addition to this husband and wife, forgiveness tends to follow their decision to sympathize with their mate. A wife writes, "It's so much easier to forgive when you understand the why behind your spouse's behavior."

Understanding is the key. As you try to understand your mate, you will be able to sympathize. (For pointers on how to sympathize with your spouse concerning any offense, mild or serious, see Appendix A, p. 327.)

2. As You Work Toward Forgiveness, RELINQUISH the Offense to Your Heavenly Father.

When you relinquish the pain within you to God, you surrender to Him whatever it is that you have against your spouse in your heart. Such relinquishment does not mean you let your spouse off the hook (see Appendix B), but you surrender to God this wound in your soul. Even though you have sympathized with your spouse, resentment can fester inside of you. So you must let go of your unforgiving spirit by giving it to God. For many people this sounds good in theory, but not at all within the realm of reality. Their bitterness feels like a tumor that cannot be removed. And for some people, the bitterness has even become a good friend, and they simply don't wish to say good-bye. Still other people have *become* the resentment: it is who they are. In these cases and others, the act of relinquishing the hurt and hate to God seems an insurmountable hurdle on the path of forgiveness. But what did Jesus do when He faced the insurmountable?

In the Garden of Gethsemane Jesus looked ahead to His crucifixion—to the shameful treatment, the agonizing pain, and, worst of all, humanity's sins being placed squarely on Him. Facing the unimaginable, Jesus prayed, "Father, if you are willing, take this cup from me; yet not my will, but yours be done" (Luke 22:42 NIV). Clearly, Jesus let go of His own will, which shrank from what lay ahead, and surrendered to His Father's will.

Are we supposed to do the same? Peter tells us:

> *Relinquishing is praying, "Our Father . . . your will be done" (Matthew 6:9–10).*

Christ suffered for you, leaving you an example that you should follow in His steps. "He committed no sin, and no deceit was found in His mouth." When they hurled their insults at Him, He did not retaliate; when He suffered, He entrusted Himself to Him who judges justly. (1 Peter 2:21–23 NIV)

We are to imitate Jesus. Just as Jesus relinquished the right to retaliate and trusted His Father for the outcome, so should we.

When you relinquish an offense, you need to send that offense somewhere. So follow Jesus' example and release it to your heavenly Father. Like Jesus, you must talk to the Father. You must pray, "Not my will be done." When you do so, you relinquish your will to resent and your will to be unforgiving. So let Him hear you honestly pray this way. This is a crucial step toward forgiveness. Keep in mind also that Jesus taught that you must forgive "from your heart" (Matthew 18:35). This demands an honest appraisal of what is in your heart, of what you have against your spouse. Before you can surrender or give anything to God, you must be in tune with what is going on inside of you.

You may not want to admit it, but the reason you are having to work toward forgiving your spouse is because you have bitterness in your heart. Remember Paul's words from Ephesians 4:31? He tells all believers to "let all bitterness and wrath and anger and clamor and slander be put away from you, along with all malice." I used to think Paul's comments on putting away bitterness sounded rather simplistic, but over the years I have seen that people have far more control over their emotions than I was willing to admit. God does help you forgive when you feel helpless to forgive, but other times He reveals to you the need to put away bitterness.

A husband writes: "I tried to release my anger, forgive her, and move beyond the bitterness to healing. I truly do not feel anger or bitterness now, only sadness and disappointment. I've tried to keep revenge and bitterness out of my life since the Word tells me that it will eat you up inside." (What? He released the bitterness and is keeping it out of his life? Yes!)

A wife writes: "God has shown me the need to let go of my bitterness and resentment for what I interpreted as lack of loving/caring behavior on my husband's part." (What? She simply let go of the bitterness? Yes!)

Paul knew what he was talking about. We can get rid of bitterness—*if we want to.* I have seen that the ultimate reason a lot of people are bitter is that they *want* to be bitter. They welcome bitterness because it energizes them. However, when they finally realize bitterness is contrary to God's will, that it is self-destructive and ineffective in changing the other person, they choose to stop.

I used to be baffled by how some people could simply let go of their bitterness and cease hostilities. *Surely they are in denial,* I thought. *These people cannot move beyond bitterness to healing by simply putting it all away.* Yet, that is exactly what they did, and I stood corrected by the Lord again. I have concluded that many who are bitter have chosen bitterness; bitterness has not chosen them. We all have a choice: keep manufacturing your bitterness or, one day, simply shut down the plant!

Please take note: the bitter anger of a husband or wife does not achieve the righteousness of God (see James 1:20). Responding to offensive words or actions with your own offensive words or actions is damaging and unproductive. The pot is simply calling the kettle black. Fighting fire with fire can help put out a forest fire, but in a marriage it only fuels the flames. (For communication pointers on how to relinquish the offense and at the same time confront the other person's sin, see Appendix B, p. 338.)

3. The Final Step Toward Forgiveness: ANTICIPATE.

To anticipate means having hope and trusting God to work. When Jesus prayed, "thy will be done," He believed His Father's will would be accomplished. This is why "He entrusted Himself to Him who judges justly" (1 Peter 2:23 NIV).

This kind of anticipation follows relinquishment. When you say, "Not my will," you will naturally want to follow that prayer with, "Your will be done." You can no longer feel vindictive or revengeful if you are anticipating God's perfect care and righteous judgment. We might say that, to the extent you are willing to relinquish the situation you need to forgive, to that extent you can anticipate God's intervention and help to forgive.

A husband wrote to tell me he had been at his wit's end with marital troubles:

After much praying, I just let go. I said, "God, this whole thing is in Your hands." A few days ago, my wife and I went to the Christian bookstore to get a Bible for a co-worker of hers, and while we were there, she found your book *Love & Respect*. Since she started reading it, she has made more positive changes than in all the two years we have been married. What is really incredible is that when she shows me respect, my feelings of love and affection start to sputter back on, like an old motor that has been left sitting for a long time. You're right. When she respects me, it makes me WANT to work so hard I could die, just to please her.

When this man put "the whole thing" in God's hands, he halted his ineffective attempts to solve his own problem, and he turned to God for help. As he came through with faith in God, he opened the door to having God come through for him. Their marriage turned the corner after he entrusted it to the Lord.

I know of a wife who was wronged by her husband. She became angry and unforgiving, but she knew this was destroying her. As a believer, she knew she needed God's help. She also knew that if she were

> *Let it go. "Don't try to get even. Trust the LORD, and he will help you" (Proverbs 20:22 CEV).*

to experience God's help, she had to do her part. So she decided to extend some sympathy to her husband and listen to his side of the story. As she did, she understood him better and felt freer to relinquish her anger. She also decided to seek her husband's forgiveness for her wrong attitude. It was then, to her joy, that "God showed up." She writes:

A friend was specifically praying that I would be willing to do whatever God wanted me to do. After tremendous conviction and a broken, humbled spirit, I knew I had to write Blake a letter apologizing to him, not only for not respecting him like I should have, but also apologizing for not handling my anger in godly ways. I also included some other things, such as telling him some things I appreciated about him. Until that day, I didn't even realize how angry I was. After I wrote the letter, I felt like a heavy load had been lifted, and I had tremendous peace. It was the most supernatural thing I had ever experienced. I had no idea what was going to happen from there, but I just acted out of obedience, and it has been amazing how God has blessed me and also brought some healing to our marriage.

This wife acted out of obedience and faith, anticipating (trusting and hoping) that God would work in her marriage, and He did. Notice what she did that contributed to moving things along. Because she had sympathized and relinquished her bitterness, she found herself wanting to do something positive for her husband. She blessed her husband by telling him some things she appreciated about him. Her husband may have deserved cursing, but this wife chose to bless instead. She lived out Peter's advice, "not returning evil for evil or insult for insult, but giving a blessing instead . . . that you might inherit a blessing" (1 Peter 3:9). Did she inherit a blessing? Her own words say it well: "it has been amazing how God has blessed me."

If you have been angry and unforgiving but have slowly moved through the steps of sympathizing and relinquishing, I pray that you will move forward, anticipating God's touch on your marriage. Yes, perhaps your spouse should make the first move and ask for your forgiveness. But what if your spouse is not as mature as you are or is more rebellious than you are? Will you remain an unforgiving soul? Is it worth forfeiting the power of God in your heart? (For pointers on how to anticipate God's help, see Appendix A, p. 327.)

Not a Formula but a Path

I realize that anytime something is described in terms of three steps, it can sound like a formula to be followed to the letter if it is to work. I want to emphasize that these three steps offer guidance on a path toward forgiveness. Some people are able to forgive by stopping to sympathize. Many need to consider relinquishing whatever has them struggling in the throes of unforgiveness and resentment. Others especially need the encouragement of anticipating that God will honor their step of faith and act in their lives.

All three of these steps are extremely useful in building better communication with your mate.

1. If you have sympathized, you will talk to your mate with more understanding instead of always making your case about why you have been hurt. Remember, mutual understanding is the key to good communication.

2. If you have relinquished your resentment, your spouse will detect a different tone and attitude in your words and, in all probability, will talk to you with a better attitude. Remember, bitterness shuts down your spouse. When bitterness leaves, your spouse will open up to you more.

3. To anticipate is to have hope in God. When your expectations are centered on what God will do, you will not place unrealistic expectations on your spouse. Remember, your heavy expectations will defeat your spouse, and healthy communication will go out the window. When you place your deepest confidence in God, you are free to be kinder to your mate, and this friendliness opens the lines of communication.

All three of the above steps put you in a more open frame of mind. They give you the attitudes you need in order to reach out to your spouse across the communication gap and make a connection. And connecting is what communicating is all about, as the following letter demonstrates.

As they looked forward to their twenty-fifth anniversary, this wife and her husband were torn apart by a catastrophe she feels was orchestrated by Satan himself, and they separated. She was almost to the point of suicide, and he was miserable too. When a friend told her about *Love & Respect,* she immediately bought a copy. After reading several chapters she began to sympathize with her husband's need for respect. Her letter continues:

> It was enough to let me realize that this was all the work of Satan because God is not a God of confusion and lies, but a God of truth and love. I e-mailed my husband and told him, in spite of all the hateful words and actions, I had always respected him— how he lived his life and the way he cared for me and my children, and I never wanted him to think that I had no respect for him regardless of what happened. He called me immediately and apologized for his part in the situation, and I apologized for mine. I came home the next day, and we have been happy ever since.

This story is only one of hundreds I hear every year. The Crazy Cycle is always there, ready to spin, but by communicating with love, demonstrating respect, and choosing forgiveness, you can slow it down or even stop it completely.

All of us may get on the Crazy Cycle from time to time, but there is a very effective preventative. It's called the Energizing Cycle, where her respect motivates his love and his love motivates her respect. *But to motivate, you must understand your spouse's need. The key to motivating another person is meeting that person's deepest need—love for her and respect for him!* In Part IV the focus will be on proactive ways to communicate positively, to speak and act with Love and Respect, and to enjoy each other to the full extent God intended.

PART IV

⟨⟨⟨⟨⟨

The Energizing Cycle:
To Better Communicate, Meet
Your Spouse's Needs

⟨⟨⟨⟨⟨

I hear from a lot of couples who have figured out how to stop the Crazy Cycle, but they still struggle to maintain a happy communicating relationship. There is an answer to this problem. It's called the Energizing Cycle, which is described this way:

HIS LOVE MOTIVATES HER RESPECT.
HER RESPECT MOTIVATES HIS LOVE.

And around you go in reciprocating fashion and in a win-win situation. When you are on the Energizing Cycle, the Crazy Cycle has no chance to spin unless you forget to use the tools at your disposal. Those tools will be discussed in the following chapters.

In chapter 8 you will learn how to communicate better by applying the principles of C-O-U-P-L-E (six steps to help husbands express love to wives) and C-H-A-I-R-S (six steps to help wives express respect to husbands).

In chapters 9 and 10, you will learn how to use decoding to deal with angry or unhappy comments that both of you are bound to make from time to time. (In chapter 5 you got a broad-brush look at the importance of decoding for good communication. Decoding is a skill that you must continually develop.) Chapter 9 (for wives) and chapter 10 (for husbands) will explain how to use C-O-U-P-L-E and C-H-A-I-R-S to decode messages your mate may send from time to time to let you know she is not feeling loved or he is not feeling respected.

In chapters 11 and 12, you will learn how to deal with the challenge of everyday communication. So much of life is very daily, very basic, and very routine. Miscommunications and misunderstandings happen at this level all the time. These chapters will teach you simple but all-important skills for dealing with communication glitches *before* they become Love or Respect issues.

CHAPTER EIGHT

Enjoy Win-Win Communication on the Energizing Cycle

I hear from many couples who read *Love & Respect* and get it concerning how to slow down and even stop the Crazy Cycle, but then they struggle with how to keep it from starting up again. They try to react less negatively to each other, but it's like turning down the settings on their flamethrowers. They don't consume each other, but they don't give each other cups of cold water too often either. Their marriage may be a little less crazy, but it's not as enjoyable as the words *Love* and *Respect* would seem to promise. Here are just two examples.

One wife explained that in the past she had conditioned her husband to respond defensively by rolling her eyes and sighing even when they were trying to communicate about the simplest of things. They have been trying to practice Love and Respect, but old habits die hard. She writes:

Wednesday night he attended a church meeting with me at the last minute. I had assumed he wasn't going because he had been battling a cold, but he came because he assumed I wanted him to come. I did not. I told him it was totally his call. Afterward he told me he would have stayed home with his cold had he really believed that I did not care if he attended or not. Clearly, we have some damage to undo before we can communicate effectively.

A husband reported that, after watching our *Love & Respect* video, he and his wife saw a marked improvement in how they communicated. He was trying to listen more, and she was trying to signal him more often when he started stepping on her air hose. He realized he had to work on saying "I'm sorry" sooner, and he also found himself "listening to understand." All of this was good, but then he added:

> I still need to improve, though. Last week she pulled out a past event from her "bowl of unresolved conflict." (I still think she was wrong on that one.) I decided to clam up to keep peace and ended up dwelling on a past event from my own "bowl of unresolved conflict."

These two letters illustrate that learning about how Love and Respect can stop the Crazy Cycle is only the beginning. Every couple needs to realize they must consciously make the effort to get on what we call the "Energizing Cycle" and apply its principles, which provide tools they can use to communicate better and more effectively.

I want to emphasize that slowing and even stopping the Crazy Cycle doesn't result in automatically experiencing the Energizing Cycle. Putting out the negative doesn't kindle the positive, nor is success merely the absence of failure. What you and your spouse must do is go beyond being *reactive* (using Love and Respect to stop the Crazy Cycle as it begins to start up) and be *proactive* (practice specific Love and Respect principles to breathe new life into your marriage).

As I have already explained (see chapter 2), I discovered the Energizing Cycle one day as I made a connection between Love and Respect that I had not seen before in Ephesians 5:33. The verse clearly says the husband *must* love his wife as much as he loves himself and the wife *must* respect her husband. Long before the day I made my discovery, I had been teaching Love and Respect as two of many important biblical responsibilities to be fulfilled by husbands and wives.

As I was reading Ephesians 5:33, I believe God prompted me to ask: "What would happen if a wife met her husband's need for respect?" The answer seemed obvious: "He would be energized. That is, he would be motivated to love her in return." As I pondered that, another question arose, and its answer became obvious: "What would happen if a husband met his wife's need for love?" Of course "She would be energized and motivated to respect him in return."

> *To stop the Crazy Cycle and get on the Energizing Cycle, "put off your old self, which is being corrupted by its deceitful desires . . . and put on the new self, created to be like God"* (Ephesians 4:22, 24 NIV).

Having seen this positive energizing connection between Love and Respect as stated in Ephesians 5:33, I decided it was like a cycle—an Energizing Cycle:

HIS LOVE MOTIVATES HER RESPECT.
HER RESPECT MOTIVATES HIS LOVE.

As I thought about my new discovery, I found myself asking, "How does this Energizing Cycle work? What can husbands and wives *do* specifically to proactively stay energized?" The answer to that came almost immediately.

As I mentioned, before my day of discovery, I had included Love and Respect as just two of a number of responsibilities that husbands and wives have toward each other in their marriage. I had been teaching and preaching on these responsibilities for a number of years and had actually built several sermon series on them. For example, the Bible teaches—and these are the salient passages for husbands—that a husband is to understand his wife, honor her, and be gentle (never bitter) toward her. Scripture also teaches him to lead her, to provide for her, and, of course, to love her. Responsibilities for the wife, according to scriptural teachings, include deferring (submitting) to her husband as well as being uncontentious and helpful. In addition she is to be a friend, quiet in spirit, sexually open to him, and, of course, respectful toward him. As I thought about how to fuel the Energizing Cycle, it became obvious that the best way to do that is to fulfill all your responsibilities toward your mate.

> *He builds her up with Love, she builds him up with Respect—the Energizing Cycle! Always, "let us pursue what makes for . . . mutual upbuilding" (Romans 14:19 ESV).*

C-O-U-P-L-E: Six Ways Husbands Can Love Their Wives

Using one of my favorite teaching and learning tools, I developed acronyms to help husbands and wives remember what God calls them to do. I experimented with several different combinations of biblical principles and finally settled on a plan where Love and Respect would be the capstones of my system. To help the husband remember how he is to Love his wife by being connected to her, I used the acronym C-O-U-P-L-E. It's quite likely you have seen C-O-U-P-L-E before, but here it is one more time, complete with each principle and the Scripture behind it:

C — Closeness: A loving husband is to cleave to his wife, taking time to talk, being affectionate, close to her heart—and not just when he wants sex (see Genesis 2:24).

O — Openness: A loving husband is to be kind and gentle, opening up to his wife, sharing his thoughts and ideas, instead of acting preoccupied, disinterested, or as if he is mad at her (see Colossians 3:19).

U — Understanding: A loving husband is to live with his wife "in an understanding way" (see 1 Peter 3:7), willing to listen when she is concerned or has a problem instead of trying to fix her. As he listens, he lets her know he is interested by paying attention and giving appropriate feedback.

P — Peacemaking: A loving husband is willing to say, "Honey, I'm sorry. Please forgive me" because he knows that he and his wife are to no longer be two, but one, living in peace and harmony (see Matthew 19:6).

L — Loyalty: A loving husband is always assuring his wife of his love and commitment, making her feel secure in the covenant they have together because she knows he would never "deal treacherously" with her (see Malachi 2:14–15).

E — Esteem: A loving husband honors and cherishes his wife in specific ways, making her feel she is first in his heart and honored as a "fellow heir of the grace of life" (see 1 Peter 3:7).

When a husband says loving things related to his wife's desires concerning C-O-U-P-L-E, she will be motivated and energized. Love is definitely more than words, but as you recall, the mouth speaks out of that which fills the heart. When love fills a husband's heart, his wife keenly wants to hear it or read it. Some husbands are self-conscious when expressing themselves face to face because it makes them

> *Husband, to energize your wife, "just talk about love. Put your love into action. Then it will truly be love" (1 John 3:18 NIRV).*

feel awkward. If you are a fairly typical male, you may have trouble expressing your emotions verbally. Earlier in our marriage I had this problem and would often resort to writing Sarah notes. Over the years I have learned to talk to Sarah openly about my feelings for her, but I still take opportunities to write something to her as well.

For example, while we were working on this book, Mother's Day rolled around, and on a greeting card I got for Sarah, I wrote:

> Sarah, thanks for being a mother who prays. When all is said, when all is done, when the earth is no more, when the seas disappear, and when the present age ends, God will speak. At that moment we will know your petitions on behalf of Jonathan, David, and Joy made all the difference in this world. Thank you for carrying this load on this one-time journey. Your husband, who loves you! May 14, 2006

In that note there were elements of Closeness and Openness and a great deal of Esteem. I wanted to honor Sarah for being the incredible mother and wife that she is. Did my words of esteem for her make her feel loved? Was she energized? Her face said it all as her eyes moistened and she held back her tears. Later, she wrote me a note:

> Your Mother's Day card and note meant so much. It encouraged me to persevere in prayer and made me remember about how you would encourage me along the way when I felt so inadequate as a parent. You gave me a sense of purpose and accomplishment—then and now. You're the best!

While many wives would respond to a written note as Sarah did, there are others who might say, "If he loved me from his heart, he would let me hear it from his lips." I have counseled many wives with this attitude, and I try to explain it's a case of Pink and Blue. As a rule, Pink can express her emotions easily, while Blue often struggles. If you have this problem with the man you love, I encourage you to cut him some slack.

Many men feel deeply about their wives, but they need help with expressing it. (For ways a husband can communicate love to his wife, see Appendix C, p. 341.)

C-H-A-I-R-S: Six Ways Wives Can Respect Their Husbands

C-O-U-P-L-E nicely sums up the connection to their husbands that wives long for, but what about husbands? What do they long for? As I searched for the right acronym, I thought of how God has created the husband to lead, protect, and serve his wife. In a word, the husband sees himself as one who "chairs" the relationship. To help the wife remember that she is to Respect her husband by acknowledging how God has created him, I used the acronym C-H-A-I-R-S. Here are the six principles in C-H-A-I-R-S, with the scriptural basis for each one:

> *Wife, follow your highest calling. No matter how difficult, unconditionally respect your husband so "that the word of God will not be dishonored" (Titus 2:5).*

C — Conquest: Because God made man to work (see Genesis 2:15), the respectful wife is called to appreciate his desire to do a good job and achieve in his field of endeavor. She does this by thanking him for his efforts and letting him know she is behind him (see Genesis 2:18).

H — Hierarchy: Because Scripture states the husband is the head of his wife as Christ is head of the church, the respectful wife is called to submit to her husband by appreciating his desire to protect and provide for her and the family, thanking him for his efforts (see Ephesians 5:22–25).

A — Authority: Because Scripture makes the husband responsible for loving and caring for his wife, she is called to respect his authority, not being contentious and combative, but appreciating his desire to serve and lead her and the family as she supports, and never undermines, his position (see Ephesians 5:25–33; Proverbs 21:9).

I — Insight: Because Scripture indicates that a woman can be tricked by cunning voices of the culture and led astray by carnal desires and intuitions (1 Timothy 2:14; 2 Corinthians 11:3), the respectful wife is called to appreciate her husband's desire to analyze and counsel, always listening carefully to what he has to say to guard or guide her. If she disagrees with his ideas, she differs with him respectfully.

R — Relationship: Because Scripture teaches that a wife should *phileo* her husband (love him as a friend [see Titus 2:4]), the respectful wife is called to appreciate his desire for shoulder-to-shoulder companionship, realizing that she is be her husband's friend as well as his lover (see Song of Solomon 5:16).

S — Sexuality: Because she understands that her husband needs her sexually, the respectful wife does not deprive him, but appreciates his desire for sexual intimacy, knowing that sex is symbolic of his deeper need for respect (see Proverbs 5:19; Song of Solomon 4:1–15; 1 Corinthians 7:5).

Whatever You Do, "Just Don't Change the *S*!"

As I developed my acronym material, I surveyed married couples by meeting in private homes with small groups to get feedback. I asked them, "Does this make sense, especially C-H-A-I-R-S?" I knew wives would resonate with C-O-U-P-L-E because it encouraged and instructed men to do all the things that are near and dear to a wife's heart. But I wondered if women—or men, for that matter—would respond positively to the more abstract and bolder ideas in C-H-A-I-R-S.

I asked one group of wives I knew were deeply influenced by feminism if such words as *hierarchy* and *authority* were offensive. I was amazed when they said, "After hearing how you define each term and apply it to our daily lives, it all makes perfect sense to us. Don't change a thing." Still doubtful, I said, "But I can rework this if you feel the words themselves will turn women off before they give me a fair hearing."

All of them told me to keep the hot-button words and teach them. One gal commented, "Don't water this down. This reflects how guys really are." Their husbands chimed in, echoing their wives: "Don't change a thing. What you teach is how we feel." One husband said for all to hear: "I don't care if you change any of the first five letters in C-H-A-I-R-S. Just don't change the *S!*"

The result of my years of research and biblical study, C-O-U-P-L-E and C-H-A-I-R-S are what I use to teach the Energizing Cycle today. Each letter in each acronym stands for a specific principle based on Scripture, a principle God commands husbands and wives to practice in their marriage. By applying these scriptural principles to their lives, couples can learn to communicate with each other in ways that energize, not de-energize!

C-O-U-P-L-E paints a picture of the wife's inner world. Her thoughts and feelings revolve around C-O-U-P-L-E. She thinks pink and when her husband speaks the language of pink—remaining fully a man of honor, never becoming effeminate—his wife feels loved. Likewise, C-H-A-I-R-S paints a picture of a husband's inner world. His thoughts and feelings revolve around C-H-A-I-R-S. He thinks blue, and when his wife speaks the language of blue—remaining fully a woman and never becoming masculine— her husband feels respected.

These two acronyms outline various truths that teach us how to love our wife

> *The teaching of unconditional Love and Respect helps your marriage when you accept it "for what it really is, the word of God, which also performs its work in you who believe" (1 Thessalonians 2:13).*

or respect our husband, as you will see in the many examples discussed in the rest of this chapter.

The "If-Then" Principle Drives the Energizing Cycle

As we have seen, the Energizing Cycle is based on the Love and Respect Connection, which operates according to the "if-then" rule: if she does something respectful, then he is likely to do something loving; if he does something loving, then she is likely to do something respectful. The two acronyms C-O-U-P-L-E and C-H-A-I-R-S provide a framework of six loving principles a husband can practice and six respectful principles a wife can practice to make Love and Respect happen between them.

But there is still more for a husband and wife to understand about the Energizing Cycle. The "if-then" rule also comes into play to connect the principles in C-O-U-P-L-E with the principles in C-H-A-I-R-S. Years of study and counseling have led me to see marriage as a living, growing organism, like a fruit tree. With this analogy in mind, I like to describe the Energizing Cycle by saying the principles in one acronym cross-pollinate the principles in the other acronym. Cross-pollination, as you know, is the process that causes plants to be fruitful and productive. And that's exactly what C-O-U-P-L-E and C-H-A-I-R-S will do for your marriage.

Just about any set of combinations will work, and in the rest of this chapter I will show you just one set of examples that demonstrates how the principles can combine (cross-pollinate) to cause a marriage to become more fruitful. In addition I will share stories of couples who have experienced this cross-pollination for themselves and have been amazed at how it has strengthened and energized their marriages.

How C-O-U-P-L-E and C-H-A-I-R-S Feed Your Marriage

As the following set of combinations will show, there is a specific connection between the two acronyms. Letters in C-O-U-P-L-E connect with letters in C-H-A-I-R-S. One action causes the reciprocation of another action. But both actions must be communicated in words, deeds, and facial expressions. The beauty of it is that the relational power of these two actions—one from the man's side (C-O-U-P-L-E) and one from the woman's side (C-H-A-I-R-S)—flows freely back and forth. Also, nobody has to "go first," but both spouses should be quite willing to make the first move. For example:

How CLOSENESS connects with RELATIONSHIP: When a husband chooses to be close and talk face-to-face with his wife, then his wife is motivated to be in shoulder-to-shoulder relationship with him without talking. Conversely, if a wife chooses to be in a shoulder-to-shoulder relationship with her husband *sans* talking, then her husband is motivated to be close and talk face-to-face with her.

> *Get energized! Speak words of Love or Respect. "Words satisfy the soul as food satisfies the stomach; the right words on a person's lips bring satisfaction" (Proverbs 18:20 NLT).*

From what couples tell me, they instinctively see the obvious connection. What goes around, comes around! One wife said, "We even make sure that we spend face-to-face time and shoulder-to-shoulder time together." Result? "My husband and I have seen a change in our marriage. We communicate with each other on a much deeper level than just talking. We hear our mother tongues. I can't believe how much more in love with each other we are."

Another wife relates that her husband is now warm and friendly instead of cold and distant, and it has all come about because they have started showing interest in each other's activities. She used to be irritated by his requests to come look at what he had discovered on the Internet. Now she not only looks, but talks with him about what he has found and compliments him on his knowledge of various subjects. He in turn enjoys joining her in hunting for antiques on eBay. "It keeps the communication so much more open between us," she says. "When he is on the computer now, he is still accessible and will talk to me when I need to, when he wasn't before."

How OPENNESS connects with SEXUALITY: If a husband chooses to be open, heart-to-heart with his wife, then she is motivated to be open to him sexually. And of course the reverse is true. If she is sexual with him, he will be willing to open up to her. In an e-mail, one wife relates that she knows sex is very important to her husband and that God created sex to bind husband and wife together. She continues:

> Over the past few months I have been praying, "Lord, help me be a responsive, fun wife in the bedroom." Praying like this . . . knowing I am honoring God (He created sex anyway) as I'm honoring my husband has been very freeing. . . . I know my husband has noticed a difference because he is more available to me emotionally and conversationally. We are more "one"—and not just in the bedroom. We fight less and enjoy each other more.

Here's something you husbands may want to try. Invite some married couples over for dinner (check with your wife first, of course) and, as you dine, ask them to share the story of how they met and eventually got married. Draw them out and let them talk. Then share how you met your wife and describe what you felt about her as you dated and courted her. Assuming you can say it honestly, express that you feel the same way about her today and, if you could go back in time, you would pursue her again for the same reasons. After your guests leave, notice the spirit of your wife. She will be energized. This is why women love attending weddings. It takes them back and ignites their romantic feelings again.

If having dinner guests seems like a lot of work, try just talking with your wife about your love for her. Avoid impatience, anger, or irritation of any kind, which is always a turnoff for her sexually. But talking about how much you love her is a turn-on.

One major proviso: you are not to be open just to get sex. In fact, it is possible that you can be open about your love for your wife, and she may not always respond sexually. But as you openly share with her about your love and how you enjoy life with her, you will meet her emotional needs and find her much more open to your sexual needs. God designed her this way.

Over the years I have heard many women tell me, "I enjoy sex, but I cannot respond to his harshness. If he would not angrily react to me in ways that hurt, and if he would just tell me he loves me, I would be far more responsive."

How UNDERSTANDING connects with INSIGHT: If a husband chooses to listen to his wife's concerns and problems in an understanding way, then she will be motivated to appreciate his insights. And as a wife listens to her husband's insights, views, and opinions, he will be motivated to listen to her with understanding instead of immediately trying to fix her problem.

I get many letters that affirm this is really a no-brainer. Before Love and Respect, one husband found himself quickly riding the Crazy Cycle when he responded to his wife's problems and hurts with solutions and advice. He had the best intentions, but his wife lashed out, asking him not to preach to her or try to fix her. He explains:

> I would then be frustrated, thinking, "What did *I* do? This is the same advice I would give anyone who comes to me for help. Why is she trashing it?" Thus, she did not feel loved and I did not feel respected. Now I understand the need to listen and literally ask the question: "Do you need solutions, or do you need me to just listen?" It has opened up communication and strengthened the bonds between us.

A wife wrote to confess that she had planned their daughter's wedding and left her husband out of the loop about the expenses, which were considerable. He became angry and started complaining that everyone just ignored what he might think and that, basically, he got no respect. Before Love and Respect, his wife would have just fired back, telling him it was her only daughter and she wanted her to have a nice wedding, etc., etc. Instead, she kept the Energizing Cycle humming by looking at the situation from his standpoint. She apologized and admitted she was wrong in the way she had been handling the plans. Her letter continues:

We talked over the wedding budget and agreed on how much we would contribute to it. He settled right down, and we were able to discuss the expenses clearly and rationally. . . . In the past I would try to get him to settle down by telling him I love him, and he would say, "I know that! But you take me for granted!" He doesn't use the *respect* word, but he does use the *taken for granted* phrase, which is the same thing. I never understood why telling him of my love wasn't enough. After [our discussion about the wedding expenses] was over, we were also closer, and it felt like we were a team working together on the problem.

How PEACEMAKING connects with AUTHORITY: If a husband chooses to be a peacemaker, taking the needs and concerns of his wife totally into account during any kind of argument or conflict, his wife will be motivated in turn to respond to his authority during stalemates. By the same token, if a wife chooses to respect her husband's authority (desire to serve and lead), he will be motivated to make peace with her and try to meet her needs and concerns during conflict at any level.

> *"The mouth of the righteous flows with wisdom . . . The lips of the righteous bring forth what is acceptable"* (Proverbs 10:31–32).

A husband wrote to tell me that using the Love and Respect communication tools had been paying off. He is more aware of when his wife is hurt by something he did or said that she felt was unloving, and he is quite willing to ask her forgiveness so they can "move ahead in a more productive manner." And he adds, "My wife has been blessing me through telling me often that she respects me for the ways that I lead and love our family. This really makes me feel good."

I have often counseled with couples where the wife is the demanding, authoritative one, which almost always causes trouble. One wife shared that she and her husband had totally different approaches to solving problems or settling arguments. She came from a family who were "great arguers," and they thrashed everything out as they shared feelings and dealt with differences. Her husband came from a family that tended to ignore problems and pretend they weren't there. She saw him trying to do the same thing until she read *Love & Respect* and realized she had been trying to be the authority over him, demeaning him harshly for what she saw him "doing wrong." Since she has tried to be more respectful, she has "noticed a great difference in the way he responds to solving problems when I come to him humbly. He becomes more willing and honest."

This wife finally "got it." When she tried to be the authority, her husband was anything but a peacemaker. It was flight or fight. When she abandoned her disparaging, strident style and began being friendly and acceptant, he stepped up to the plate and faced problems instead of seeming to ignore them. She feels loved, and he feels respected. Instead of remaining opponents, they have become a team.

How LOYALTY connects to CONQUEST: If a husband chooses to be loyal to his wife and family and constantly lets her know it, she is motivated to be supportive of his career conquests outside the family. And when a wife backs her husband in his desire to work and achieve in his field of endeavor, it motivates and encourages him to remain loyal to her and the rest of the family.

It can be a delicate balancing act to make this connection work. An FBI agent confided in me that the amount of time he spent on his job was causing his wife to complain and question him even though he actually thought he was balancing things "pretty well." He would get defensive and lash back at her, saying he was trying his best to do a good job and he didn't appreciate her questioning. They would slip onto the Crazy Cycle from time to time because he heard her questioning the manner in which he tried to do his best at work, and he felt disrespected. His wife, however, was simply feeling unloved because she saw him spending inordinate amounts of time away from her. His letter continues:

This got us into the Crazy Cycle with a lather! Not until we discussed it in the light of our Love and Respect study did we truly understand the feelings of each other on this issue. While I couldn't do much to readjust my schedule (as a matter of fact, it soon got even more demanding time-wise), what changed for us was the ability to understand each other's intentions, and with that understanding came a release from the tension that blocked our communication.

With mutual understanding came better communication! The FBI agent and his wife made two crucial choices. She chose not to interpret his long hours as abandonment, and she learned to trust that he was making it a high priority to arrive home as early as possible considering the unpredictability and high demands of his job. He chose to accept her occasional words of admonition reminding him to prioritize family and home time because he could see she was consciously speaking words of affirmation and respect for his position and decision-making responsibilities. He adds, "When the light bulb turned on . . . we literally laughed with relief at having our impasse defined so clearly. Since our problem was 90 percent attitudes and 10 percent circumstances, we now find ourselves dealing with the 10 percent without much difficulty."

A wife wrote to tell her story of the conflict she had been having with her husband because he put in such long hours. One day she happened to be near where he worked, and she dropped in to talk for a few minutes. Her husband was swamped with answering phones that were ringing off the hook. He barely acknowledged she was there as she waited uncomfortably for about ten minutes, hoping to talk with him. Finally, unable to get his attention to even wave good-bye, she slipped out.

As she drove down the road, she knew she had to make a decision. They had studied *Love & Respect* together, and she knew that her old response to what just happened would have been "You're always putting work before me! I never see you anymore. Don't you even care?" She had gone to his office looking for a simple form of love—his attention and a little conversation. She didn't get it, and the Crazy Cycle could have easily spun that night when he got home because there had been many Crazy Cycle arguments over how cold he would be when she dropped by to see him at work.

But then God started reminding her of something I had said about how He has called husbands to be in the workforce and that wives should respect their husbands' desire to work hard and excel. Just as she made the decision to take that kind of stand rather than get angry, her cell phone rang. It was her worried husband. "Kath? I'm sorry. . . . The phones were so busy." "It's okay," she answered. "I'm not mad! I respect how hard you work, and I'm behind you 100 percent. Because of you, our family has all of our needs met. You are an awesome provider. Thank you!"

In shock, he said, "I'm so glad you understand . . . Phone's ringing again. Gotta go! Love you!" Her letter continues:

> Well, I just cried all the way home because I knew God was changing my heart. I loved the fruit I was seeing. That night, when he came through the door, he grabbed me and kissed me like it was our first time. He said, "I couldn't wait to get home to you. Let's go out, no kids, and just be together."

Round and round it goes in a joyful dance. When she respected his conquests in the workplace, he demonstrated his loyalty and love. When he assured her of his commitment to her, she was willing to support him in his work so much so she had to write and tell me!

How ESTEEM connects to HIERARCHY: If a husband chooses to esteem or honor his wife and her role in the family, then his wife is motivated to accept and respect his role as head of the family hierarchy and his desire to protect and provide for her and their children. When a wife is content with her husband as the head who protects and provides for the family, he is motivated to esteem, honor, and respect her by treasuring her as first in importance to him.

Stories come to me from all directions as couples get the connection between the powerful concepts in C-O-U-P-L-E and C-H-A-I-R-S. I heard from a wife who got the message after reading *Love & Respect* made her aware of how unfulfilled her husband was in their relationship. She admits that, although she deeply loved him, she never understood him. The daughter of a domineering father, she had seen her mother struggle as he "kept his wife in her place," and she determined this would not happen to her. After getting married, she and her husband both had careers, but she had the better job, which paid well. When children began to arrive, she went to part-time and, because her husband had a rotating schedule, she could schedule herself to work when he could be at home. She felt proud that she could show her husband she could be independent of him and show him it was her choice—not his choice—to be with him. She had no idea of how he felt until they learned about Love and Respect. Her letter continues:

> I didn't want a man to lord it over me like my father had, but this has brought about in my husband intense feelings of disrespect and of not even being needed in his own home. Also, he has chosen to work at a job that is not fulfilling nor financially rewarding, but one that allows us to raise our children without day care. He has stayed at this job to allow me greater freedom to be home, and I never looked at this as a tremendous sacrifice. I just thought he was too afraid to try anything else. We bought *Love & Respect* and read through it together. When I saw the tears flow from years of misunderstanding and pain, it crushed me. I feel an immense freedom now when I'm with my husband because he knows that I understand and can respond in his native tongue.

When this wife understood that her husband was honoring her by holding a lesser job, she became fully aware of how he was practicing headship of his family in a humble, sacrificial way, and she honored him by showing her deep respect. They had been on a Crazy Cycle for years almost without realizing it. Love and Respect put them on the Energizing Cycle and, as she says in closing, "saved our marriage."

Sometimes It All Works Out Beautifully

The set of comparisons that I have just shared illustrate a few of the ways C-O-U-P-L-E and C-H-A-I-R-S can affect your marriage with positive energy. In some marriages it's as simple as stopping one thing and starting another. Presto! The Energizing Cycle kicks in.

One husband related that, before he attended a Love and Respect Conference, his marriage was breaking down and he did not even see it. Both powerful firstborns and successful career people, they could not communicate without one trying to force his or her will on the other. The conference helped the husband see that every time he insisted on his own opinion or wishes, he was crushing his wife's spirit. He mistakenly thought he was simply establishing the fact that he was in charge and things would get better with time. He decided to stop coming across in an authoritarian manner, and now peace reigns in their home. He writes:

> *To practice the Golden Rule of marriage, give Love and be given Respect; give Respect and be given Love. As Jesus said, "Give, and it will be given to you" (Luke 6:38).*

> When I come home or talk with her during the day, I talk to her in a loving way. I communicate that I love her and respect her opinion. If things get out of hand—which they sometimes do—I reflect after the fact and approach her in a loving way. We talk back over the incident and move forward, usually in agreement. Even if one of us has to give in, we are both comfortable with the outcome. The principles taught in your seminar have helped us through some very tough times.

When another wife stopped communicating to her husband that he was an idiot with no insights worth sharing, *then* he started to be more understanding. She also sees a real improvement in her ability to express her needs to him instead of "becoming so hurt he just can't figure me out." Her e-mail continues:

> If I need something from him like time or attention or specific encouragement, I have the confidence to bring those requests to him because I know his greatest desire is to be my knight in shining armor. This seems like such a simple principle, yet it has freed me from the huffing and puffing and waiting for him to get a clue. Now I have the freedom to request respectfully things I need and not set him up for failure. (Mind reading is a terrible way to make a marriage.)

Sometimes spouses may think they are making all the right energizing moves, but they are overlooking one simple thing. One husband admits:

> When I heard the title of your seminar, I asked my wife if she felt loved. (We have been married thirty-seven years, and I have even done some teaching on marriage relationships.) Because I do so many things to demonstrate my love for her, I expected to hear a hearty "Of course, Jim!" so I was shocked when she was just silent. I reminded her of all the things I do to show her love, and I told her I couldn't understand why she wasn't giving me an answer. When she finally did answer, it changed my entire approach to demonstrating love to my wife. She said, "I do appreciate all the things you do for me, but the way I feel loved is . . . by the way you talk to me. When you talk to me the way you do to your men friends, I don't feel loved." Wow! What an eye-opener that was!

Jim reports that, in response to his wife's comment, he began speaking to her with kindness, tenderness, and thoughtfulness, not in the hurried and direct way he speaks to his male friends. Recently she told him, "Jim, you have been speaking so lovingly to me the last few days. That means so much to me. Thank you."

C-O-U-P-L-E and C-H-A-I-R-S Are Not Twin Vending Machines

I always caution spouses not to use C-O-U-P-L-E or C-H-A-I-R-S like they are vending machines—just put in a coin and out comes whatever you want. For example:

- "If I ride horses with my husband, he'll drink lattes with me and gaze into my eyes all evening."
- "If I open up emotionally to my wife, she will buy skimpy lingerie and even wear it to bed."
- "If I have more sex with my husband, we will become instant soul mates."

It could go on and on, but only if you want to use Love and Respect like a child wanting a candy bar. C-O-U-P-L-E and C-H-A-I-R-S should not be practiced to manipulate a husband into being loving or a wife into being respectful. I say this because I have seen far too many husbands and wives try to use this kind of information to change their spouse instead of trying to meet their spouse's needs. They seek to *get* Love or Respect, but not *give* it.

For example, I get e-mails from gals who give me glowing reports about how their husbands responded to their words and actions of respect—for a day. These guys help around the house, offer to do errands, and even give back rubs, but then it all stops by the next day—or so it appears. These wives ask, "Now what am

> *"Flattery is nothing less than setting a trap" (Proverbs 29:5 CEV). Your spouse will rebel against your manipulation and control.*

I supposed to do? This isn't working. Do you have any advice? What am I doing wrong? He was great for a day, but it didn't last."

When I get letters like these, my first thought is "Yes, I have advice. You are a gal who doesn't have a mean bone in her body, but you don't get it. This is not a vending-machine approach to marriage: 'I will show him a little respect each day, and then he must love me every day in ways that energize and pamper me. If he doesn't do it every day, this thing isn't working.' My advice is: Be realistic—respect him *unconditionally*—and be more patient."

I have the same advice for husbands who are trying to be loving after making a number of Crazy Cycle mistakes. Maybe you had some success, but lately your wife has pulled back and is her old critical self. Welcome to reality. Be patient and keep trying to love her *unconditionally*. If you wade into a dark swamp for two hours, it will take you at least two hours to wade out—and maybe longer. Likewise, if you have seriously wounded your wife several times over the years, she will need to see firsthand that she can trust you and open herself to you again. This takes time; there are no shortcuts. And you must love her regardless of her response.

Remember, *unconditional* means unconditional! What would you think of a person who announced the following? "I'm putting conditions on loving and respecting unconditionally! I will only do this unconditional thing under the condition that my spouse responds—and responds right now! If my spouse does not fulfill my conditions, then I'm stopping this unconditional stuff!" All of us laugh at this glaring contradiction of terms—the conditional unconditional! Yet all of us must admit we feel just this way when our spouse isn't responding to our gracious efforts!

But doesn't the Energizing Cycle promise a positive response from one's spouse? No! The Energizing Cycle is simply the best of all alternatives. It is more likely that a husband's love will motivate his wife's respect than his hate will. And it is more likely that a wife's respect will motivate her husband's love more than her contempt will. However, there is no guarantee that love or respect will motivate, and that is the reason the word *unconditional* must be put in front of *Love* or *Respect*. In fact, the paradox is that Love and Respect can only really work if it is unconditional!

The Energizing Cycle Has Long-Term Potential

Following is an e-mail from one fellow who really "gets it." For the first seven to nine years of their marriage, he spent a lot of time standing on his wife's air hose, criticizing her for most things he did not agree with. He was simply reflecting how he was raised in a family where "everyone was always at each other's throats." His wife could not handle it and she just clammed up on him.

Learning about Love and Respect turned him around, especially the "Love" part. He writes:

> I realize how important it is to love my wife in a special way. The positive thing is that we are not spending as much time on the Crazy Cycle as we did before. Patience is the key. I have chosen to stop criticizing my wife and spend more time praising her. I've seen small strides since going on your program, which has given me a better picture of how marriages are to look biblically. I'm excited about the long-term potential in following this approach.

I especially like this husband's reference to long-term potential. As two goodwilled people run the marriage marathon, a wife will want to respond respectfully when her husband loves her. At the same time, when a wife respects her husband, he will want to respond more lovingly. And the beauty of it is that the concepts in C-O-U-P-L-E and C-H-A-I-R-S can cross-pollinate in any number of combinations, not just the ones I used for my examples in this chapter.

A husband, for instance, can practice closeness as his wife responds positively to his authority and leadership. A wife may offer praise and admiration for how hard her husband works while he makes peace by apologizing for a sharp word he spoke earlier. A husband listens to his wife's concerns with understanding, and she responds with a special note thanking him for protecting her and providing for her.

Opportunities for practicing the Golden Rule Love-and-Respect style are everywhere. Anything can happen and the sky's the limit. The good news is that, nurtured faithfully and patiently, the Energizing Cycle works beautifully. But there is a bit of bad news: C-O-U-P-L-E and C-H-A-I-R-S are very effective tools, but they are not a magic bullet. As hard as you try to communicate in an energizing, positive way, there are bound to be those moments when one of you says something that sounds slightly (or more than slightly) negative. If the Energizing Cycle is to keep going, this kind of message needs decoding. In chapter 5 we saw how a couple can use decoding to stop the Crazy Cycle. But, as most couples realize, there is a fine line between the Crazy Cycle and the Energizing Cycle. To keep the Energizing Cycle going strong, you can't get too good at decoding. In the next two chapters, I will explain why decoding is a skill you will need as long as you are married and give you sample ideas of what to say to keep both of you energized.

CHAPTER NINE

Decode—and Then Use C-H-A-I-R-S to Energize Him

(Note to husbands: This chapter is for wives only, but you are invited to read along.)

While writing this book I had one of those days when I simply couldn't get anything done—or so it seemed.

Months before starting on this book, I had agreed to speak at a prayer breakfast that was two hours away. I decided to drive over the night before, check in at a motel, and be rested and ready to go the next morning. The prayer breakfast went well, and as I was driving home, my cell phone rang. It was Sarah telling me she had just made an appointment for me at a clinic where I could get my knee examined and X-rayed. The knee wasn't seriously sore, but it had kept me from my daily jogging routine.

Sarah had made the appointment for me because she was concerned (and tired of hearing me complain, but not do anything about it). I arrived at the clinic just in time for my appointment, and like countless others who have gone to the doctor, I waited. And I waited. Then I waited some more.

After a three-hour comedy of errors that included meeting two doctors (neither of whom was the doctor I was supposed to see); finally having my doctor arrive an hour and a half late, give me a shot, and then vanish; a fruitless attempt to get the X-ray technician to come back from lunch; and eventually having a nurse take the X-ray with coaching over the phone, I was told the knee was okay and just give it more rest before exercising again. I left, making a mental note to tell Sarah not to schedule me at this particular clinic again.

I went home with a knee that was still sore enough to keep me off the jogging track, a huge pile of e-mails that had to be answered, and not one word written for this book. My frustration increased when I learned that Sarah wanted to go out to dinner with Kathy, a friend of hers who was visiting from out of state. She hoped I could go too, but if I had no time due to my workload, she understood. Feeling obligated to play the role of gracious host, I went with them to dinner, and when I got back to my desk, there were still more e-mails screaming to be answered. I excused myself while Sarah went off with Kathy to chat for a while before bed.

Finishing the urgent e-mails, I decided to e-mail Sarah, who has her own computer in another part of the house. We are both on our computers a great deal, responding to e-mails from people who have attended a conference or read some of our materials. Often it's just quicker and handier to communicate briefly with in-house e-mail messages. This time my message was brief: "I'm getting frustrated. I've done no work on the book. It's been all e-mails."

That's what I said, but it was not exactly what I meant. Actually, I was wanting to send Sarah a message that *really* said, "I am frustrated because everything that happened today kept me from getting any writing done and meeting an impossible deadline—especially that doctor's appointment you set up and going out to dinner this evening."

Not content, however, with sending her an e-mail, I walked over to our "Four Seasons" room where Sarah and her friend were talking. Managing to get in Sarah's line of vision, but where her friend could not see me, I said, "I've done no work on the book today. It's been all e-mails." I did not sound or look angry, just rather matter-of-fact, but I was sure she would decode my real message: my conquests were not succeeding! Sarah looked back at me but gave no reply. She just kept talking with Kathy while I turned and went back to my computer.

In a sense I was trying to blame Sarah for the fiasco, but more accurately I just wanted to voice my frustration about not achieving my work-related goals and move on. Over the years, I have told Sarah that there would be moments when I might be upset about something, but if she would give me a little time, I would drop it and move on. Whatever upset me was my issue, not hers, but admittedly there might be times when I would try to entangle her in my issue and get her upset too. Of course I knew I should not have said anything about being frustrated over my horrible day. It was, after all, *my* issue. But because I was feeling sorry for myself, I could not resist the temptation to whine a bit even though I was writing a book on communicating lovingly with one's spouse!

> *"There is no one on earth who does what is right all the time and never makes a mistake"* (Ecclesiastes 7:20 GNB). *This includes your husband!*

What I did not realize as I headed back to my computer was that, even though Sarah had not yet read my e-mail to her, she was indeed angry about my boorish interruption of her conversation with Kathy to say, "I've done no work on the book. It's been all e-mails." And she *had* discerned that I was wanting to blame her for scheduling my three-hour doctor's appointment and taking Kathy out to dinner. Although she was angry, she told herself, "This is his issue. I will respond respectfully at the proper time and then drop it."

But later, after our houseguest had retired, Sarah read my e-mail for the first time: "I'm getting frustrated. I've done no work on the book. It's been all e-mails." This only irritated her all over again, but she reminded herself that in the past she had watched me vent and then move on. Controlling her anger, she answered my "I'm frustrated and it's kind of your fault" message with her own e-mail that said:

> Might I say that I am so sorry about your doctor ordeal today, but I would like to share with you that I woke up in the night with the idea to get you to a doctor so you wouldn't have to wonder and keep worrying about not exercising. And I gave you the option of not going to dinner tonight, and I truly meant it when I said you didn't need to go. So I do feel bad for you not getting anything written, but I am convinced this book will get done.
>
> Further, let's rejoice there is nothing wrong with your knee. We can look at the glass half-empty or half-full. As you have often said, "It is your choice. Choose wisely." You could be scheduling surgery, which would have taken at least another full day and maybe a couple weeks to recover.
>
> I will do what I can to support you—like make doctor's appointments, get you directions, make hotel and plane reservations, and tell people we can't get together with them, but other than that I don't know how else to help but to pray.

Sarah had, indeed, correctly decoded my frustration about getting no work done. She had not, however, allowed me to put her on a guilt trip for my very bad day, although it would have been easy for her to feel that way after my brief outburst. She also could have drawn both verbal pistols from her holsters and started blasting away, but she didn't. Or she could have just rolled her eyes in disgust as she told her friend that "Emerson sometimes feels a bit overwhelmed when he is writing a book." But she didn't do that either. Instead, she responded to my irritating e-mail message, plus the interruption of her conversation with her friend, with maturity, patience, and compassion.

After many years of working on our communication as a couple, Sarah knew this was an instance when I would receive her e-mail with the same goodwill that prompted her to send it. While my "It's been all e-mails" venting could be called childish, from our perspective it was more about Emerson being open about his feelings (*very* frustrated) about not achieving his personal goals for the day and Sarah responding respectfully and honestly. I was able to express what was on my chest, she shared her heart, and that was all that was needed. Sarah had confidence that I would receive her respectful exhortation and move on, which I did.

> *A respectful wife understands that "whoever forgives an offense seeks love, but whoever keeps bringing up the issue separates the closest of friends" (Proverbs 17:9 GW).*

Later, as I went to bed, Sarah said she needed to stay up to work on some things for the next day. She did not mention what had happened or her e-mail, and neither did I. Were we letting the sun go down on anger?[1] Not in this instance because I had vented my anger over a bad day and moved on, while Sarah had contained her anger and responded to me respectfully and had moved on as well.

There Is a Fine Line Between Energizing and Crazy

The next morning Kathy was laughing and having fun with Sarah, while I was my usual positive, cheerful self, ready to move forward with the many items on our Love and Respect Ministries agenda. Before getting into the daily routine, though, perhaps I should have said something to

Sarah like "Thanks for your e-mail last night. It was by far the best one I got all day." That would have been a perfect light remark to make, but to be honest I didn't think of anything like that at the time. The entire experience served as a reminder that Sarah and I are all still in process. We may never get this thing perfect, but we can make our communication less imperfect by learning from our mistakes.

A few days later, as I was working on the book, I realized that my "no good, very bad, horrible day" was actually a great example of decoding your spouse's negative message, but not stepping on his air hose in return. I wrote a rough draft of what had happened and showed it to Sarah. Then, and only then, did I learn that she had been upset by my "It's been all e-mails" antics.

"You did make me angry when you interrupted our conversation so rudely," Sarah admitted. "I almost said something, even with Kathy sitting there, but I contained myself because I realized it was your issue, not mine. And that's what I tried to say later when I wrote you my e-mail."

Sarah's comment completely surprised me. I had honestly not detected any irritation in her e-mail to me (although now that I look at it again, I can see that she was a bit angry but still trying to be firm and respectful). The entire incident was another instance (there have been many) when I was in my typical blue fog. I had been frustrated by my nonproductive day, so I had vented in my usual low-key manner and then gone back to work.

To put the whole incident in Love and Respect terms, what was really going on was that I was feeling disrespected by the incompetent treatment (three hours of sitting!) I had received at the clinic and frustrated by the impact this incompetency had on my work schedule. (Didn't those people know I had no time to waste while they tried to get their act together?) I had to vent my frustrations somewhere, so I did what husbands are often prone to do: I went home and wound up venting to my wife and coming across unlovingly toward her at the same time.

If Sarah had reacted disrespectfully, she would have slowed or even stopped the Energizing Cycle and started us moving toward the Crazy Cycle. I was already pushing us in that direction, but she defused things because she chose to address issues respectfully (and as the mature one!), while at the moment I was not being the poster child for Love and Respect—or maybe I was modeling for a poster you could throw darts at.

My point is that there is a fine line between the Energizing Cycle and the Crazy Cycle. All married couples have frustrating days as they try to keep the Energizing Cycle humming. When those days (sometimes they are moments) happen, it is more important than ever to decode each other and act in a mature manner. If you don't, the Energizing Cycle will slow and eventually stop, and the Crazy Cycle will kick in. You won't reach your goal of staying on the Energizing Cycle.

Obviously, I cannot give specific help for handling the endless variety of remarks that need decoding in any marriage. Each couple is unique; each spouse has his or her own way of sending messages. I can, however, lay down some biblical guidelines that will help us satisfy each other's basic needs for Love and Respect. In the rest of this chapter, I will discuss typical negative remarks that need decoding and then offer positive suggestions for what to say in response that will keep the Energizing Cycle going.

Whatever offensive words might have been spoken, always listen for your spouse's basic need. At the very bottom of things, in every case and in every conversation, you can do your marriage a huge favor by assuming she is seeking to feel loved or, in the case of this chapter, he is seeking to feel respected—and then give your spouse some grace!

> *All of us are talking back and forth, but "everyone enjoys a fitting reply; it is wonderful to say the right thing at the right time!" (Proverbs 15:23 NLT).*

How to Use C-H-A-I-R-S to Decode Your Husband's Cries for Respect

Does the Bible provide any tools husbands and wives can use to decode each other's words? Absolutely. In chapter 8, we looked at a general description of the two Energizing Cycle toolboxes: C-O-U-P-L-E for use by husbands and C-H-A-I-R-S for use by wives. In the rest of this chapter, we will look at how a wife can use the scriptural principles in C-H-A-I-R-S to decode (and possibly defuse) negative comments her husband might make. In chapter 10 we will see how a husband can use scriptural principles related to C-O-U-P-L-E to decode and defuse his wife's negative comments.

More often than a wife may realize, her husband will make an unloving comment that is really a cry for respect that needs decoding. His remark may be directed at something she has said or done, or it could refer to something else that has happened. We have just looked at one such instance. I had a very bad day and sent Sarah a coded message sort of blaming her for many of my problems, when I was actually more upset with the fiasco at the clinic and how it kept me from working.

> *The wife who decodes her husband's complaints and energizes him with Respect is indeed "a gift from the LORD" (Proverbs 19:14 CEV).*

Instead of feeling hurt by her husband's seemingly unloving words, a wife can look for possible explanations for his behavior and seek to fulfill God's call to her to give him the gift of unconditional respect, which he does not deserve (Ephesians 5:33).

To show her husband unconditional respect, a wife is to practice C-H-A-I-R-S.

- **C**onquest — She appreciates his desire to work and achieve.
- **H**ierarchy — She appreciates his desire to protect and provide.

- **A**uthority — She appreciates his desire to serve and to lead.
- **I**nsight — She appreciates his desire to analyze and counsel.
- **R**elationship — She appreciates his desire for shoulder-to-shoulder friendship.
- **S**exuality — She appreciates his desire for sexual intimacy.

My experience confirms that most husbands send their wives messages from time to time concerning their six basic needs. Following are ideas on how to decode these messages and respond in a way that improves communication with your husband.

CONQUEST: If he feels his work is unappreciated, you'll hear about it.[2]

Beginning with Adam, God designed man to work. We read as much in Genesis 2:15—"Then the LORD God took the man and put him into the Garden of Eden to cultivate it and keep it." But God had still more plans for Adam's work: "Then the LORD God said, 'It is not good for the man to be alone; I will make him a helper suitable for him'" (Genesis 2:18).

When his wife is his suitable helper, his companion to stave off loneliness, and a supporter of his pursuits in the workplace, a husband feels respected. But when a wife's attention and energy are drawn away from her husband, she may hear him saying: "The kids . . . Your focus is always on them. I'm happy you're a great mom, but what about us?" It would be easy for a wife to think this remark sounds unloving, even selfish (when he says *us*, he is usually thinking, "What about *me?*"). She would do well, however, to decode these words to get at the real meaning behind them—a cry for some respect.

It will do little good for a wife to say, "It's all about you," "I'm doing the best I can," etc. Her husband's comment sounds critical, but his heart is saying, "What happened to the cheerleader I knew during our courtship—the girl who believed in me and made me feel as if I could conquer the world?" When a wife senses that her husband is feeling less than respected and supported—that he's wondering if he is just a meal ticket for the family—she could try or adapt some energizing remarks like these:

- "Honey, you're right. I get too preoccupied with the children. Will you forgive me?"
- "You've made it possible for me to be a full-time mom. I am so sorry if I ever make you feel like only a meal ticket. How can I change?"
- "I'm so proud of what you are doing at work. I tell everybody except you. That will change—starting right now."
- "Let's set aside some time tonight just for us. I want to hear about what's happening at work."
- "The Bible says Eve was Adam's suitable helpmate. Am I your suitable helpmate? What could I do to be better at that?"
- "I feel bad that you are frustrated at work, but I believe in you and I am behind you all the way."

Note how this last sample comment corresponds to what Sarah told me in her e-mail: she felt bad that I had been frustrated by getting no work done on the book, but she was still convinced I would finish it.

There are many ways to send an energizing message; it is simply a matter of personal taste as to how it should be expressed. (Reviewing the questions under "Conquest," chapter 1, p. 24, may prompt more ideas for energizing remarks you could make to your husband about his need for conquest.)

> *For mutual understanding and good communication, "pleasant words are like honey from a honeycomb—sweet to the spirit and healthy for the body" (Proverbs 16:24 GW).*

HIERARCHY: If his desire to protect and provide is being squelched, he may send a coded message.

In Ephesians 5:22–23 Paul lays down a dimension of God's call on the wife that can be controversial in a present-day culture significantly influenced by radical feminism. He writes: "Wives, submit to your husbands as to the Lord. For the husband is the head of the wife as Christ is the head of the church . . ."(NIV). As I explain in *Love & Respect,*[3] when a wife willingly places herself under her husband's protection and provision, he feels respected. But when a wife complains that her husband is not providing what she wants or blames him for her fears and insecurities concerning the finances, he may come back with remarks about "Quit complaining. You're a nag. Nothing I do is good enough. You are never satisfied" or even "You are a worrywart. If you don't like what I earn, then you go back to school and improve your career options so I can live off you!"

Comments like these usually sound unloving, especially if the husband is not doing a great job of providing all that is needed and he knows it. A wise wife, however, realizes her husband is simply sending her a coded message that is asking her to come across more respectfully (just as she sends him coded messages from time to time asking him to come across more lovingly). He may sound over the top for saying or even intimating that she is a nag, but when his words are decoded, what he is really trying to say is "I'm supposed to be the head of this family, and it is often a little scary. I'm trying to be responsible, and you could help me by telling me that you respect my desire to provide for you."

Headship can be a touchy subject in some marriages, but a wife who is willing to decode her husband's words may figure out that he feels like his position as head of the family is being threatened or ignored. In that case, she might use or adapt any of the following to keep the Energizing Cycle going:

- "Honey, I'm sorry for coming across in a way that belittles you. This has nothing to do with you. These are my fears rooted in my childhood. Will you forgive me?"
- "Have I ever told you how safe I feel with you? I like that feeling a lot."

- "I often thank the Lord for how you protect and provide for me and the kids."
- "When I realize that you would die for me if necessary, I am overwhelmed. Thank you!"
- "I am so thankful I am married to a responsible man. It means a lot to me."
- "Honey, I complain too much and don't say I respect you often enough. I apologize."

What I say above only scratches the surface of how a man might voice his need to be seen as protector and provider for the family and what a wife can say in response. But no wife should ignore this need; it is deep within her husband and must be met. (Reviewing the questions under "Hierarchy," chapter 1, p. 25, may prompt more ideas for energizing remarks you could make to your husband about his desire to protect and provide.)

AUTHORITY: Listen for and respect his desire to serve and to lead.

Scripture clearly teaches that a wife should not be contentious. Consider Proverbs 21:9: "It is better to live in a corner of a roof than in a house shared with a contentious woman." There are many ways a wife can be contentious, but disrespectfully challenging her husband's God-given authority is one that can slow up the Energizing Cycle in a hurry.

As I said in *Love & Respect*, the way to make your husband feel respected is to tell him that because he has at least 51 percent of the responsibility, he also has 51 percent of the authority.[4] But what happens when the two of you face a difficult choice and your husband is not allowed to make the final decision? That is when the wife might hear "Do you want me to be the leader or not?" Or, if the husband is really exasperated, he might say, "Quit trying to wear the pants in this family!" Comments like these often sound harsh and unloving, but that is probably not his real intention. A wife must decode his words and understand he is not saying,

"I don't love you." He is really saying, "When I am held primarily responsible and then you exercise veto power, I feel disrespected."

In a Love and Respect marriage, there should be give-and-take about decisions that affect both spouses, but when a husband has to make the call, he appreciates a wife who respects him even if she strongly disagrees with what he is doing. When a wife decodes her husband as feeling frustrated about not being allowed to fill his leadership role, she can make respectful, energizing remarks like these:

> *"As charcoal fuels burning coals and wood fuels fire, so a quarrelsome person fuels a dispute"* *(Proverbs 26:21 GW).*

- "Lots of times when I complain or criticize, I really need assurance. But I know this is a put-down to your leadership. Please forgive me."

- "God made us equal, but you are the one He made responsible for me and the kids. Forgive me for ever failing to respect your authority."

- "Honey, I know you have a lot of pressure on you as you lead our family. Tell me how I can pray for you and help you."

- "I really feel secure because of your strength and authority, especially with our teenage sons. I just want you to know that."

- "When I argue or disagree with you, I am not trying to wear the pants. I am simply trying to help. Please trust my heart."

- "I have been convicted lately about my contentious spirit. Please forgive me for not respecting your leadership."

Again, I want to emphasize that a man's desire to serve and lead is not one he can easily express. Instead of being harsh and unloving, his comments may be more in the line of trying to joke about it, as one husband did when he said his wife was "the neck who turns the head." Fortunately, she decoded his "joking" and changed her ways. (Reviewing the questions under "Authority," chapter 1, p. 25, may prompt more ideas for energizing remarks you could make to your husband about his desire to serve and lead.)

INSIGHT: *Don't let your woman's intuition make you deaf to his desire to analyze and counsel.*

A wife should have a healthy dependency on her husband's advice and insight, but I have counseled many wives who reject this idea and therefore are in danger of being deceived. As Paul wrote, "it was not Adam who was deceived, but the woman being quite deceived, fell into transgression" (1 Timothy 2:14). Feminists might call this passage "a chauvinist put-down," but there is wisdom here for the wife who will see it. Women are remarkably gifted with intuition, but often they can depend too much on their own opinions and reject their husbands' insight.[5]

Part of the problem is that the typical woman doesn't want advice or solutions; she wants empathy, a listening ear. When a husband tries to share his insights, he may hear, "Quit trying to fix me!" And she may hear in return, "Why tell me your problems if you don't want my help?" This remark can sound unloving to a wife unless she decodes her husband's words and realizes he is doing what almost every man does when he sees a problem: he is trying to help by offering solutions. When a wife senses she has acted disrespectfully toward her husband by rejecting his suggested solutions, she can use or adapt any of the following statements and be energizing and encouraging instead:

- "Honey, I'm sorry. I know you are trying to help. It's just that I need you to listen for a while. That is what will make me feel better."
- "I know I can depend too much on my feelings. I thank the Lord He has given you to me because I need your insight."
- "You know, honey, we make a good team. With my intuition and your insight, we can handle a lot of problems."

- "I apologize for acting like I don't want your opinions on how to deal with the kids. I need your input. It's just that sometimes I get so frustrated. I feel like nothing is working, and I take it out on you. Please forgive me."
- "Honey, please forgive me for making you guess when I want your listening ear and when I want your solutions. I need to let you know."
- "Honey, would it be okay if I asked you for some advice?"

As we saw in chapter 8, there should be a balance between the man's need to give insight and the woman's need for understanding. It is true that often she doesn't want advice; she wants a listening ear. At the same time, however, the wise wife will realize her husband's desire to help and advise is strong. She should refrain from getting angry and humor him a bit, as one wife did by saying, "Thanks for the input. I know I am not the brightest bulb on the tree when it comes to certain things. I am glad we have each other." (Reviewing the questions under "Insight," chapter 1, p. 25, may prompt more ideas for energizing remarks you could make to your husband about his desire to analyze and counsel.)

"Anything you say to the wise will make them wiser. Whatever you tell the righteous will add to their knowledge" (Proverbs 9:9 GNB).

RELATIONSHIP: His desire for shoulder-to-shoulder friendship may seem a bit odd, but keep your ears open for it anyway.

To get a clue about how a wife can fulfill her husband's need for a shoulder-to-shoulder relationship with her, turn to Paul's advice to Titus, which includes having the older women teach the younger women "to love their husbands and children"(2:4 NIV). In most cases, when Paul teaches his readers to love, he uses the Greek word *agape,* but here he uses *phileo*, which essentially means a woman should be a lover/friend to her husband.[6]

When a wife is friendly and shows that she likes her husband, particularly by doing shoulder-to-shoulder activities with him, he will feel respected. But when she becomes so immersed in her own schedule and duties she seems to have no time for him, then she might hear something like "Can't you let that go for a few minutes? Come sit with me and watch the last two minutes of the game." A wife could respond to this request with "Don't you know I have a lot to do?" or she can decode her husband's message, put her duties on hold for a little while, and say, "Sure, watching with you will be fun."

The key, however, is to respond in a truly friendly way, not resignedly like a martyr or in the slightest way begrudgingly. Being friendly to her man is one of the most effective things a woman can do to strengthen her marriage. When wives write to me out of desperation because their marriage is going under, I give them a quick assignment: "You can do three things to turn this marriage around. 1. Be his friend. 2. Be friendly. 3. Be his friendly friend. P.S. In case I forgot to tell you, be his friend." I also ask them to list seven things they can do to be more friendly, to start putting these things into practice, and then to write in six weeks to tell me what happened.

Typically, after all this friendliness on the part of their wives, husbands make comments like these: "Who are you—and what have you done with my wife?" and "I don't know what drug you are taking, but don't kick this habit."

If being friendly can help a wife halt the Crazy Cycle, it can be even more effective in keeping the Energizing Cycle rolling. Just remember, when it comes to being friendlier, it is always wise for a wife not to make direct remarks about "being a better friend to you." Instead, actions speak volumes as you simply seek opportunities to be with him in a friendly way. For example, if he is working on something around the house, just sit by and watch for fifteen or twenty minutes. If he asks you why you are sitting there, just say you wanted to be with him and reassure him that you did not come because you "need to talk." If you are a typical woman, the silence may be almost unbearable, but resist the temptation to say something. Instead remember that one of the best ways to communicate with your husband is by not trying to communicate with your husband! Notice his demeanor later on! (Reviewing the questions under "Relationship," chapter 1, p. 26, may prompt more ideas for energizing remarks you could make to your husband about his desire for shoulder-to-shoulder friendship.)

SEXUALITY: *Listen carefully. His desire for sexual intimacy is much deeper than merely physical.*

A husband has a need for sexual release that only his wife can meet, and when she does so, he feels respected and honored.[7] By the same token, a wife has a need for affection and emotional closeness that only her husband can meet, and when he does so, she feels loved and cherished. These two major needs can cause a standoff that will definitely keep the Energizing Cycle from spinning unless someone makes the first move.

When a wife shames her husband, she is "as rottenness in his bones" (Proverbs 12:4), and one of the ways she can shame him is sexually. If she seems to deem his sexual need contemptible ("Stop it! I'm not in the mood!"), he is crushed and provoked to respond, "You never seem to be in the mood anymore," and he might even add, "Are you trying to punish me?" or "I'm tired of this sexual blackmail." At this point, the Energizing Cycle has stopped, and the Crazy Cycle has already made a few revolutions. A wife can let her husband stew in his own frustration, or she can try to decode his cry for respect. The wife who is willing to honor her husband's sexuality can try saying or adapting the following to keep the Energizing Cycle going:

- "I don't try to blackmail you by withholding sex. Please forgive me for coming across this way. I don't intend to."

- "I enjoy making love, but first I need you to hold me and talk to me. I'm the Crock-Pot; you're the microwave. We both have the same goal, but I take longer to warm up!"
- "I do want to satisfy you sexually. I want us both to be satisfied. Let's try to spend more time early in the evening just talking and being together. This could help both of us relax for making love later."
- "I have never tried to punish you by withholding sex, but now I see how you felt when I denied you. Please forgive me."
- "When you are more open with me about your heart and tell me you are sorry, this is a turn-on for me."
- "I'm sorry the kids and all the rest of it have left me too tired to make love at times. Why don't we leave them with my mother and get away for a weekend?"

When wives are using the principles embodied in the C-H-A-I-R-S acronym, Sexuality messages can be the easiest and the hardest to decode. Some husbands will be very up-front, and their complaints don't really need much decoding. Other men may be too proud to say anything obvious, but they will send other messages that voice their frustration. Regardless of how a husband communicates his need for sex, the best approach for a wife is to realize that his need for sexuality is usually one of his strongest and she should try to meet that need even if she doesn't feel like it.

Michele Weiner-Davis is one of an increasing number of sex therapists who would agree. She has helped many couples achieve better communication and put new spark in their marriage by advising them to not only talk about sex together, but also—in the words of the Nike commercial—to "Just Do It!" (For more on the "Just Do It!" approach to improving the sex in your marriage, see *Love & Respect Workbook* [Nashville: Integrity, 2005], Appendix V, pp. 218–222.)

Ms. Weiner-Davis speaks from experience gained in her own twenty-five-year marriage. There was a time when she was less interested in sex than her husband, but they worked through the problem and deepened their bond with each other. When a woman client might balk at having to be more sexual in order to get her husband to be more loving and attentive, Weiner-Davis simply asks her, "What if your husband complained when I sent him home with the assignment to talk to you more, go out more, and be more romantic in order to get you to be more physically intimate?" If this sounds like the "if-then" principle discussed in chapter 8, you are right: it is. Weiner-Davis says that good marriages are based on the idea that people who love each other take care of each other's needs and desires, and when they do, reciprocity happens![8] (Reviewing the questions under "Sexuality," chapter 1, p. 26, may prompt more ideas for energizing remarks you could make to your husband about his desire for sexual intimacy.)

Decoding His Desires in Each Category of Needs in C-H-A-I-R-S Is Only Half the Story

In this chapter we have focused on how a wife can use C-H-A-I-R-S to decode any negative messages her husband might send that could slow down the Energizing Cycle if she doesn't respond to those messages in a mature and respectful way. Thousands of women have discovered that C-H-A-I-R-S does work once they understand that the male needs I have described are legitimate and very real for most men.

But what about the needs of the wife? They are described in acronym C-O-U-P-L-E, which covers six of a woman's most basic desires. Every husband should master decoding the needs described in C-O-U-P-L-E because this is the secret to connecting with his wife and making her feel loved. We will look at how this is done in the next chapter.

CHAPTER TEN

⟶⟶

Decode—and Then Use C-O-U-P-L-E to Energize Her

(Note to wives: This chapter is "for husbands only," but you are invited to read along.)

When Sarah and I were in our late thirties and early forties, our three children were pretty much into their teen years, and we experienced the same tensions most families encounter, all of which put a strain on our marriage. In my journal I described one such evening, which offers a microcosmic glimpse of what life was sometimes like for us back then:

> Sarah is discouraged. She is feeling our family is not close. One of the boys has been gruff and distant; the other expresses disinterest in being home at all. Both of them have gone out with their buddies, and Joy has been invited to a friend's house for the

evening. It is plain to Sarah that fun is outside of this home, and this disappoints and saddens her.

As I recall, I penned those brief lines on a Friday night. I tended to make notes in my journal at times when I was heavyhearted, and this was one of them. While Sarah and I had eaten dinner alone, she had verbally dumped what felt like an attack on me when she commented that our family situation was so "boring." Sarah was not attacking me as much as she was venting her disappointment, but her words were still hard to accept. I sat there eating, feeling blamed, but not knowing how to respond. My heart was heavy, so I searched for some way to lighten things up a bit. Looking down at the dog, I said, "And I suppose you ran away today too!"

> *The right word matters! "A person's anxiety will weigh him down, but an encouraging word makes him joyful" (Proverbs 12:25 GW).*

Sarah's response was quick, but I wasn't sure she was joining me in being light. She said, "I'm the one who needs to run away."

We sat there looking at each other, both aware that parenting is not a popularity contest and that it is much more a marathon than a sprint. You want to trust your heavenly Creator and His promises, but in those frequent moments of uncertainty, you can have feelings of panic. We were having one of those moments then, on a Friday night, when it felt like all the children had gone AWOL.

Guilt flooded over me, and I began telling myself outlandish things like "The kids are all gone because you are a horrible authority figure. If you had done something different when they were in diapers, your teenagers would be home roasting marshmallows in the fireplace, singing 'Kum Ba Ya,' and sharing their passion to go to the mission field to die a martyr's death—after they finish Harvard Medical School." Feeling cornered by Sarah's comments, I thought to myself: *Does my lousy parenting*

disqualify me from the ministry? What am I supposed to do? Tender my res-
ignation from the church and sell Bibles door-to-door?

Afraid I might say something more that could be misunderstood as
my trying to be glib, I remained subdued, observing how ironic it was
that when the children were young, our home was Grand Central Station. In fact, I was the Pied Piper. Neighborhood kids would knock on
our door and ask, "Can Mr. E come out and play?" But when our children entered the teen years and especially when Jonathan and David got
driver's licenses, it was a whole new (parenting) ball game.

Although our home was still open to their friends, and we encouraged our kids to invite them over, we experienced what almost every parent of teenagers encounters as they break away to become independent.
Being home is not cool; being out—anywhere—is the goal. This is normal, but not always enjoyable for parents who wait—and watch the
clock. On this particular Friday night, Sarah had pictured all the kids at
home, having their friends over and enjoying laughter in the air. Instead,
it was just the two of us, having very little fun—and no laughs.

Ironically, with all the kids out of the picture, it would have been a
perfect evening for us to enjoy each other by going out for ice cream, talking together, or maybe calling spontaneously and meeting up with some
friends—something we like to do—and then later, back home . . . who
knows? But that didn't happen. Instead Sarah spent the evening cleaning
the garage, while I went down to the athletic club to swim laps.

"Do You Not *Care* Where Your Son Is?"

Sarah's discouragement over our teenagers continued. . . .

On another Friday evening our son David had stayed out too long.
We didn't know where he might be, and Sarah was getting worried. As
the hour grew late, she confronted me in my study and asked in an accusing tone, "Do you not *care* where your son is? You haven't asked all
evening."

Startled out of my concentration on something I was writing for an

upcoming board meeting at the church, I
responded as best I could: "Because I don't
ask doesn't mean I don't care." Back then
I had not yet preached my series on marriage, and I had not discovered the Love
and Respect truths in Ephesians 5:33. My
reply was mildly defensive, but I wasn't
trying to hurt Sarah at all. I did care about
David—a great deal—but it did not appear
that way to Sarah. She turned on her heel
and quickly left the room. A few minutes
later I followed and found her with a look
on her face that showed she was greatly
burdened, but I didn't know what to do
or say.

> *Husbands, even
> Jesus Himself was
> asked by a woman,
> "Do you not care?"
> (Luke 10:40).
> When your wife
> accuses you of not
> caring, decode her
> deeper meaning.*

Now, years later, I know that a proper Love and Respect response
would have been to give her a hug and say simply, "Yes, I care, a great
deal. I'm sorry I came across as uncaring. Let's pray for David right now
and then talk about how to deal with this." But in those years I had not
yet made the Love and Respect Connection. I knew a little bit about
Love, and I realized that Sarah was crying out for something loving from
me. But during such instances, her negativity and confrontational questioning often left me tongue-tied or saying something that made me
sound unloving.

What I knew much less about was Respect and how I, as a man, need
it. I sensed Sarah was not really trying to attack me by being confrontational, yet I felt something that I now recognize as disrespect. I couldn't
articulate this feeling, but it was there, and one way or another I communicated my sense of not being respected in a way that made me look
unconcerned or unloving. I suppose, in a way, I was stonewalling. I just
locked up, trapped in a feeling of helplessness.

An important concept I had not yet discovered was decoding. Sarah's question, "Do you not care where your son is?" sounded accusing, but she was simply venting her frustration over feeling helpless as a parent. She wanted our family to be loving and fun; she wanted the home to run smoothly. Teenagers have a way of messing that up, and it left both of us feeling helpless at times. And because I was not aware of decoding or how it worked, I could only respond as best I could.

Later that evening, after Sarah had gone to bed, I stayed up to write reflectively in my journal:

> As a wife ventilates her deep burden as a mother, she will express things in a very negative way. If I am mature, I will not personalize. In some ways God has created the male to personalize less. Perhaps the Lord designed us this way because of a wife's ongoing need to release her negative emotions! But . . . how is a guy to respond to the claim he doesn't care?

When feeling provoked, remember "he who is slow to anger has great understanding, but he who is quick-tempered exalts folly" (Proverbs 14:29).

I suppose, in a certain sense, I was decoding Sarah's words and actions, but I didn't know what to call it. At least I had tried to be understanding. Sarah would often say—and still often says—I am the most understanding person she knows. And even back then I did have one thing down: Sarah needs to release her negative emotions. But when she did, they flooded over me, drowning me in what seemed to be a situation I could not handle.

When Sarah confronted me about David and asked, "Do you not care?" she was sending me the message "Tell me you care about David *and me*. Do or say something to *help me*." While I was trying to understand and not personalize her remarks, I wasn't at the place where I could decode her words and do something helpful. All I could do was wonder how I was supposed to respond to her over-the-top remark that I did not seem to care at all.

Over the Years I Have Gotten Better at Decoding

These scenes from earlier in our marriage are typical of moments when I tried to understand and respond lovingly to my wife, but fell short. I couldn't—or wouldn't—do or say what was needed. Why? Perhaps it was pride that welled up when Sarah's confrontational questions left me feeling hurt and defensive. I knew she didn't mean to hurt me, but her words hurt anyway. I have a hunch that many husbands will identify with my struggles in these scenes, which dramatize how important it is to be aware of the need to decode your wife's words and to continue to learn how to do it better.

In more recent years, I have become able to use Love and Respect principles to first decode what Sarah is saying or asking and then respond in a way that helps her feel better, at least to some degree.

For example, I have been trying to phone my son David every night to have prayer together because we agree it is important to ask God to guide us in what we are doing. He does video production for Love and Respect Ministries and has also launched his own video production business as a sideline. Sometimes he answers, but usually I call after he has gone to bed, so I leave my prayer on his voice mail. He will play the message the next morning as an encouragement to start the new day.

I must confess, however, that writing pressures sometimes cause me to forget to call. Sarah seldom forgets, and when I slip up, she invariably asks, "Did you call and pray for David?" This past week I forgot to make the call two nights in a row, and by the time Sarah reminded me, I felt I was too weary to be much of an encouragement. On the third night, Sarah waited until well into the evening and, noting that I was deeply engrossed in writing (as usual), she walked into my study and asked, "Are you *ever* going to call David again?"

There was a time when I would have taken that *ever* as a disrespectful insult and said something sarcastic like "As a matter of fact, I haven't—and I don't think I will ever call him again." And then I would have stonewalled her the rest of the evening and maybe into the next day. Now, because we practice Love and Respect and because I know how Sarah thinks, I refused to become irritated by her words, which I could have easily interpreted as chiding and scolding me for being irresponsible. Instead, I decoded her question to simply mean she was very concerned about David, and because of years of living with me in ministry, she truly believes that my prayers have the power to impact David's life. She wasn't trying to put me down; she was wanting me to lift David up! Yes, her use of *ever* was an overstatement, but I know she talks like this when she is anxious and needs reassurance.

All of this crossed my mind in the space of a second or two. I turned to Sarah and said, "Wow! Here I am, with a commitment to pray for our son every evening, and I get so busy I forget. Thanks, honey, for reminding me. I'll do it right now. And please keep asking me about David. With this deadline pressure, I need all the help I can get."

No matter how often I decode Sarah, I keep working at it and finding there is always something new to discover about my wife and how to read her as the person I love. Over the years I have talked to hundreds of husbands who are often baffled or angered by what their wives are saying. Believe me, I empathize because I have been there many times myself. We Blues can't bat a thousand percent when decoding our Pinks, but we can do a *lot* better. The rest of this chapter will help the typical husband decode what his wife is saying and use the C-O-U-P-L-E principles for spelling love to a wife—and keeping the Energizing Cycle going.

Do these six principles cover *every* instance a husband needs to decode the message his wife is sending? No, because—as I said in chapter 9—there is no way to give specific help for every situation. Each couple is different, and each wife has her own way of sending messages. But the six principles in C-O-U-P-L-E do give a husband a framework that helps him listen for his wife's basic needs. And whatever a wife might say that sounds negative or critical, underlying her words is her primary need for love, which can usually be met by practicing C-O-U-P-L-E: Closeness, Openness, Understanding, Peacemaking, Loyalty, and Esteem.

> *"The tongue that brings healing is a tree of life" (Proverbs 15:4 NIV). Words of love from a husband are like good medicine that brings life to the marriage.*

How to Use Scripture to Decode Your Wife's Cries for Love

Often a wife will make comments that sound disrespectful to the husband. Many of these remarks are really cries for love that need decoding. She talks this way because she sees—or *thinks* she sees[1]— that her husband is not fulfilling God's call to "love his wife as he loves himself" (Ephesians 5:33 NIV). As we saw in chapter 8, God commands him to practice C-O-U-P-L-E. The reason I say God is calling husbands to practice C-O-U-P-L-E is because all six principles come out of Scripture. So let's look at examples of how a husband can use C-O-U-P-L-E to decode and respond to negative comments by his wife and keep the Energizing Cycle going.

CLOSENESS: *If you're not close, you'll hear about it.*

A husband "shall cleave to his wife; and they shall become one flesh" (Genesis 2:24). A simple and somewhat limited interpretation of this verse is the physical sense "to have sex with her." But sex will not be ultimately meaningful to her if the husband makes no effort to be close to her emotionally, to be connected. That's why he may hear her say, "Sex and food—that's all you really want" or "The only time I seem to be interesting is when you want to make love." These comments are critical, but her heart is really saying, "You mean more to me than any other adult, and only you can meet this need I have for your love. I need you."

If a husband hears words from his wife that he can decode as meaning "I want you to be closer to me—in every way," what can he say? Here are a few simple ideas—words that energize—that you can use or adapt as you see fit:

- "After dinner, let's have coffee and you can tell me how your day went."
- "I'm sorry for being preoccupied. Please say that again."
- "I am sorry. I don't want you only for sex. Please forgive me for coming across as selfish."
- "I'm going to make changes in my work schedule. We need to spend more time together."
- "What would you say to getting our date night going again regularly?"
- "I really like planning changes in the house together. Let's do more of that."

Note that many of the above suggestions focus in one way or another on talking or situations that encourage conversation. As chapter 8 pointed out, when a husband talks to his wife as he practices Closeness or Openness, his wife is much more likely to want to be sexually intimate later. I can recall one husband, who had been introduced to C-O-U-P-L-E and his wife's need to be close, saying, "I wish I had figured this out years ago. I wouldn't have spent all those nights on the living room sofa." (Reviewing the questions under "Closeness," chapter 1, p. 21, may prompt more ideas for energizing remarks you could make to your wife in response to her need for closeness.)

OPENNESS: *Act distant or irritated and she may think you are mad at her.*

God commands husbands to "love your wives, and do not be embittered against them" (Colossians 3:19). Several translations substitute the word *harsh* for embittered, and one version advises husbands to "love your wives and be gentle with them" (NCV). When a husband's look and voice are harsh or even less than gentle, his wife will not feel loved and energized—no matter how fervently the two of them may have pledged themselves to ride the Energizing Cycle. If he continues to sound angry or disgruntled, he may eventually hear "What have I done now? You sound mad at me"; "Why are you so touchy? It seems like I need to walk on eggshells around you lately"; or perhaps "My, we seem to be a grumpy bear today." Wise is the husband who can decode any words like these and realize his wife is not being disrespectful; she simply wants him to reassure her that he is not angry with her and that he loves her.

> *"An angry man stirs up strife" (Proverbs 29:22)—and so does a husband who appears angry!*

When a husband gets the message that he could be a little (or a lot) less harsh and seemingly angry, what could he say to come across more gently and lovingly with words that energize? Try or adapt any of the following:

- "I'm sorry for sounding angry. Will you forgive me?"
- "I'm not mad at you; I'm actually mad at myself. I'm sorry."
- "It is easier for me to think my thoughts than talk about them, but that leaves you in the dark. I will try hard to include you more."
- "I heard somebody say that a wife will give her husband time to process things if he promises to talk later. I promise to talk later!"
- "Starting today, I am going to respond lovingly when you ask me what I am thinking, and I want you to check me on how well I am doing."
- "What would you think of taking a few minutes every evening to talk about our day? If it's okay with you, I'd like to start tonight."

If the two of you have been humming along nicely on the Energizing Cycle and your wife makes a remark that is letting you know you need to "show a little kindness," try to approach it with a little humor: "I am

NOT angry! Gimme a kiss" or something else off the wall that lets her know you are kidding but still getting the message. Do this, of course, only if the two of you like to communicate in this fashion. (Reviewing the questions under "Openness," chapter 1, p. 21, may prompt more ideas for energizing remarks you could make to your wife in response to her need for openness.)

UNDERSTAND: *She prefers that you listen, not lecture.*

First Peter 3:7 instructs husbands to "live with your wives in an understanding way." Mark it down, men! When a woman feels understood, she feels loved. And when she doesn't feel understood, her husband might hear "You just don't seem to understand"; "You just don't seem to get it"; or perhaps "Why can't you just *listen* to me?" The woman who makes these kinds of remarks needs to be decoded, not accused of being disrespectful or contemptuous. She is trying to get a message through that says, "Please love me by showing a little empathy, that you know how I feel." If a husband wants his wife to feel he understands her or at least that he is trying to, he might say energizing words like these:

- "I'm sorry for not being understanding. Will you forgive me?"
- "Please tell me again what you said. This time I promise to listen."
- "This is what I hear you saying. Tell me if I'm getting it."
- "I'm sorry I seem so dense. I want to relate to what you are saying."
- "I haven't experienced this, but I feel bad about what you're going through."
- "I'm sorry. Is there anything I can do to help?"

Remember, all of these suggestions are only that—suggestions. You can word your remarks any way you like. Just be sure you are caring and empathic. Your best approach, however, is often simply to listen and be genuinely interested. One wife wrote to tell me how learning about Love and Respect had affected her husband: "He has been forever touched. I notice him really trying to tell me he loves me and serving me. Just last

night he asked me if I wanted him to listen or fix it. That was so cute."
(Reviewing the questions under "Understanding," chapter 1, p. 22, may
prompt more ideas for energizing remarks you could make to your wife
in response to her need to be understood by you.)

*PEACEMAKING: If she feels she is "one" with you, all is peace-
ful.* When the Pharisees came to Jesus to ask Him if divorce was legal for
any reason at all, He referred them back to Genesis and pointed out that,
because man and woman were created male and female, a man is to
"cleave to his wife and the two shall become one flesh . . . What, therefore, God has joined together, let no man separate" (Matthew 19:4–6).
Jesus is saying that God's ideal is that a couple is not to "separate," that
is, divorce. Because God joined them together, they are no longer two but
one.

Husband and wife are a team, and as a team they are to live in harmony, working to resolve their conflicts so that their relationship does
not come to an end. Living in peace with her husband is a gigantic value
to a wife. When she feels they are at peace
with each other, that they are "one," she
feels loved and energized.

On the other hand, when a wife feels
lack of harmony between them, she might
say, "Why am I usually the one who has to
say, 'I'm sorry'?"; "Is it my imagination, or
am I usually the one who has to take the
blame?"; or, spelling it out a little more
disrespectfully, "Sometimes you seem so
clueless about what it means to be a couple." When a wife sends messages about
her need for peace and oneness, she is
telling her husband he is the only man with whom she wants to be inti-
mately at peace, but something has come between them. In reply, husbands should use or adapt the following words that can energize a wife.

> *After his instruc-
> tions to husbands,
> Peter writes, "To
> sum up, all of you
> be harmonious . . .
> Seek peace and
> pursue it" (1 Peter
> 3:8, 11).*

- "I am sorry for what I said. I was wrong. Will you forgive me?"
- "Let's come at this again. I apologize. I was thinking about what I was going to say, and I think I caused a misunderstanding."
- "I shouldn't get defensive. This ends up hurting you, and I don't intend to hurt you. Do you believe me?"
- "This week let's set aside $40.00 for the one who is quickest to take responsibility for the problem instead of placing blame. I could use a little more pocket money!"
- "Let's see how our disagreements can be used by God in our marriage. I want to spend a few minutes praying together, asking Him for wisdom."
- "Let's join that new couples' class at church on creating win-win situations in your marriage."

Of all the suggestions above, the most powerful and usually most effective is the first one. If you sense any kind of rift that could slow the Energizing Cycle, use this tried-and-true approach: "I'm sorry for what I said. I was wrong. Will you forgive me?" There is no better way than this to act on Solomon's insight: "A gentle answer turns away wrath" (Proverbs 15:1). Over the years, husbands have told me, "I thought if I said, 'I'm sorry,' she'd keep after me, rubbing it in. But it was like you said. She felt bad about her part and even apologized to *me*." (Reviewing the questions under "Peace-making," chapter 1, p. 22, may prompt more ideas for energizing remarks you could make to your wife in response to her desire for peace with you.)

LOYALTY: Is she sure you'll always be there?

The prophet Malachi comes down hard on certain husbands who have treacherously divorced their wives. Malachi is appalled that any man would do this to his wife "though she is your companion and your wife by covenant" (Malachi 2:14). Some wives have reported to me that their worst fear is being abandoned by their husbands. They would rather die of cancer with a loyal and committed husband at their side than live a healthy life and be traded in for a new model.

Loyalty spells love to a wife, but if she lacks assurance because her husband's actions or words make her feel even vaguely insecure, she might say things like "Do you *really* love me? I sometimes wonder"; "Do you want me for *me*? Sometimes I'm not really sure"; or, perhaps trying to mask her feelings with a joking question, "Tell me. Will you stay with me when I'm old and gray?" With these remarks she is not trying to be disrespectful or suggest you are disloyal. She simply longs to know that only death will ever separate you.

When a wife comes up with any kind of "Will you always love me?" comment like those above, a husband can use or adapt any of the following to reenergize the situation:

- "Honey, you are stuck with me. I am not going to go away until I go six feet under."
- "You are the only woman for me. Please always believe that."
- "We can grow old and gray together, and I'll love you all the way. Let's go shop for matching wheelchairs."
- "I often thank God for giving you to me. In fact, I rejoice!"
- "Sweetheart, I'm sorry if I have done *anything* to make you wonder if I love you. I have always loved you and always will."
- "Will I always love you? Let's go for a walk and talk about renewing our vows."

It's sometimes tempting for a husband to think, *Loyalty? That's no problem for us. She knows I love her, and that's that.* Don't be too sure. Our swimsuit-issue culture puts the marriage bond under constant attack.

One discouraged wife who clearly was riding the Crazy Cycle wrote:

I could probably deal with a lot of it if he at least made me feel secure in the marriage, but he doesn't tell me I'm beautiful, that he's still attracted to me, nothing to make me feel that he won't leave me. Instead, like any man, he looks at other women. Often the thought has crossed my mind, *Maybe if I had a breast augmentation done, or perhaps 120 pounds is too much and I need to lose some weight . . . Maybe then he'll love me.* I know these are ridiculous thoughts, but I just don't know what to do any more. I'm only twenty-seven. Life shouldn't be like this.

Indeed, life shouldn't be like that for any wife. Hopefully, you are on the Energizing Cycle, and your wife is not struggling like this woman, but her words reinforce a truth that every husband committed to Christ should heed: *every* wife appreciates compliments about how she looks as well as those other little comments that reassure her of your commitment. Give them often. (Reviewing the questions under "Loyalty," chapter 1, p. 23, may prompt more ideas for energizing remarks you could make to your wife in response to her need to know you're in the relationship for the long haul.)

ESTEEM: A wife needs respect too.

The last part of 1 Peter 3:7 clearly decrees "grant her honor as a fellow heir of the grace of life." Women need respect, too, and when a woman is respected (honored) by her husband, she feels loved. But when a wife is feeling like she is second-class, she might get to the point where she will comment, "So often there seems to be a double standard." Or perhaps she may say something like "Okay, honey, you do what you want. I'm only your wife." And if she is really irked and the Energizing Cycle is in danger of grinding to a halt, a husband might hear "I'm not sure why, but lately I feel like a doormat." Any comment that suggests a wife feels less than equal to her husband must be decoded for what it is: not an attempt to show him disrespect or contempt, but an effort to motivate him to treat her more lovingly. Only he can make her feel loved the way she wants to be loved.

> *"Her husband praises her. He says, 'Many women are good wives, but you are the best of them all'"* (Proverbs 31:28–29 GNB).

Oddly enough, sometimes the more negative a wife's words sound, the more she is seeking her husband's positive love!

A wise husband decodes his wife's negative words; a foolish husband just gets angry and lashes back or goes the other direction and stonewalls her with silence. A wise husband would try to assure his wife and energize her by saying:

- "Honey, for whatever I have done or said to make you think you are a doormat, I apologize. Please forgive me!"
- "I am really sorry you feel there is a double standard in our family. What can I do to change that?"
- "I don't want to do whatever I want. I want to do what you and I want to do together."
- "You're the best thing that ever happened to me. Let me tell you why."
- "You are fantastic! I see God using you in so many ways, especially in our family."
- "What have I or the kids done to make you think that? You are the best wife and mother any family could ask for!"

I often tell husbands they should never put off esteeming their wives and instead take every opportunity to make them feel they are first in importance. So often we have a compliment or a word of praise on the tip of our tongue, but then we let it go because "She knows how I feel. I don't have to tell her." But you do have to tell her—and the more often the better. I have heard men who suddenly lost their wives make tearful admissions. One broken widower confessed, "I wish I would have told her how much she meant to me. How can you live so long with a person and not see the treasure in front of your eyes?" (Reviewing the questions under "Esteem," chapter 1, p. 23, may prompt more ideas for energizing remarks you could make to your wife in response to her need for honor and respect.)

Continue Honing Your Decoding Skills

What I have been trying to stress in this chapter, as well as in chapter 9, is that when your spouse gets negative, you both can fall off the Energizing

Cycle. It is crucial to understand that your spouse's negativity is rooted in feelings of being unloved or disrespected. When you decode your spouse's messages and become aware of these deeper needs, you can say something that is loving or respectful and keep your marriage moving forward.

As valuable as decoding can be, though, it is not the only skill you need to stay on the Energizing Cycle. Not everything that happens in a marriage is a Love or Respect issue that needs decoding and straightening out. Much of life consists of doing simple everyday things like washing dishes, cutting grass, buying groceries, getting the car serviced, and on and on. You and your spouse must communicate in this everyday world, and while it involves the simple and mundane, this does not mean that you won't have communication problems.

As everyone knows, miscommunication happens all day long. She says something that is not clear or seems to have more than one meaning. He doesn't listen carefully when she explains what she needs. She forgets to make a phone call. He forgets to tell her about a call that came in. On and on it goes. These minor matters aren't Love or Respect issues to begin with, but they can quickly escalate if not dealt with skillfully and positively. In the next chapter Sarah and I will demonstrate how miscommunication can easily happen—and how to deal with it when it does.

CHAPTER ELEVEN

Dealing with the
Everyday Challenge

We have seen how the principles in C-O-U-P-L-E can cross-pollinate with the principles in C-H-A-I-R-S, creating an "if-then" effect that can enable you and your spouse to practice the Golden Rule toward each other in all kinds of ways (chapter 8). And we have considered how husbands and wives can use the principles in C-O-U-P-L-E and C-H-A-I-R-S to decode each other's negative or critical remarks and make positive responses that keep the Energizing Cycle humming (chapters 9 and 10).

As I have stressed in chapters 8–10, decoding is the skill you implement *after* your spouse makes a remark or several remarks that suggest she is feeling unloved or he is feeling disrespected. There might be some issue on the table, such as when to leave, what to buy, or how to do something, but at this point that matter is not the *real* issue. The real issue is lack of love or respect, and you need to decode this.

As important as decoding is, another skill—what I call *clarifying*—is just as important. Clarifying is what you need to do *before* the conversation reaches a point where your spouse feels unloved or disrespected.

> *The Bible recognizes common sense in communication: "If you don't speak in a way that can be understood, how will anyone know what you're saying?" (1 Corinthians 14:9 GW).*

Clarifying is a must as you deal with a huge area of communication that all married couples face every day—the small issues such as little differences of opinion, minor conflicts, or miniscule misunderstandings. Something is said that is not clear or perhaps not heard correctly. The two of you must clarify what was said or what was meant, or this small issue will turn into the Big Issue of someone not feeling loved or respected.

I call this area the "Everyday Challenge." Every married couple knows what I mean because among all lovers misunderstandings are inevitable. Miscommunications happen. It is what life is made of when two human beings interact. Here is an example of how Sarah and I miscommunicated recently.

All I Said Was "I'm Leaving"

It was a beautiful June morning where we live in Michigan, a great time to be eating breakfast on the patio in our backyard filled with colorful flowers and overlooking a beautiful watery marsh covered with lily pads and cattails. I was just finishing my bowl of cereal when Sarah came out, her Bible and devotional books in hand. The moment I saw her, I said, "I'm leaving." No "Good morning" or even a "Hi." Just "I'm leaving."

Was I angry with Sarah or something? Not at all. I was just remembering other occasions when she had found me on the patio and had said lightheartedly, "I find a spot I enjoy, and then you take it." Anticipating she was about to say this again, I quickly sought to reassure her that I was about to make my exit and not usurp her precious quiet-time retreat. I saw no need for any formalities like "Good morning" or even "Hi!" Besides, I was sure she would know exactly what I was talking about, so I just said, "I'm leaving."

But what did Sarah hear when I announced, "I'm leaving"? She wasn't thinking of how I might intrude on her quiet time; she interpreted my words much differently and simply replied, "Don't worry. I'm not coming out here to talk to you."

Was Sarah offended because I had uttered "I'm leaving" so abruptly? She wasn't offended. Instead she was remembering many other occasions when I had to dash off, so she thought I was letting her know I did not have time to talk to her at that moment. In other instances, this could have bothered her, but in this instance she was trying to assure me that having a conversation was not on her mind.

But Sarah's response was not what I expected. I thought she would say, "Thanks for giving up the patio. I was planning to have my quiet time now." Instead she had told me not to worry because she had not come out to talk to me. She had misinterpreted what I meant by "I'm leaving," and I was taken aback. I could have reacted in different ways, a lot of them negative. Such small, seemingly meaningless remarks can cause questions to leap into one's mind: *What did she mean by saying she didn't want to talk to me? Was that some sort of subtle dig? Or was I in trouble and didn't know it—again?* On the spot I decided to clarify things, so I looked at her and said casually, "Why did you say that? Did you think I said, 'I'm leaving' because I didn't want to talk to you?"

My remark, in the form of a question, can be called feedback. I fed back in my own words what I thought she seemed to be saying to me. The fact that my feedback was in the form of a question is important. I was inviting Sarah to speak—to tell me why she had said what she said.

And Sarah did just that: "Well, that's why you told me you were leaving, wasn't it?"

Note that Sarah gave me feedback with a question of her own. By listening carefully, I quickly saw she had completely misread my "I'm leaving" remark. Now I had a choice: get defensive ("How could she even think such a thing!") or gently try to correct the misunderstanding.

> *Don't get defensive and argue. "Patience and gentle talk can convince a ruler and overcome any problem" (Proverbs 25:15 CEV).*

I chose Door Number Two and carefully clarified: "No, that's not what I meant at all. I know you have been having your quiet time out here. You have kidded me about moving in on your favorite spot. When I saw you coming, I wanted to assure you I wasn't taking your spot at all and, in fact, I was just leaving. Can you see this is what I meant?"

I paused to let Sarah respond, and her puzzled look turned into a big smile as she said, "Oh! I'm sorry. I shouldn't have said that. Thanks for thinking of me. I do love it out here. Just sitting here makes me feel so blessed."

With clarification made and possible conflict averted, I finished my last bite of All-Bran, arose—bowl in hand—and went into the house to go to work on this book. Sarah settled down with her Bible and devotional books to share the patio and backyard solely with some birds that had landed on some cattails in the marsh a few yards away.

The scene I just described is a simple one, but not unfamiliar. In this case both of us had misunderstood the other's intentions, quickly done a bit of mind reading, and jumped to certain conclusions. Welcome to marriage! Welcome to the Everyday Challenge to communicate successfully with your mate!

Rule No. 1 for Good Everyday Communication

There are many theories about communication, some of them rather complex and difficult to practice. But, after more than twenty-five years of counseling married couples and hearing their tales of miscommunication and misunderstanding, my first and most important rule for better everyday communication is simply *Take time to be clear.* And to be clear, learn to *speak carefully* to be understood—and, just as important, to *listen carefully* to understand. This rule is easy to say, but not always easy to remember to do—as my "I'm leaving" remark to Sarah on the patio illustrates. It is all too easy to mind read or jump to conclusions, and sometimes you can just be plain lazy in expressing yourself (as I was with Sarah), assuming your partner will know what you mean. But your spouse doesn't always know what you mean, and the possibilities of a tiny misunderstanding growing into something a lot more serious are legion.

One innocent remark prompts a retort of some kind, which leads to another sharp response. Back and forth it can go, feelings flare, and soon you and your spouse are having "heated fellowship"—and you have no idea why. When that happens, you two have obviously stepped over the line between an issue and a Love or Respect issue. At least one of you is suffering from a pinched air hose and is feeling unloved or disrespected. The Energizing Cycle has ground to a halt, and the Crazy Cycle is ready to spin—or is already turning.

> *Here's a goal for the tongue-tied: "Even though I'm not good with words, I know what I'm talking about . . . I have made this clear to you in every possible way"* (2 Corinthians 11:6 GW).

There Is a Difference Between Decoding and Clarifying

Right here, it might be helpful to spell out the difference between decoding and clarifying in more detail. Decoding is what you do *after* you step on your mate's air hose and deflate his or her spirit. Decoding is what you do when you strongly suspect—or can clearly tell—that your mate's air hose has been pinched. Either she is feeling unloved or he is feeling disrespected. At this point, the Crazy Cycle has begun.

The wife will react in a way that feels disrespectful, but she really wants her husband to understand she is feeling unloved. Her disrespectful actions or words are her coded message. She is saying, "I need to feel your love."

The husband will react in a way that feels unloving, but he is hoping his wife will understand he is feeling disrespected. His unloving actions or words are his coded message. He is saying, "I need to feel your respect."

So, what about clarifying? Clarifying is what you do *before* you step on your mate's air hose and deflate his or her spirit. For example, you are having a typical conversation, but you can tell there is a misunderstanding. One of you isn't being clear or isn't hearing correctly. Then and there you clarify the misunderstanding before your spouse's spirit deflates. You *lovingly* or *respectfully* clarify matters so that your spouse will not feel unloved or disrespected. The reason you take pains to clarify a seemingly small matter is to prevent the situation from becoming a Love or Respect issue that needs decoding. Clarifying is what you do to stay off the Crazy Cycle and keep positive energetic feelings flowing between the two of you, to keep yourselves on the Energizing Cycle.

To illustrate the difference between clarifying and decoding, let's go back to my original remark to Sarah: "I'm leaving." Because I had not made myself clear regarding what I was thinking, Sarah could have interpreted "I'm leaving" as some kind of rejection of her. Had she actually wanted a little conversation—as is often her desire—my remark could have made her feel unloved. She could have lashed out sarcastically: "Okay, don't take time for your wife. Just rush off to work on your new Love and Respect book that tells couples how to talk to each other." That kind of remark would have been a clear indication that I had deflated her spirit and needed to decode what she was saying. I would definitely have had a lack-of-Love issue on my hands.

Fortunately, my "I'm leaving" remark had not offended Sarah. Her response—"Don't worry. I'm not coming out here to talk to you"—was her way of saying she was trying to be respectful of my need to get started on my workday. She was letting me know she didn't have any expectations about taking my time to talk, but I had no way of reading Sarah's mind. I felt I needed to clarify things because I thought I sensed a tiny bit of defensiveness when she said, "Don't worry. I'm not coming out here to talk to you." Perhaps I was programmed to sense something because over the years she would walk up and her first words would be "Can we talk?"

Further complicating the dynamics of this brief exchange, though, was the fact that for many years I have done most of my studying and writing at home in my study, which serves as my home office. I am often preoccupied with some new idea or thought even while eating my breakfast on the patio. Sarah is very respectful of my privacy while I am working in my study, but on the patio I am supposed to be available.

So what was Sarah *really* saying? Was she telling me she hadn't come to bug me by wanting to talk? Was she really hurt but acting as though she didn't care? Or was she just telling me she had other things to do? I had to get things straight, and that's why I was quick to give her feedback designed to clarify what each of us had meant. And because my feedback statement had sounded friendly and nonthreatening, she felt free to admit that, indeed, she thought I was leaving because I didn't want to take time to talk. She simply wanted to respect my desire to get going with my workday. Once I had that straight, I was able to explain what I had meant by "I'm leaving."

Perhaps all of this sounds like I am making a lot out of very little. That is just the point. Couples continue to get into arguments and fights because they wind up making a lot out of what seems to be nothing. In the daily interactions you have with your spouse, subtle meanings and nuances are often easy to misinterpret if they're not clarified. Our patio exchange sounds so simple and insignificant, hardly worth mentioning, but it could have gone in a much different direction. Stopping to give Sarah feedback and to receive feedback from her helped us avoid a potentially big bump and kept us on the Energizing Cycle.

> *Just as writers of Scripture must clarify, so you must make things clear by saying, "What I mean is . . ."* *(1 Corinthians 1:12 ESV).*

Sarah and I have a wonderful marriage. We are great friends, but we still experience small misunderstandings that could easily turn into conflicts if we did not clarify what was meant when who said what. To clarify, we must go back and come at the conversation again, carefully speaking and carefully listening to each other. A big part of being careful to clarify is to get and give clear feedback to ensure that each of us understands what the other one meant. Most of us are not born with this ability. It is a skill we acquire, and we can always learn a bit more about doing it better. (See Appendix D, "Using Feedback to Clarify Your Conversations," p. 346.")

How I Learned to Listen and Speak More Carefully

I began learning about the need for listening carefully to understand and speaking carefully to be understood at age thirteen when I enrolled in the Missouri Military Academy. Except for the summers when I went home, I spent the next five years there. As a cadet and then as a cadet leader, I experienced day in and day out interaction with other people. From 6:20 a.m. when I was jolted awake by a bugle playing reveille until 9:45 p.m. when I crawled wearily into bed to the sound of "Taps," I lived in community.

Not surprisingly, when you live in community, you learn a great deal about communicating—and you learn most of it by trial and error! For example, one day as a cadet leader, I was in charge of a unit of over one hundred cadets. I had just brought them to attention in formation when suddenly I saw a cadet break ranks in the rear and start walking away. "Private," I said sharply, "get back in line. This unit has not been dismissed yet." Much to my chagrin I later learned that the commandant had walked up in the rear and directed the cadet to go back to the dorm and get the belt he had forgotten. Because the commandant was not that tall, I had not seen him through the several ranks of cadets before me. All I had seen was a cadet bolting formation. I could have stopped the cadet, spoken quietly with him, and learned the reason for his actions. Instead I barked like any Marine drill sergeant and wound up getting a very disapproving look from my commandant—and feeling foolish and embarrassed.

This incident was a small item in the Great Scheme of things, but it taught me there is a right way and a wrong way to interact with people. At the heart of the right way to communicate is listening carefully and speaking carefully.

Over the decades since I attended the academy, I have met and ministered to thousands of people, many of whom have never learned to listen and speak with care. All of us like to think we do, but we blunder on, sure that we understand what someone just said and assuming that others understand what we mean. I have learned that, no matter how long I study communication and work at doing it better, nothing is more important than trying to understand and be sure you are understood. To assume that understanding is automatically taking place is folly, especially in a marriage.

After graduating from the military academy, I enrolled at Wheaton College, a small Christian liberal arts school just west of Chicago. I was a new believer in Christ and longed to communicate effectively with people about my newfound faith and on important topics to me but I knew I had much to learn. After taking some core courses, I came upon a class called "Interpersonal Dynamics." The course description talked about principles that would help me understand other people and enable me to be understood. I was hooked! Hardly believing my good fortune, I signed up and sat spellbound under the teaching of Dr. Lois LeBar, and her teaching literally changed the way I communicated.

I recall her saying: "Before you talk with another person, especially if the topic is at all emotional, ask yourself: 'Is that which I am about to say going to build trust or undermine trust between this person and myself?' " That single question revolutionized the way I interacted because it made me see the crucial importance of being aware of how I was coming across. Dr. LeBar challenged me to watch the facial expressions of others around me and to determine if my communications tended to draw them closer or drive them away.

A Scriptural Short Course on How to Communicate

I never forgot what Dr. LeBar taught me, and, as I graduated from college, went on to grad school and seminary, and then returned to grad school, I kept finding confirmation for her words in Scripture passages that spoke about the importance of communicating by seeking to speak carefully and listen carefully. For example, these three proverbs provide thought-provoking word pictures about what it means to speak and listen carefully:

> Proverbs 18:13—"He who gives an answer before he hears, it is folly and shame to him."
>
> Proverbs 15:28—"The heart of the righteous ponders how to answer, but the mouth of the wicked pours out evil things."
>
> Proverbs 16:23—"The heart of the wise instructs his mouth and adds persuasiveness to his lips."

If you listen before you answer . . . *if* you think before you speak . . . *if* your heart instructs your mouth . . . *then* what you say will make your wife feel loved or your husband feel respected.

And from James 1:19 comes advice no husband or wife can overlook: "Know this, my beloved brothers: let every person be quick to hear, slow to speak, slow to anger" (ESV). James's words, plus proverbs like those quoted above, have stuck in my mind and positively impacted my marriage. It is as if the Lord is tapping me on the shoulder, saying in that inaudible but very clear way, "Listen first, Emerson. Be as quick to listen as you are to speak. In fact, *listen first a lot more often.* And keep your temper. Be slow to get angry because what you think Sarah might have said or done isn't as bad as your first impulse might tell you."

Ever since the Love and Respect Connection clicked in my mind, I have seen a practical application of what I learned under Dr. LeBar and from Scripture that can help husbands and wives. The goodwilled husband who wants to improve communication with his wife can do so rather quickly by asking himself, "Is what I am about to say going to result in my wife feeling loved or unloved?" The goodwilled wife who wants to improve communication with her husband need only ask, "Is what I am about to say going to result in my husband feeling respected or disrespected?"

Pausing to ask these questions can do wonders for your marriage, as Sarah and I well know. Try it and you will notice that you soften your voice, you select your words more carefully, and you listen to your spouse more patiently. In many cases, your spouse responds in kind with softer tones, words that build you up, and patience to hear you out. Amazingly, mutual understanding happens, and mutual understanding leads to good communication.

Tone of Voice and Facial Expression Are Crucial

In our conferences, we stress how crucial it is to communicate with the right tone of voice and the right expression on your face. This is a problem for men and women, but for different reasons. I have counseled many couples where the wife complains that the husband comes across as harsh and unloving. From her pink perspective, he is frowning with disapproval or sounding stern, even angry. According to his blue point of view, he is simply making his point firmly and accurately. Obviously, he needs to put on his wife's pink sunglasses and pink hearing aids and see how he really looks and sounds to her. A guy can be oblivious to the damaging effects of his angry glare. This can feel abusive to a wife. Though this fellow can glare at his buddy in a way that angrily declares, "Back off and drop it," and his buddy will not break down and cry, God has not designed a wife or daughter to be looked at with such a glare. She is not wrong for her hurt feelings, just different from a male.

I have talked with many wives who would like to tell their husbands, "Please turn down the volume. And, please, more than anything else, realize how I feel when you speak to me harshly or look at me with an angry glare. Few things hurt me so badly. Sometimes my heart pounds; other times I feel myself going numb. I feel devastated. More than anything, I want to talk things through with you, but when you scowl and growl, like I've done something wrong or really dumb, I want to shut down or just scream."

> "Why do you have such an angry look on your face?" (Genesis 4:6 CEV).

At the same time I have had many wives tell me they know they are guilty of a negative tone of voice and a sour look on their faces. They don't necessarily sound harsh; theirs is more a tone of contempt, often accompanied by a rolling of the eyes. The pink wife who is guilty of this kind of behavior needs to put on her husband's blue sunglasses and blue hearing aids so she can realize how disrespectfully she is coming across to him. Many women think they are saying what needs to be said; they even think they are doing a good job of saying it respectfully. But they don't see or hear what their husband sees and hears. In our Love and Respect Conferences, I tell wives this: "After your next 'lively' discussion with your husband where you think you have respectfully said what needed to be said, go into the bathroom, shut the door, and re-enact your part. Try to use the same tone of voice, body movements, hand gestures, and facial expressions you used when talking to him." I see wives out in the audience sort of sucking in their breath as they remember a recent scene at home. And

I have had many wives tell me they tried my suggestion and what a stunning revelation it was. Did these wives intend to communicate disdain earlier? Rarely. The point here is not to suggest these wives are mean-spirited. The aim is to point out the appearance of disrespect and its ill effects on the male spirit.

Obviously, the harsh or contemptuous tone and the angry or sour look are mortal enemies of the Energizing Cycle and great friends of the Crazy Cycle. Marital researchers agree that a huge percentage of communication problems between husband and wife are due not to *what* is said but to *how* it is said—the attitude and tone of voice. To keep the Energizing Cycle going and the Crazy Cycle at bay, you must make attitude adjustments and break old habits. Difficult, yes, but it can be done *if you truly want to make these changes.*

One Love and Respect wife wrote:

> [I think daily about] learning to be soft in my speech to my husband so I am being respectful, not only with my words, but the tone of my voice and my body language. IT ABSOLUTELY WORKS AND IS FREEING FOR BOTH OF US. And the remark . . . about thinking about how you want your son's wife to talk to him . . . THAT really was something to think about, and I've never forgotten it. I would want her to be kind, loving, soft, and respectful in her behavior toward him. I always think of that when I'm speaking to my husband.

I have not written at length about the importance of tone of voice and facial expressions, but please do not take this to mean I give them less than major importance. In the following letter a wife expresses my concern perfectly:

> I think the reason many women fly right by this "negative tone and facial expression thing" is that it seems such a small thing compared to the problems they are experiencing. They have a hard time believing that making this small adjustment could

really make that much of an impact. To them, they see mountains of problems: he's not an involved father, he's not a spiritual leader, he lets things go around the house, he works too much, he doesn't "date" me anymore, etc. So it's hard for them to believe that a small adjustment like this could really get them past these major issues.

I agree completely and would only add this encouragement: try making this "small adjustment" and see if those major issues don't improve.

This chapter has emphasized clarifying the little things and shown how this simple approach can lead to good communication and help you avoid problems. But there is more to dealing with the Everyday Challenge. So in chapter 12 we will look more closely at clarifying and how to use the "Is what I'm about to say . . ." question. In addition, I will share other important strategies that can help you either avoid or get rid of your communication problems as you stay on the Energizing Cycle.

CHAPTER TWELVE

More Strategies for Dealing
with Communication Glitches

In chapter 11, I introduced the concept of clarifying and how important it is in keeping some minor issue from escalating into a more serious problem because someone starts to feel unloved or disrespected. I also encouraged you to ask yourself, "Is what I'm about to say going to make my spouse feel loved or unloved, respected or disrespected?" In this chapter I want to share some additional insights on how clarifying works with the "Is what I'm about to say . . ." question to bring about mutual understanding and better communication.

Like so many strategies in the Love and Respect approach to marriage, asking yourself the "Is what I'm about to say . . ." question is simple, but not necessarily easy to do consistently. Do I ask myself this question every time I have some kind of conflict or potential conflict with Sarah? No, because sometimes I forget; other times I may be irked and just plain not want to! But I can tell you this with certainty: When I ask myself this question and come across lovingly to Sarah—and when she asks herself this question and comes across respectfully to me—we stay firmly on the Energizing Cycle. But when we fail to ask this question and when I come across unlovingly to Sarah or she comes across disrespectfully to me, we jump off the Energizing Cycle, and the Crazy Cycle starts to spin.

If you use the "Is what I'm about to say . . ." question consistently, I can guarantee that two things will happen: you will *speak* more carefully and *listen* more carefully.

How can I guarantee this? Because of personal experience. When I listen more carefully, I tend to understand Sarah much better. In turn, she feels understood and is far less likely to be defensive. *She feels loved.* And when I speak more carefully, Sarah tends to understand me much better. When I feel understood, I am far less likely to be defensive. *I feel respected.*

When Glitches Come Up, Use Feedback to Clarify

Despite your best intentions, however, minor breakdowns or glitches in communication do occur. When they happen, don't accuse your spouse of not listening carefully or speaking clearly. Instead, make your own move to clarify things. If your spouse seems unclear, say, "I'm sorry. I guess I didn't understand. What I thought you said was . . . [Then state what you heard as best you can.] Is that correct?"

Or, if it is apparent that your spouse either did not hear you correctly or has misinterpreted your words, say, "I'm sorry. I was not as clear as I could have been. What I meant to say was . . . [Then restate what you are trying to convey as best you can.] Is that what you heard me saying?"

Be patient as you start to use these simple feedback questions. I recall that when I began doing this on a consistent basis, I was stunned by how poorly people listened. I wanted to get defensive, say I had been very clear, and ask them to please get the wax out of their ears! But I realized that would be useless and nonproductive, especially with Sarah, so I just smiled and kept at it, restating what I had said and refusing to be irritated. And it has paid off. I have found great joy in being able to guide a conversation so I am not a victim of misunderstanding, and neither is the person with whom I am conversing.

Why I Have Learned to "Listen Up" More Often

One reason I have learned patience with others is that I have my own problems with listening, especially to my wife. Seemingly, about once a month, I don't listen carefully enough to what Sarah says. For example, she recently told me she was going to her friend's home for several days to help her with her new

> *During times of misunderstanding, what would happen if you responded "with all humility and gentleness, with patience, showing tolerance for one another in love" (Ephesians 4:2)?*

baby. When the time neared for the child's birth, Sarah reminded me of her plans, but I could not recall anything at all about her telling me she was leaving for several days. In past years I would have said, "You never told me that." Not anymore. I have learned that, when it comes to relationships or emotions, Sarah knows precisely what she has said. In fact, her memory of this kind of conversation is practically infallible. I have often heard her repeat a conversation word for word, in exact chronology, and with appropriate inflections!

Based on my own experience, I suggest to husbands that you refrain from arguing when your wife says, "I did, too, say that." Instead of claiming she didn't tell you clearly, admit that you probably didn't listen carefully enough. Trust her heart and give her the benefit of the doubt. If anything is to be doubted, it is probably your memory because the typical male does not listen carefully to his wife. Fortunately, when I don't listen, Sarah cuts me some slack. If I ask a question that she has just

> *Husband, when you interact or disagree with your wife, does she still feel "the heart of her husband trusts in her" (Proverbs 31:11)?*

answered, it frustrates her to no end, but she patiently repeats it. Instead of getting into a childish "did so—did not" routine, she gives me grace.

To sum up, when it seems that somebody didn't listen or speak clearly, don't waste energy getting defensive or angry. Instead, get feedback and repeat what you said or let your spouse do the same. Clarify the issue and don't let it become The Big Issue. As I often say, there is no point in being *right but wrong at the top of your voice.*

Words of Caution for Talkative Wives . . .

As important as clarifying is, there is one danger. I have counseled many wives who feel their husbands don't understand them. This kind of wife can mistakenly think "clarifying things" must mean talking and listening to each other at great length to achieve mutual understanding. What I say seems tailor-made to help the talkative wife put pressure on her not-so-talkative husband to converse with her more and thus make her feel more loved. Truth be told, many husbands will not automatically want to clarify things as readily as I tried to do with Sarah on the patio. I can relate because earlier in our marriage I was in that very same boat. It took me a number of years to put together what I learned at military academy and in college and apply it to being a loving husband. The typical man is not as ready to talk about things the way a woman can.

Scripture speaks to this problem in 1 Peter 3:1–6. There Peter instructs wives to respect their husbands not by being talkative but by reflecting a quiet spirit. In fact, he says that the wife with a husband who is "disobedient to the word" (which could mean a carnal Christian or an unbeliever) can win him "without a word" by living a pure and respectful life before him (vv. 1–2). While this passage is pointed more toward the couple on the Crazy Cycle, I believe it can also be applied to a couple who is trying to keep the Energizing Cycle humming. In many a marriage that is firmly on the Energizing Cycle, the husband can still be on the quiet side while the wife is a real talker. That is why, when I stress the need for husband and wife to speak and listen carefully, the wife should not interpret my teaching to mean she can demand that they talk every time she feels the need.

When women get together, they typically feel free to talk about their burdens and relationships. Many wives have a natural tendency to do the same with their husbands. Their idea of how to keep the Energizing Cycle going is to talk about things—lots of things. You see, even if a couple is on the Energizing Cycle or at least trying to be, many women are never satisfied. She may assume, "If we talk about things, I can point out how I feel to help him understand me and change so he can better love me."

As she tries to increase talking *with* him, she can wind up talking *at* him. Now the Energizing Cycle is slowing down in a hurry. Even though it seems he is not trying to understand her and the needs of the marriage as much as she would like, she is wise to say less, especially if her tendency is to say too much. She is not to think she will start respecting her husband more as soon as he begins talking more. In fact, it's almost a sure bet that if she moves toward him with too many words, he will feel disrespected.[1]

The too-talkative approach closes off most husbands, especially the less talkative ones. When pressed to talk more, this kind of husband loses energy. He pulls back and may even revert to stonewalling, to not talking at all. Now the Energizing Cycle has stopped, and the Crazy Cycle is starting up.

The woman's need to talk, talk, talk is

Ladies, be careful. "A nagging wife goes on and on like the drip, drip, drip of the rain" (Proverbs 19:13 CEV).

often a major reason why couples struggle to stay on the Energizing Cycle. Many women find it hard to practice what Peter says about "without a word." Their feelings tell them they must talk to their husbands and even point out (in a loving way, of course) things that can make their marriage healthier. These wives just know, if they can have a good talk and if their husbands will respond to their requests to work on the marriage, they will feel wonderful.

I realize that some wives may read this and protest, "But we *have* to talk. How can we resolve anything if we don't talk?" My advice is this: you must choose between resolving what you don't think is perfect and trying to stay on the Energizing Cycle. Even if you believe what you want to say is necessary and true, pressing him too hard to talk about it can come across as being disrespectful and contemptuous—precisely what the Lord instructs you not to be.

Ultimately, you must choose: believe that, because you have a God-given need to talk, more talking is necessary *or* accept your husband's God-given need to do less talking and be patient with him.

I strongly encourage you wives to follow the instruction in 1 Peter. It protects you from your natural tendency to end up talking in ways that guarantee to shut your husband down. When you see your husband's spirit deflate, you need to apply Peter's command: win him "without a word." Am I saying you should never, ever say anything? Of course not, but as you show a gentle and quiet spirit *and* as you learn to address issues respectfully, you will be able to see your husband open up again, and communication will happen.

But many women have been conditioned by our feminist-influenced culture to believe that if they remain quiet and don't share their feelings as much as they think is necessary, they will lose their power and sense of self, nothing will ever be resolved in their marriage, and no improvement will ever happen. The wife who has these fears should remember that God's instructions always have a profound purpose. From what we hear at Love and Respect Conferences and by e-mail, many husbands are convicted and motivated to change far more quickly when a wife comes across respectfully with a gentle and quiet spirit as 1 Peter 3:1–6 teaches. My word of encouragement to all wives married to a goodwilled man is this: as you practice quietness and unconditional respect, your marriage will improve, issues will get resolved, and your sense of self and power will increase.

The gentle, quiet, and respectful spirit *does* work. As one wife wrote to tell me: "I'm more aware of how I can misunderstand my husband when he communicates, so I take time to listen more carefully and ask questions. I am more patient and less offended. I also dwell less on hurts . . . and am experiencing more peace."

So try the gentle, quiet spirit for three months and see what happens in your marriage. Remember that the key to motivating another person is meeting that person's deepest need. When a wife meets her husband's need to feel respected, he is motivated to meet her deepest need—to feel loved. Note carefully that having a quiet spirit does *not* mean you can never say one word about your need for love. You can mention your love needs, but you must communicate them respectfully and at a pace that he can handle. When you seek to point out your love needs (spelled out in C-O-U-P-L-E), keep his respect needs (spelled out in C-H-A-I-R-S) ever before you. Your goal is mutual understanding, not just being understood.

Admittedly, this is a faith venture for a wife. So, to keep the Crazy Cycle contained and the Energizing Cycle turning (if ever so slowly at times), "pray without ceasing" (1 Thessalonians 5:17). And keep your sense of humor, especially when you become discouraged and frustrated. As one wife prayed, "Dear Lord, I pray for wisdom to understand my man; love to forgive him; and patience for his moods . . . because, Lord, if I pray for strength, I'll beat him to death!"

A Word to the Wise for the Non-Talkative Husband

Having warned the wives of possible pitfalls of talking too much, I want to turn to the husbands who may be guilty of talking too little. What I have said to urge wives not to talk so much is not to be taken by the silent husband as confirmation that he is off the hook and doesn't need to try to improve in the talking department. Note that after Peter instructs the wives to do less talking and more quiet, respectful living before their husbands (1 Peter 3:1–6), he goes on to say, "You husbands likewise live with your wives in an understanding way, as with a weaker vessel,[2] since she is a woman; and grant her honor as a fellow heir of the grace of life, so that your prayers may not be hindered" (v. 7 NASB 1977).

There is much here for the less talkative husband to ponder. As a way of honoring Christ, he is to obediently attend to his wife's concerns. He is to work at being understanding by moving toward her to listen and empathize. He must realize that when he moves away and hardly talks to her, she is threatened. Peter specifically instructs husbands to live with their wives in an understanding way because, by nature, the typical male neglects trying to understand. He tends to move away from his pink wife to go do his blue thing. Few things hurt her more or make her feel more unloved.

Since starting our Love and Respect ministry, I have thought a great deal about what Peter might have meant by "live with your wives in an understanding way." And if a goodwilled husband wants to treat his wife like porcelain, not cast-iron, and if he truly wants to esteem her as a fellow heir in Christ, I have a prescription for staying on the Energizing Cycle. If I could talk man-to-man with such a husband, here is what I would say:

- When your wife comes to talk to you, listen to her. Realize she is coming to you because you matter more to her than anyone else. She has certain emotional needs, and only you can meet them. Sometimes she may say things that don't make sense to you, and she is apt to misspeak and exaggerate when she is upset, but don't put her down. Instead, listen to her heart. Give her a chance to express her concerns and, as she does so, don't try to fix her. Don't give her your solutions unless she asks for them.

- At times invite your wife to make suggestions or even offer constructive criticism about how you are doing as a husband. This will probably be no fun. You are apt to hear "You always . . ." or "You never . . ." Take the hits like a man of honor. Realize you can crush her spirit very quickly if you get defensive or push her away. Sure, you have lots of that kind of power, but you never want to use it. Instead, be humble. Apologize and seek to make adjustments.
- When your wife is being inaccurate and needs better information, calmly explain the facts. Do not be patronizing or arrogant. Let the truth carry its own weight.
- Coach your wife on saying things respectfully. You don't need to explode or lash out to get respect. Just tell her when something sounds disrespectful. At the same time, don't be a Mr. Milquetoast or a wimp. If she gets too emotional, lovingly ask her to calm down. Be firm but tender, and over time you will have a very happy wife—and you will be a very happy man.

> *Gentlemen, when your wife is disrespectful, even insulting, which of the following describes you? "A fool's anger is known at once, but a prudent man conceals dishonor" (Proverbs 12:16).*

One husband compared where he and his wife are now to where they were before discovering Love and Respect: "When Teresa would come to me with a problem, I would listen, but then I would most often come back with 'Well, I'll tell you what I would do.' I was always listening so I could be heard. I very rarely listened to understand." The result was predictable. They were on the Crazy Cycle a great deal of the time, but now they enjoy the Energizing Cycle as they consciously apply Love and Respect principles. He adds, "Now I find myself listening more closely to what she means when she comes to me with a problem and wanting to understand her feelings. It's no longer, 'Hurry up and say it, so I can tell you what I think.'"

Try to Keep Spiderwebbing Under Control

The goodwilled husband who is willing to work at listening better must remember he will face obstacles, and one of the most intriguing that he should be ready to deal with is spiderwebbing. You won't find a formal definition of this term in the dictionary, but most married couples will recognize what spiderwebbing is. Someone starts with this point and goes to that point but doesn't finish that point before going on to another point, not finishing that point but doubling back to an earlier point. Multitasking women are masters of this art. They can get together and start talking about things. They never finish one point because that reminds them of some other point. They can go on for half an hour, but somehow they always bring the conversation full circle and eventually finish all the points! For husbands, however, this kind of conversation is usually not that simple. Here is a typical conversation with a spiderwebbing wife:

She: "Honey, did you hear what happened? At the middle school today, the fire alarm went off, and all the kids were herded outside. Joey didn't have his coat on, and they stood outside in the snow for twenty minutes. Now he's got a bad cold. So I took him to the doctor."

He: "Oh, so that's what happened? There was a fire?"

She: "No. It was a fire drill."

He: "So Joey got a cold?"

She: "Yes, but that's not what happened. What happened is that Dr. Smith is getting a divorce. He's leaving his family. I talked to Mary, his receptionist. You know Mary. I went to high school with her brother. I went out with him a couple of times. He was so cute . . . Remember he flunked out of school? But she told me he's now a millionaire in construction. Can you believe that? He built a huge mall in Peoria. He's married and has four kids, and one of them has disabilities—I feel so badly about that. The next time we travel through Peoria, we need to stop at that mall. By the way, did you pick up my dress at the cleaners in the mall on the way home? And we need to be at that party tonight no later than 7:30. Can we be ready by 7:10? I have a new babysitter. They just moved in from Tucson, and they seem to be such a sweet family. Emily told me about them the other day when we worked out together. By the way, my back pain went away. Did you send in the check for the monthly dues at the club? Last month it was so embarrassing when I handed the girl my card, and she told me we were overdue."

Now if two women were having this conversation, the one who heard this monologue could quite likely repeat it almost word for word. But the average male? His eyes are glazed and his head hurts. He lost her back there somewhere when somebody built a mall in Peoria. The reason the average husband is totally confused by spiderwebbing is that God designed him to be *linear*.

Consider a board meeting of a group of men. They have an agenda that includes Points A, B, C, and D. They begin with discussing Point A, and they stay on the topic. They take a vote, it comes out 9–3, and they are done with that item. Then the men move on to Point B and do the same thing. They are usually bulldogs about staying on the point. They are wired to finish one point completely and then move on to the next. It's called linear thinking and the typical male is completely at home with that approach to conversation. But when he gets together with his wife and she starts bouncing from one point to another—fully intending to come back and finish each point—he gets that blank, faraway look in his eyes. The wife notices this and says, "You're not listening to me."

Some males get so entangled in her spiderwebs all they can say is "Huh?" Others smile sheepishly and admit, "Well, honey, you're right." And some, not at all amused, reach for the TV remote. Whatever the reaction, the Energizing Cycle slows down—fast.

Some wives think their husbands don't care if they spiderweb. Not so. Men simply can't absorb all that information given in that way. So what's the answer? Should women try to totally give up spiderwebbing and become linear thinkers and talkers? That's not likely to happen this side of the Promised Land. So what couples must do is give each other a measure of grace. Husbands need to let their wives release their emotions and share their reports. Wives need to do this with as little spiderwebbing as possible, saving the longer versions for girlfriends.

Mundane Misunderstandings Don't Equal a Bad Marriage

Advice for overly talkative wives: "The more words there are, the more pointless they become" (Ecclesiastes 6:11 GW). Advice for men with a hair-trigger temper: "You should be quick to listen and slow . . . to get angry" (James 1:19 CEV).

Spiderwebbing is an amusing example of the trivial and mundane things that can cause problems when husbands and wives try to communicate, so please don't take any of this small stuff lightly. Perhaps I sound like I may be overemphasizing the importance of the trivial and mundane, but I can't help it. I have counseled too many couples whose conflicts, arguments, and fights start with what seem to be trivial and mundane remarks. My advice to all husbands and wives is to accept the fact that misunderstandings over mundane issues are inevitable. Conversations like the patio exchange between Sarah and me are typical of *all* couples! Sarah and I have our particular quirks and characteristics that can get us going—and you have yours. The sooner you accept this fact, the sooner you can start using the wisdom in this chapter to build a stronger marriage.

What you must not think, even a little bit, is that your minor misunderstandings mean your marriage is not working. You can wind up feeling defeated by what appears to you to be a bad marriage when your marriage is as normal as the next couple's.

One reason that a lot of wives, in particular, may think their marriage is unfulfilling and not romantic enough is because of what they see on the screen—the small one in their living room as well as the big silver one at the local theaters. Please do not fall into this foolish trap. The romantic episodes you see in a film are fictional scenes played out by expert actors to produce something with box-office appeal.

But why be influenced by actors who will play a passionate romantic scene before the cameras and typically fail miserably at relationships in real life? The truth is, behind closed doors actors are no different from anyone else. We all have the same basic needs: love for her, respect for him. Sarah and I *know* you can experience a richer, more fulfilling, and, yes, more romantic marriage if you and your spouse practice Love and Respect.

But it will only happen as you accept the fact that a marriage becomes good *through* conflict, not apart from it. Scripture tells us that we "will have trouble in this life [of marriage]" (see 1 Corinthians 7:28), but Scripture also gives us the wisdom to deal with marital problems, conflicts, and misunderstandings with the mundane things that come up during daily life together as well as the more serious issues. Since 1973, when Sarah and I said, "I do," we have been learning how to apply scriptural wisdom to the everyday challenges that come our way. And when we do, we are never disappointed.

For us, staying on the Energizing Cycle doesn't mean we need to be constantly on a real high (although we have our share). And we stay away from any real lows as I seek to be quietly loving and Sarah seeks to be quietly respectful. Things purr along fairly smoothly as we go about our daily duties, but when we have trouble—when misunderstanding happens or conflict comes up—we deal with it lovingly and respectfully. My love motivates her respect; her respect motivates my love. The cycle of energy flows back and forth. *It works.*

There Is One More Cycle Every Couple Must Ride

We have looked at how to use the right words and attitudes to both stop the Crazy Cycle and get the Energizing Cycle up and running smoothly. But biblically inspired communication is the driving force for one more cycle. We call it the Rewarded Cycle because it points to how God will reward you no matter what is happening in your marriage. If your mate is refusing to communicate with you at the moment, you can still communicate with God. And if you and your spouse are clicking on all twelve cylinders of the Energizing Cycle, you also need to be aware of the Rewarded Cycle, which teaches that everything you do to Love or Respect your mate, you do first out of obedience to God. In chapter 13 I will explain how the Rewarded Cycle works and why it is vital to good communication.

PART V

The Rewarded Cycle:
The Unconditional Dimension
of Communication

In the introduction to this book, I made the point that the key to marriage is not communication per se. The real key is mutual understanding, which is gained by learning to speak each other's language, with the husband speaking love to his wife and the wife speaking respect to her husband. And as they better understand each other, better communication has to follow.

While all of that is certainly true, there is a dimension to marriage that goes beyond mutual understanding and good communication. In an ultimate sense, this book is not primarily about either one because your marriage is not only about your relationship to your spouse. First and foremost, your marriage is about your relationship to God and communicating the way He commands. God's way of communicating in marriage is to talk with words of unconditional love and respect. When you speak words of love and respect, God rewards you. In fact, He rewards you even if your spouse does not respond positively to your words of love and respect. This is what the Rewarded Cycle is all about. I have used the word *unconditional* often in this book. In the next four chapters, I hope to help you understand it at an entirely different level. In communication terms the Rewarded Cycle teaches:

HIS LOVING WORDS BLESS REGARDLESS OF
HER RESPECTFUL WORDS.
HER RESPECTFUL WORDS BLESS REGARDLESS
OF HIS LOVING WORDS.

In chapter 13 you will see the importance of realizing you are in the unconditional dimension of life called God's kingdom, which means you are to speak loving or respectful words to your mate unconditionally as unto Christ. You are enabled to speak this way through your faith in Christ and desire to follow Him. The Rewarded Cycle is about your Lord and your relationship to Him, and He commands you to express yourself lovingly or respectfully and always unconditionally. Because a husband reverences Christ, he seeks to speak in loving ways to his wife. Because a wife loves Christ, she seeks to speak in respectful ways to her husband. Whether your mate responds in kind is not your primary concern. Following Christ out of love and gratitude is your first priority, and as you do so, you will reap rewards in this life, yes, but in limitless measure in eternity.

Again, unconditional words of love or respect do not mean you turn a blind eye to your spouse's wrongdoing. You may need to confront the sinful behavior. Truth must not be compromised. However, you speak the truth lovingly or respectfully. This is the gift you give your spouse. Your spouse has not earned this gracious confrontation, and it certainly isn't in your nature to give such a gift! Your propensity, if you are like the rest of us, is to give your spouse a well-deserved tongue lashing—a lashing that is biting and insulting. But you pull back from this manner of scolding because of the Lord's commandment to you not to talk this way. God has revealed a different way to communicate, and He rewards this way of talking.

In chapters 14–16, you will learn five specific, biblical ways to speak unconditional love or respect to your mate. Though we learn about Love and Respect in Ephesians 5:22–33, nowhere in this passage does Paul specifically address the use of the mouth. Why? Because he wrote in detail about how Christians are to use the mouth in Ephesians 4:24–5:21, giving us five golden nuggets of wisdom that he expects his readers to apply to marriage. The husband seeking to love his wife and the wife seeking to respect her husband will speak words that are *Truthful, Uplifting, Forgiving, Thankful, and Scriptural.* To speak these kinds of words unconditionally is to honor God by speaking His way. And when you honor God, He honors and rewards you in this life and eternal life to come.

---·······⊶⊷·······---

CHAPTER THIRTEEN

Why the Rewarded Cycle Is for Every Marriage— Hot, Cold, or Lukewarm

As we come to the last and most important part of *The Language of Love & Respect*, it's time for a brief review of Parts III and IV:

1. How do you slow or stop the Crazy Cycle?

Gain mutual understanding by learning each other's language—loving words for her and respectful words for him. This mutual understanding leads to better communication.

2. How do you keep the Crazy Cycle in its cage?

Get on the Energizing Cycle and stay there by speaking words of Love and Respect as you practice the principles in C-O-U-P-L-E and C-H-A-I-R-S.

Those who learn about Love and Respect and seek to practice it usually have no trouble mastering the concept of the Crazy Cycle or understanding why it is a constant threat that must be kept contained and not allowed to run amok. The Energizing Cycle is also simple enough to understand, and it is the way to stay off the Crazy Cycle as husbands practice Love for her with C-O-U-P-L-E and wives practice Respect for him with C-H-A-I-R-S.

But everyone, including Sarah and me, soon discovers the Energizing Cycle does not work perfectly. More correctly, no one can practice C-O-U-P-L-E or C-H-A-I-R-S perfectly because we are all human. Remember, no one can speak perfectly (see James 3:2). You or your mate will also fail to love perfectly and respect perfectly—and what then? We hear from many couples who slow and stop the Crazy Cycle, but they struggle to keep the Energizing Cycle going full speed, and because their communication isn't going perfectly, they grow discouraged.

This is where the Rewarded Cycle comes into play because it teaches:

HIS LOVE BLESSES *REGARDLESS* OF HER RESPECT.
HER RESPECT BLESSES *REGARDLESS* OF HIS LOVE.

In other words, the Rewarded Cycle is where the rubber meets the road. No matter how negative a marriage may be at the moment—seemingly stuck in the Crazy Cycle—the husband must choose to love *unconditionally* and the wife must choose to respect *unconditionally*. There are no ifs or buts, no setting a human standard or bargaining along the lines of "I'll start talking respectfully when he starts to deserve it" or "I'll use more loving words when she starts showing me a little respect." (For more on what it means to extend Love and Respect unconditionally, see Appendix E, "Unconditional Love and Respect Do Not Operate on a Scale of 1–10," p. 351.)

The Rewarded Cycle is not primarily about you and your marriage; it is about you and Jesus Christ. You understand that your first task is to love, reverence, and serve Him no matter how negative things might get with your spouse. In these final chapters I want to emphasize that being on the Rewarded Cycle means communication with God is actually more important than communicating with your spouse. It may well be that your spouse is not even interested in communicating with you at the moment. That is why much of this chapter will focus on the need for prayer—for constantly talking to God, sharing your burdens, and getting His support and strength to love or respect your spouse unconditionally. Keep in mind, however, that as you speak words of unconditional love or respect in service to Christ, a wonderful thing often happens. Your marriage is happier, you communicate with each other better, and you share true oneness and genuine friendship.

Notice I said a wonderful thing *often* happens. Not always. One spouse may want to live by Love and Respect principles, but the other is not interested at all or is downright hostile, ready to leave, separate, or divorce. Or both may commit to Love and Respect, but one party is far less fervent or disciplined about it. No matter what the specifics, getting on the Rewarded Cycle becomes imperative. The husband or wife with the rebellious or disinterested spouse knows that the first goal is serving and honoring the Lord no matter what is happening in the marriage, and from that the rewards will follow.

> *For all those on the Rewarded Cycle: "Do not lose your courage, then, because it brings with it a great reward" (Hebrews 10:35 GNB).*

The Rewarded Cycle Is for Happy Couples Too

Am I saying that the Rewarded Cycle is only for marriages where there are problems and one mate is just not cooperating? A major concern for Sarah and me as we teach Love and Respect Conferences is that couples understand that the Rewarded Cycle also applies to the marriage that is—at least for the moment—humming along nicely on the Energizing Cycle. We know from personal experience that no couple can keep the Energizing Cycle going without a hitch. Just because Sarah speaks respectful words does not guarantee I will be motivated to respond with a love song. I might be having an "It's been e-mails all day" kind of a day, and I could respond with words that are not all that loving. To paraphrase James 3:2, never being at fault in what you say means you have to be perfect, and perfection is in short supply this side of heaven.

So what happens when the Energizing Cycle does not work as expected on a 24–7 basis? It's not easy to keep priming the Energizing Cycle pump particularly if you just made it a point to say something loving or respectful and your spouse did not reciprocate. Getting back to the example where Sarah speaks respectfully, but I do not answer lovingly, the Energizing Cycle has slowed, possibly stopped. Sarah could easily say, "Well, I've done my part. Now it's his turn to make the first move and get us back on track." But suppose I'm stubborn and don't make any kind

> "By your teachings, Lord, I am warned; by obeying them, I am greatly rewarded" (Psalm 19:11 CEV). God rewards your obedience to Love and Respect—even if your spouse does not respond!

of move, such as saying, "I'm sorry"? Maybe I am so wrapped up in my own thinking I'm not even aware of what I have said that is so unloving. Or I could have made a very loving remark to Sarah and, for any number of reasons, gotten disrespect in return. This kind of less-than-perfect talking and acting happens in the best of marriages.

But it is at just this point that the Rewarded Cycle helps followers of Christ choose to look at marriage differently. If you take the Rewarded Cycle seriously, you know there is a greater motive for how one acts in a marriage than simply loving your wife to get respect or respecting your husband to get love. The more mature you are in Christ, the more you are able to understand you do not give in order to get. The Love and Respect couple does not operate on a manipulative basis: "If you give me sex, I will talk lovingly with you" or "I'll give you sex if you let me spend more money."

So, what have Sarah and I concluded should be the primary motive for loving and respecting? The Rewarded Cycle reminds all of us that the most important motive for speaking lovingly or respectfully to each other is because you want to obey Christ.

The Rewarded Cycle—Restated

Let me now state the Rewarded Cycle in communication terms:

HIS LOVING WORDS BLESS REGARDLESS
OF HER RESPECTFUL WORDS.
HER RESPECTFUL WORDS BLESS REGARDLESS
OF HIS LOVING WORDS.

I know of one husband who was exposed to Love and Respect principles four times, including two full conference experiences, before he really understood the importance of the Rewarded Cycle. Ted and his wife, Tammy, had been practicing Love and Respect with mixed results, often "repeating the same dumb mistakes and falling into the Crazy Cycle again and again." It seemed that whenever they had any conflict or confrontation, he preferred to run and hide instead of trying to apply the principles in C-O-U-P-L-E.

During two years of trying to Love and Respect each other, the arguments never seemed to change. Ted found it easier to just dismiss their problems with "that's-the-way-I-am-quit-trying-to-change-me" excuses. Fortunately, he kept listening to the Love and Respect message, and the fourth time was the charm. He writes:

During the Rewarded Cycle part of the conference, you asked, "What is the purpose of marriage?" To procreate, to train up the next generation of leaders by modeling Christian values in the home—these were some of my answers. Your answer, however, was that marriage is the testing or proving ground, the developmental process to prepare us for the ultimate relationship with God the Father, and that we can glorify God by our marriage. This hit home, and, when looking at marriage from my perspective, I was convicted of how I have fallen short.

Ted was a successful salesman who treated prospects and customers with Dale Carnegie charm as he gave them a high level of service. The result was plenty of referrals, more customers, and a good book of business. As he listened to the Rewarded Cycle teaching for the fourth time, he finally realized that, when it came to serving Tammy and their children, he usually threw all of his people skills out the window, acted unlovingly, questioned her motives, and read into everything she said. It struck him that if Tammy were a prospect or a customer, he would never hear back from her or get any more of her business because of how he sometimes acted.

Tammy was the one person God had given Ted as a gift to honor and cherish and love unconditionally, but he treated his customers better and more patiently! As the Rewarded Cycle principles began to sink in—when he heard that his marriage was supposed to be preparing him for a closer, more intimate relationship with God and the ultimate reward—Ted decided he needed to go to God *first* and *then* seek to love his wife unconditionally.

Ted says in closing:

God changed me during your conference, and I'm glad to say that this time I heard His message in the Rewarded Cycle. I have made some changes in my priorities and strive to live by them. Tammy and I have been communicating better than ever, and although we still get on the Crazy Cycle once in a while, we both are quick to realize this and jump off at the next rest stop.

What I like best about Ted's letter is that now he sees the rewards from Christ are very real right here and right now as well as in heaven for eternity. The Rewarded Cycle is not fairy-tale stuff, nor have we added it to give our Love and Respect Conferences a spiritual touch. The premise of the Rewarded Cycle—Love and Respect are rewarded by God even when your spouse is unresponsive—is instead the most important concept that we teach. Because your words of Love or Respect might be going unrewarded in your marriage does not mean those words will go unrewarded by God. Your marriage matters too much to Him for that. Every word you speak to your mate provides you with the opportunity to show your heart to God. To paraphrase Ephesians 6:8, whatever good words you speak to your spouse, you will receive rewards back from the Lord.

The Rewarded Cycle Puts You in the Unconditional Dimension

When any couple—very happy, so-so, or miserable—grasps the real meaning of the Rewarded Cycle, they move into what I call the "Unconditional Dimension." This is not some esoteric or mysterious state; it is simply being aware in a new and fresh way that, as a believer, you are part of the kingdom of God. As a member of His kingdom, you are to act and surely to speak in ways that honor Him, no matter how difficult doing so may be. As Sarah put it that day when I discovered the three cycles of marriage, "The Rewarded Cycle isn't saying there is a magic formula for marriages. Sometimes we must do what we do out of love and reverence for God."

Sometimes I am asked, "So, where do

> *Has your mate turned against you? "God will bless you when people insult you, mistreat you, and tell all kinds of evil lies about you . . . You will have a great reward in heaven" (Matthew 5:11–12 CEV).*

the rewards come from? How does the Rewarded Cycle actually work?" Clearly, the rewards come from God as you faithfully live out your marriage as unto Him. First, you experience the presence and power of God right here, right now, as He sustains you and answers your prayers on a daily basis. Second, infinitely greater rewards wait in heaven. Whatever you may go through here on earth will seem like a small matter compared to heaven's joys.

Actually, Jesus taught all Christians to live in the Unconditional Dimension when He said, "For if you love those who love you, what reward do you have? Do not even the tax collectors do the same? If you greet only your brothers, what more are you doing than others? Do not even the Gentiles do the same?" (Matthew 5:46–47).

Peter echoed Jesus' teaching as he wrote to Christians who were being persecuted:

> Servants, be submissive to your masters with all respect, not only to those who are good and gentle, but also to those who are unreasonable. For this finds favor, if for the sake of conscience toward God a man bears up under sorrows when suffering unjustly. For what credit is there if, when you sin and are harshly treated, you endure it with patience? But if when you do what is right and suffer for it you patiently endure it, this finds favor with God. For you have been called for this purpose, since Christ suffered for you, leaving you an example for you to follow . . . while being reviled, He did not revile in return . . . but kept entrusting Himself to Him who judges righteously. (1 Peter 2:18–23)

Through Jesus and Peter, God set forth His standard for living in the Unconditional Dimension: choose to be loving even when the other person is not; do what is right regardless of the treatment you receive. I believe this standard applies directly to marriage.[1] A husband who speaks lovingly to his disrespectful wife will be rewarded, and a wife who speaks respectfully to her unloving, not-worthy-of-respect husband will be rewarded. Whether you are husband or wife, the reward is what can keep you going in the midst of the craziness: knowing that God commends you, knowing that you have found His favor for your words and actions.

I hear from many husbands or wives who tell me of spouses who are speaking badly about them, betraying them, leaving them. For someone in any of these situations, Peter's words hold special meaning: "If you are reviled for the name of Christ, you are blessed, because the Spirit of glory and of God rests on you" (1 Peter 4:14).[2] For example, a wife writes:

> My husband has moved out and says he doesn't love me anymore. He claims he doesn't know what happened . . . He is not even the same person he was six months ago. The man I have spent the last thirteen years with would not let anyone or anything keep him from his kids for very long, but he isn't acting like this is bothering him at all. I love my husband, and I want him back . . . I did the Respect card[3] just like you told me. The only sign I got was the next night we had a real conversation on the phone. . . .
>
> I have given him space and let him go. He keeps saying that he just needs to be alone. I pray every day and I know God is working, but is there anything else I can do? I need my husband, and our kids need their dad. Jimmy will be eight in April, and he is having a really hard time . . . has had nightmares . . . doesn't want to go to school. Candice is four and she doesn't understand. Sometimes I find her carrying around pictures of Danny and me together, such as a snapshot taken at our wedding. We just all miss him and want him home. I don't understand why he acts like he hates me when he can't even really tell me what is wrong. Without God I would not have been able to make it to this point.

And a husband whose wife has taken up with her dance instructor writes:

No matter what I do to show love to my wife, any effort I've made over the past year and a half, I get and see no response from her. She is emotionally dead toward me. And I feel so disrespected by the ongoing relationship she has with him. She moved out of the house over a month ago by her own decision, even after the marriage counselor recommended against it. She is seeing a different counselor, for what she calls "personal counseling" . . .

Tomorrow is Valentine's Day. . . . I believe the right thing to do is call her and make some plans to see each other over the weekend, but even if we do, I will just be going through the motions because, for several months now, I have felt dead emotionally too. What you said about showing love regardless of her response has shown me a possible window of opportunity—a divine moment, so to speak—when a decision made now can possibly affect things forever. I don't know how much I have left in me, and it's not going to be easy. But I know this is what God wants me to do. Hope and trust in Him is all I have left.

> *"You never know, wife: The way you handle this might bring your husband not only back to you but to God. You never know, husband: The way you handle this might bring your wife not only back to you but to God"* *(1 Corinthians 7:16 MSG).*

Never, Never, Never Give Up!

The above two letters describe a sad reality. A husband can choose to be unloving and leave. A wife can choose to be disrespectful and take up with another man. But does this mean there is no hope for a marriage? Not at all! Note that hope and trust in God are keeping both of these hurting spouses going. So never give up hope! If the door to reconciliation is not absolutely closed by the remarriage of your spouse, there is *always* hope. If God has not closed the door, you should not close the door. Just because your marriage feels hopeless to you does not mean it is hopeless from God's perspective or in light of His power. Also, it is quite possible your spouse has inner doubts about choices made and an inner longing to return. In cases where reconciliation does happen, I have heard husbands or wives testify: "I was wanting to return home, but I never told my spouse. In fact, I was the meanest at those moments. I was fighting with myself."

We all know it is darkest just before dawn. I have seen many turnarounds. Don't give up! Remarkable stories of healing and restoration abound. One such account that came in the mail tells of how a wife restored her marriage, going from despair to the decision to delight in God's blessings. She had a nice home, three wonderful children, and a husband who kept her frustrated and angry. "I was feeling unloved and misunderstood," she writes. "I lashed out very hard, trying to get some kind of positive reaction. . . . Nothing worked. Our communication deteriorated."

Then she came across our book *Motivating Your Man God's Way* (self-published by Emerson and Sarah Eggerichs and available online at Loveandrespect.com). As she struggled with concepts like unconditionally respecting her husband and the Rewarded Cycle, she decided that, even if her life here on earth is not what she had dreamed of, she would focus on her eternal life. She knew God was calling her to make one last try, and she vowed to do the assignments in the book to the letter. That way she would be able to look her children in the face and tell them, "Mommy did all she could."

Doing "all she could" to practice unconditional respect quickly became more than she could handle on her own. She relied heavily on promises from God's Word, including "I can do all things through Him, who strengthens me" (Philippians 4:13). Several times she went out to her garage to cry out for help, begging God for strength to unconditionally respect her husband and keep her natural desires to be disrespectful under control. And as she drew closer to God, she felt Him drawing closer to her. She saw that God could speak to her husband's heart louder than she could by ranting and raving. Soon her husband began noticing her respectful approach and conversation. The arguments became less frequent, and they started to laugh together again.

Then her husband's hunger for the Lord began to grow. He made Christian friends and joined a men's Bible study and a Sunday school class. He became the spiritual leader in their home and eventually stood before over one hundred people to testify that his wife's faith in God and her unconditional respect for him had allowed God to change their hearts and their marriage. As she heard the man who several months earlier had proclaimed, "I hate living here!" now telling people how God had brought love back into their marriage, she could feel a hug from God and hear Him whisper, "Well done, good and faithful servant."

In closing she writes:

> We are still a work in progress, and God's mercies are new every day. I can honestly say that the pain of laying down my pride and going against society's way of earning respect has set me free. I am not a doormat, as Satan would like us to believe. I have been elevated to a place in my home that I used to fight for. My husband comes to me for advice if need be. That is much more rewarding than spouting it off when it is not asked for or appreciated. We communicate and we want to be together. The chemistry that I thought was permanently dead is renewed. God did it all.

I often stress that one of the greatest rewards any persevering spouse can have is being a good example and influence on the children in the family. Note that the woman who wrote the letter above knew God was calling her to make one last try. She vowed to do so, knowing that no matter what happened, she would be able to look her children in the face and say, "Mommy did all she could."

She Didn't Want a "Bible Banger" for a Husband

Sometimes a husband can be instrumental in turning his wife around. In one instance, a couple had struggled for years. Neither Elliot nor Lindsay knew Jesus as their Savior or Lord. Elliot's ongoing problems with drugs and alcohol helped contribute to Lindsay's affair with someone she met at work. When the news dropped on Elliot like a 5,000-pound bomb, he turned to a friend who had been witnessing to him about Christ. His crisis convinced him he needed God's forgiveness and help, and he became a Christian.

The change in him was so apparent it got Lindsay's attention—at first in a negative way. Because he had struggled with alcohol and drugs in the past, she saw his new devotion to Bible reading as a different kind of addiction. She "didn't want to be married to a Bible banger," yet she continued to be amazed by the difference in her husband. When the man with whom she was having the affair called to get together, she kept putting him off. Since he had taken a different job, she wasn't seeing him every day at work, and as time passed, the affair faded. Meanwhile the wall of resentment between Elliot and Lindsay slowly came down as she began to realize she needed what he had—a relationship with Christ.

Lindsay writes:

> I got on my knees, asked the Lord for forgiveness, and invited Him to come into my heart. WOW! It was then that our marriage was totally on the right track. We found a new church, got involved in a Bible study, started doing foster care, had twins of our own, adopted two more children . . . I could go on and on. God is so good!

Years later, when Lindsay and Elliot attended a Love and Respect Conference and heard about the Rewarded Cycle, they realized it captured exactly what they had experienced. The conference strengthened their marriage so much that the following Christmas Lindsay gave Elliot a new wedding band with Ephesians 5:33 engraved in it. The concept of the Rewarded Cycle provided a framework that enabled them to describe to others what had happened to them. They are hoping to start a Love and Respect ministry in their church, telling others that the first step is to totally surrender to God and, as you seek to Love or Respect unconditionally, good things happen. Elliot was rewarded with God's favor and approval for forgiving Lindsay's adultery, shaping up his own life, and hanging in there in the marriage despite her contempt for him and his faith. And then he received an additional reward when Lindsay placed her faith in Christ and they went on to enjoy a Love and Respect marriage.

Will every marriage experience a turnaround like those described above? As long as God's gift of free will is in force, no guarantees come with the Rewarded Cycle. Jesus recognized the painful potential of divorce (see Matthew 19:3–12; Mark 10:11–12), and Paul recognized that an unbeliever can leave permanently and end the marriage (see 1 Corinthians 7:10–15).

When there is no turnaround—only a turning away—is all effort wasted? Usually not. In fact, spouses who have been rejected often discover that when they walk and talk from a heart set on loving or respecting, the "Cha Ching!" effect happens. In *Love & Respect* I draw a word picture of a billion angels holding a gigantic handle.[4] Whenever a husband or wife does or says something loving or respectful to a spouse who seemingly does not care, all those angels pull down on that handle and—"Cha Ching!"—a secret treasure of blessings pours into a colossal golden bowl. No, Publishers Clearing House does not suddenly appear with a big check, but God's blessings do reward the spouse who is obedient in the face of what seems hopeless or when progress seems all too slow.

One wife wrote to tell of attending a Love and Respect Conference with her husband, and for awhile communication improved. But then she noticed that he would move toward her lovingly only when she was "good." In short, his love for her felt very conditional. But then Rewarded Cycle thinking gave her needed insight:

> What the Lord revealed to me was that my heart's desire was that my husband love me and my pain would be gone. But the Scriptures tell me that God alone should be my heart's desire. He should be the One thing I seek. Everything else I desire should be such a distant second that even if I don't get my other desires, my love for God and His love for me satisfies my deepest longing (for Him) because I have what I really desire the most.

> *Unconditional Love or Respect is never wasted. Hang on to this promise: "Let us not lose heart in doing good, for in due time we will reap if we do not grow weary" (Galatians 6:9).*

Her husband has noticed the change in her, but although he has been a Christian since childhood, he still loves her *conditionally*. She reports:

> When I'm close to God and therefore more like Jesus, my husband likes me; when I'm not, he avoids me. The trick is to be indifferent to his response either way, and be content in the situation God has placed me, because I am filled with God's love. I have made great strides, but I do fall off the wagon occasionally.

A husband who has grasped the vision of the Rewarded Cycle finds that it sustains him even though his wife of twenty-five years is moving out. She is not leaving because of infidelity, abuse, or other typical reasons. The only "reason" she can give is that she does not love him or respect him. He writes:

> In the midst of this rejection and all the pain that goes with it, I have been aghast at the thoughts of vengeance that seem ever present in my mind. My desire is to act and react toward her with

honor and integrity as Jesus would, and it is only by His power in my life that I have had any hope of doing this.

In the midst of what has been a two-year battle, this husband read *Love & Respect* and also watched the DVD. With tears he prayed the Prayer of Commitment (see page 33) and repented of his doubts that God could do anything to change his marriage. His letter concludes:

> I am thanking God for this opportunity to draw nearer to Him and to honor Him even in this. I know that my challenge is to unconditionally love her, and I pray God shows me ways to do this even as she leaves. . . . Thank you for speaking words of truth that have drawn my heart back through the fog . . . I have failed in so much and I have lost so much, but I pray that this would be one of those seven times when a righteous man would fall and get back up, looking only to Jesus.

The letters quoted above represent the hundreds I receive every year that describe what living on the Rewarded Cycle is like. Some speak of miraculous turnarounds; others sound like they are hanging on to the barest shreds of hope. But all of these husbands and wives share one vital thing: because they believe in God and His personal response, they prayed in faith and stepped out in obedience.[5] God has answered, is answering, or will answer their prayers. Right here, right now, God is honoring their faithful witness and example to their children, their friends, and anyone in their sphere of influence. The rewards are real and ongoing, but the best news of all is that the greatest rewards are yet to come.

Rewards Here Pale in Comparison to Rewards There

While rewards in this life for obeying the Lord in your marriage can be substantial, they pale next to what awaits us in heaven. There the rewards will take on a glory that is really indescribable in earthly terms. Whatever you have had to put up with on earth will be worth it a billionfold when you meet your Lord face-to-face. As Paul looked back on the horrendous struggles and suffering that had been his, he spoke of outwardly wasting away, but being renewed inwardly daily. And then he added, "For our light and momentary troubles are achieving for us an eternal glory that far outweighs them all" (2 Corinthians 4:17).

Mark it down: God will reward your words and ways. He is preparing you for what I call "the Eternal Ahhhh!" As I say in *Love & Respect,* when you wonder what heaven will be like, just think of all the wonderful, joyous occasions that have been yours—everything from your wedding and birth of your children to graduations and promotions, incredible vacations, glorious sunsets, all those times when you literally exclaimed, "Ahhhh! This is so great, so wonderful, so beautiful!" Imagine putting together the feelings of elation and sheer joy you experienced during all these glorious, happy events. Then realize that when you stand before your Lord in heaven, the joy you feel will be a trillion times greater, obviously beyond human comprehension. The "Ahhhh!" you utter then will mean infinitely more because God is rewarding you—directly, fully, and eternally.

When you stand before God after living a life of unconditional love or respect before your mate, no matter what his or her response was, you will hear, "Well done, good and faithful servant! You have been faithful with a few things; I will put you in charge of many things. Come and share your master's happiness" (Matthew 25:21 NIV). Paul speaks of this same kind of reward when he writes:

> Whatever you do, do your work heartily, as for the Lord rather than for men, knowing that from the Lord you will receive the reward of the inheritance. It is the Lord Christ whom you serve. (Colossians 3:23–24 NASB)

The Rewarded Cycle is simple enough. You speak words that bless your spouse in order to bless God, who will in turn bless you. As Peter put it, "Do not repay evil for evil or insult with insult, but with blessing,

because to this you were called so that you may inherit a blessing"
(1 Peter 3:9 NIV).

Be Holy; Then Happiness Follows

While in college I heard the expression "God does not want you happy,
but holy." I never forgot that and have often shared this saying with
those I counsel. The point, of course, is that when you seek to be holy
and to live for God, internal joy is a wonderful by-product. Many marriage therapists, however, subscribe to the notion that, above all, a person should be happy. In one survey of divorced people, 35 percent rated
their counselor as wanting to save the marriage; 41 percent were neutral; 14 percent of the counselors encouraged divorce.[6] These numbers
more than suggest that many therapists would give little support to husbands and wives wanting to stay the
course on the Rewarded Cycle, yet I
believe this is what God wants. As I have
already said, no matter how or where the
marriage is going, reconciliation should
always be the goal unless the door closes
completely.

> *Choose a marriage counselor carefully "for there are many who . . . deceive others with their nonsense . . . they are upsetting whole families by teaching what they should not, and all for the shameful purpose of making money" (Titus 1:10–11 GNB).*

There are many sobering warnings
about God's judgment in Scripture, even
for Christians whose salvation is assured.
So don't think you can speak lovingly or
respectfully for a period of time and then
decide that the voices of worldly wisdom
are right and that "being happy" is more
important than hanging in there for the
long haul. John's words of warning
against being deceived by teachers of lies
can easily be applied to married couples
today: "Watch out that you do not lose

what you have worked for, but that you may be rewarded fully" (2 John 8 NIV).[7]

There is no triteness in declaring the Christian lives for an audience of One. God is there, and He is not deaf. As Jesus Himself taught, "every careless word that people speak, they shall give an accounting for it in the day of judgment" (Matthew 12:36). And Paul speaks of how believers in Christ are building upon Him, and what they build will be tested by fire. If it passes, the believer receives rewards; if it fails, what was built will be burned up (see 1 Corinthians 3:12ff). I believe that part of what we build is made from what we say, the words we use. Our loving or respectful words—or the lack of them—do matter because all our words will be judged. Our words reflect our heart, and while we cannot lose our salvation, we can lose rewards that God would like to give us.

"Do Not Give Up, For Your Work Will Be Rewarded"

How, then, can we keep going and not forfeit rewards God wants to bestow? The following letter from a husband whose marriage is less than perfect says it well:

> God is definitely doing a changing work in me, and when I keep my eyes on Him, I do okay. But when I look at my circumstances, the bitterness wells up, and I get on the wrong path. The key for me is to read the Bible for what it says about me, not my wife. My love of God's Word has grown so much, and there are many Scriptures that speak to me, but one I carry around on an old battered index card is 2 Chronicles 15:7–8. Verse 7 says: "But as for you, be strong, and do not give up, for your work will be rewarded" (NIV). Then I personalize verse 8: "When Cedric heard these words . . . he took courage."

I would add that Jesus says personally to Cedric, "Behold, I am coming quickly, and My reward is with Me, to render to you, Cedric, according to what you have done" (see Revelation 22:12).

Friend, whether He comes in your lifetime or you go to Him first, He intends to give you His rewards. So take courage, be strong, and do not give up. Husbands and wives who seek to please Him will be rewarded for loving or respectful speech.

In the next three chapters, I will share five kinds of speech that are especially pleasing to God. As you learn to use these kinds of words, you will be rewarded in your marriage here and now and surely on that glad day when you stand before Him and hear, "Well done, good and faithful servant."

CHAPTER FOURTEEN

⟭⟭⟭⟭⟠⟭⟭⟭⟭

The Jesus Way of Talking— Part I

Communicating with Love and Respect

I was eighteen when my father placed his faith in Jesus Christ. He was fifty-one, and the first change I noticed in him was his vocabulary. He simply stopped cursing and using profanity. As I look back on my dad's almost-overnight turnaround, it reminds me of what happened after the Welsh revivals in 1904. Many of the Welsh coal miners who placed their faith in Jesus Christ were so profoundly affected that they stopped using profanity. The problem, however, was that the mules that drew the coal cars up out of the mine were accustomed to obeying only profane commands. When the redeemed coal miners tried to give them commands without cussing, the mules refused to budge! Coal production was severely impacted until the mules were retrained to obey different commands.

This is not to say that my dad had been talking to my mom as if she were a mule. In fact, most of the time he was quiet, and his language was acceptable. But if he perceived that Mom had done something contrary to his preferences (like buying furniture he thought we didn't need), he would get angry, and in his rage he would swear at her and anyone else handy. After coming to Christ, however, Dad quickly recognized the hypocrisy in saying he was a believer and going into profane rages.

> *"If a person thinks that he is religious but can't control his tongue, he is fooling himself. That person's religion is worthless"* *(James 1:26 GW).*

My father understood that if he wanted to obey and please God, he could not continue to give free rein to his anger and talk as he had before. Now that he was saved, Dad had two relationships—one with Mom and one with God—and he realized that neither was separate from the other. He could not talk to God one way and to my mother another. To my knowledge, Dad never went into another rage like the ones that were commonplace for him before he became a follower of Christ.

James wrote the early church and challenged the believing community on this very point: you cannot separate the horizontal from the vertical. You cannot talk one way to God and another way to your family, friends, acquaintances, etc. As he warned about the power of the tongue, James wrote, "With it we bless our Lord and Father, and with it we curse people who are made in the likeness of God. From the same mouth come blessing and cursing. My brothers, these things ought not to be so" (James 3:9–10 ESV).

Your Marriage Is Really a Triangle

To apply James's words to marriage, think of a triangle. At the bottom left-hand corner is the husband, at the bottom right-hand corner is the wife, and at the top of the triangle is Jesus Christ. The point is simple, but profound: however you communicate with your spouse horizontally—lovingly, respectfully, or otherwise—you are also communicating these same thoughts and words to the Lord vertically. For the follower of Christ, marriage is not a relationship of only two, but three. The husband, the wife, and the Lord are all connected.

> *"Even before there is a word on my tongue, Behold, O LORD, You know it all"* (Psalm 139:4).

After my father chose to follow Christ, he quickly seemed to understand that when his words shot across the room to my mother, they also shot heavenward. It was as though the Lord would ask my dad, "Ed, what did I just hear you say to Jay?" At first my dad would reply, "But, Lord, I wasn't talking to You. I was saying those things to my wife." Then the Lord would respond, "No, no, Ed. Your marriage is a tool that I use to reveal the condition of your heart. The way you talk to Jay shows what is in your heart, not only toward her but toward Me as well. When she is grieved by what you say, I hear her cries. We are all connected, and you cannot separate us by thinking that you can talk only to Me in one instance and only to her in another."

My father's conversion to Christ happened decades before the Lord led me to discover the Love and Respect Connection, but it didn't take Dad long to "get it" regarding how a husband should speak to his wife. He didn't become a saint or the perfect husband and father, but he became far less imperfect! As my father grew in his walk with Christ, he could have echoed the old prayer: "Lord, I am not what I want to be, and I am not what I'm going to be, but thank You, Lord, that I am not what I used to be!"

There is a wonderful truth in the principle that what goes out also goes up. As my father learned how to talk in a way that blessed my mother, he also blessed God, who was listening to every word. And the same is true for all of us. We can bless God by talking positively to our spouse. We can grieve Him by talking negatively and destructively. It is always our choice.

What If My Spouse Doesn't Deserve My Blessing?

Keep in mind that there can be no conditions on these blessings of Love or Respect you utter to your spouse. It's all too easy to bite your tongue and not talk negatively, but at the same time you may be refusing to speak in warm, positive ways that could bless your spouse because you don't believe your spouse deserves it. You are right about one thing: your spouse doesn't always deserve a blessing. But you are wrong if you think this matter is only about you and your spouse.

Remember, you are talking to Christ through your spouse. In fact, if you want to profoundly bless the heart of God, speak words of blessing to your spouse right after your spouse speaks far less than words of blessing to you. Your spouse may curse you or perhaps just be nasty. Whatever the case, your goal is to come back to your spouse with words of blessing. As Peter puts it, "not returning evil for evil or insult for insult, but giving a blessing instead; for you were called for the very purpose that you might inherit a blessing" (1 Peter 3:9).

> *"When we are reviled, we bless . . . when we are slandered, we try to conciliate"*
> *(1 Corinthians 4:12–13).*

But just how, you may be wondering, *can you give your mate a blessing, especially if the conversation has been anything but rosy positive?* By speaking words of unconditional Love or Respect. Sometimes we are tempted to think that words of blessing must sound very sacred or spiritual, like a minister's benediction following his sermon. There are times for those kinds of blessings, but in your marriage you can bless each other daily in dozens of simple ways by practicing Love and Respect.

What Exactly Is a Blessing?

One definition of a blessing is giving people something for which they can feel thankful, something that makes them feel secure, supported, content, or encouraged. In other words, you and I can bless our spouses when we are loving or respectful enough to try to decode remarks they have just made that sound like we might have a Love or Respect issue going. Or we can bless our spouses by being loving or respectful enough to clarify something that is unclear to one or both of us.

And surely we can bless our spouses with what we say—even after our spouses have been cranky or nasty—by coming back with words of unconditional Love or Respect: "I'm sorry for coming across in a way that has made you feel unloved or disrespected." In other instances you and I may be discussing sensitive subjects with our spouses. Our words will either bless or not bless our spouse. That is the time to ask ourselves, "Is what I'm about to say going to result in my spouse feeling loved or unloved? Respected or disrespected?" In either situation, we can be sure the Lord hears! Our words do not escape His notice because we are speaking lovingly or respectfully first for Him and then for our spouse. And as we speak to our husband or wife as unto the Lord, our spouse will be influenced, encouraged, and certainly blessed.

Finally, as I will explain later in this chapter, you can bless your spouse in many different ways by using the Jesus Way of Talking. The foundation of the Jesus Way of Talking is T-U-F-T-S, an acronym that stands for Truthful Words, Uplifting Words, Forgiving Words, Thankful Words, and Scriptural Words. As they come from your lips, these kinds of words can bless your spouse in many ways.

Sometimes, however, you can bless your mate by saying nothing. One couple started trying to practice Love and Respect but soon started to butt heads over something they could not agree on. He spoke in a way she thought was unloving, and just as she started to say something that would "make him get off her air hose," she remembered 1 Peter 3:9—"not returning . . . insult for insult, but giving a blessing instead." She writes:

I quickly slapped one hand over my mouth to keep from saying something disrespectful, but it really wanted to be said, so I slapped the other hand over the first one. I stood there against the cabinet, kind of squirming and grinning with my eyes, because I really wanted to respond in my usual way. He just looked at me from across the kitchen and said softly, "Thank you."

> "He who guards his mouth and his tongue, guards his soul from troubles" (Proverbs 21:23).

With those two words, all her frustration and desire to be disrespectful instantly dissipated! She was respectful, and her husband felt blessed. They ended up having a great evening—just the opposite of the night before when they went to bed without speaking. Over the last few months, their relationship has improved, they talk more, she works at letting him lead, and they both work on making Love and Respect responses to each other. Her letter concludes, "We are finally becoming friends after so many years of having walls between us."

Imagine You See Jesus Just Over Your Spouse's Shoulder

A word picture I share in Love and Respect Conferences has been immeasurably helpful to many people. I tell them this "With eyes of faith, envision Jesus standing just beyond the shoulder of your spouse and listening to every word you speak in every conversation, pleasant or tense. When you speak lovingly or respectfully to your spouse, you are speaking to Christ. Your spouse just happens to be there too." This truth has sanctified the lips of many. Instead of giving their spouse a verbal whipping or choking on the idea of saying anything positive, now some spouses are motivated to speak words of unconditional love or respect.

One husband wrote that the key point for him when he attended our conference was this word picture of Jesus standing beyond his spouse's shoulder because it reminded him of James 2:12–13:

So whenever you speak, or whatever you do, remember that you will be judged by the law of love, the law that set you free. For there will be no mercy for you if you have not been merciful to others. But if you have been merciful, then God's mercy toward you will win out over his judgment against you (NLT).

His letter concludes:

Learning how much we need Jesus and His forgiveness has enabled me to listen to and love my wife, and as I communicate more patiently, she returns the same kind of response to me. As we take ourselves less seriously and less competitively, we become freer in love, and we win.

The next time you and your spouse get into a tense conversation, you may want to envision Christ standing just beyond your spouse's shoulder. When you do, remember His words: "Truly, I say to you, as you did it to one of the least of these my brothers, you did it to me" (Matthew 25:40 ESV). Whether visiting those in prison, feeding the hungry, giving the thirsty a drink, or speaking a word of Love or Respect—everything is to be done to and for Christ.

Why We Call It the "Rewarded Cycle"

In Ephesians 6:7–8, Paul echoes Jesus' words when he exhorts believers to do the will of God from the heart "because you know the Lord will reward everyone for whatever good he does, whether he is slave or free" (NIV). Surely "whatever good we do" includes the words we speak. To the Colossians Paul wrote this:

> "Let the words of my mouth and the meditation of my heart be acceptable in Your sight, O LORD, my rock and my Redeemer" (Psalm 19:14).

Whatever you do in *word* or deed, do everything in the name of
the Lord Jesus, giving thanks to God the Father through him . . .
Whatever you do, work heartily, as for the Lord and not for men,
knowing that from the Lord you will receive the inheritance as
your reward. You are serving the Lord Christ. (Colossians 3:17,
23–24 ESV, italics mine)

These ringing words are meant for everyone in the Colossian church, but
Paul names wives, husbands, fathers, and slaves specifically (see Colossians 3:18–22). Clearly, in the marriage, in the family, and in the household, when you speak words of blessing, you are speaking to the Lord,
and for this you will be rewarded.

When you understand the simple but wonderful truth that the
believer is to do everything—including talking—in the name of the
Lord, you see why we call this part of our Love and Respect teaching the
Rewarded Cycle. When you speak lovingly to your wife no matter how
she has spoken to you, God rewards you. When you speak respectful
words to your husband no matter how he has spoken to you, God rewards
you. Whatever good things you speak, you "receive back from the Lord."

The Jesus Way of Talking Guides You to the Goal

The most beautiful aspect of the Rewarded Cycle is that God has provided
the Jesus Way of Talking to help you reach your goal of speaking lovingly
or respectfully in all situations, not just when things are going well. It is
one thing to resolve to talk lovingly or respectfully to your spouse as unto
Christ—and it is another thing to pull it off consistently. If you are like
me, you may second-guess yourself from time to time: "Am I really speaking lovingly? Should I say this or not say it? Am I saying this in a way that
feels loving to Sarah? How can I be sure which words to use?"

The Jesus Way of Talking helps you battle any tendencies to second-
guess yourself because it gives you guidelines for your words. You can
have the assurance that you are trying to speak lovingly or respectfully
even when your spouse does not respond positively. In God's eyes you can

be a loving or respectful communicator even when there is a communication glitch, even when your spouse doesn't seem to be listening or is just in a difficult mood at the moment.

Possibly of greatest value is that the Jesus Way of Talking helps you evaluate your own words when you just don't seem to be connecting with the other person or persons. In my communication with Sarah as well as others, the Jesus Way of Talking helps me determine why I am sometimes not feeling good about what I said. As I use T-U-F-T-S to remember that I am to speak Truthful Words, Uplifting Words, Forgiving Words, Thankful Words, and Scriptural Words, I have a checklist that helps me spot ways I innocently and often unthinkingly make a mess of communicating Love or Respect to Sarah.

What do I mean by "make a mess"? Simply this: Emerson has goodwill but lacks good sense on occasion, and Sarah feels unloved. Sarah has goodwill but can't see what she is doing that is so disrespectful, and Emerson feels disrespected. As well as we know the Love and Respect Connection, we still slip up from time to time. That's why the Jesus Way of Talking can be helpful. Remembering what the Bible says about our speech in these five areas helps you realize that you just weren't thinking or that you have a blind spot concerning what is going on.

> "And whatever you . . . say, do it as a representative of the Lord Jesus. . ." (Colossians 3:17 NLT).

Paul Spells Out the Jesus Way of Talking

I found the Jesus Way of Talking not in the Gospels, but in Paul's letter to the Ephesians. In chapter 4 he switches from teaching doctrine to making practical application for daily living. There Paul reminds the Ephesian believers (and us) that they are no longer to live as ungodly people do, alienated from the life of God because of their ignorance as well as giving themselves up to callousness, sensuality, and impure practices (see Ephesians 4:17–19). "That," says Paul emphatically, "is not the way you learned Christ!—assuming that you have heard about him and were taught in him, as the truth is in Jesus" (Ephesians 4:20–21 ESV). Instead they are to put off the "old self," be renewed in their minds, and put on the "new self," created after the likeness of God (see Ephesians 4:22–24).

Then Paul proceeds to spell out what putting on the new self is all about, and here is where I found the Jesus Way of Talking—five guidelines for communicating Love and Respect in the Unconditional Dimension:

TRUTHFUL WORDS—"Laying aside falsehood, speak truth" (Ephesians 4:25).

UPLIFTING WORDS—"Let no unwholesome word proceed from your mouth, but only such a word as is good for edification" (v. 29).

FORGIVING WORDS—"Let all bitterness and wrath and anger . . . and slander be put away from you, along with all malice . . . And be . . . forgiving . . . just as God in Christ has forgiven you" (vv. 31–32).

THANKFUL WORDS—"There must be no filthiness and silly talk, or coarse jesting, which are not fitting, but rather giving of thanks" (Ephesians 5:4).

SCRIPTURAL WORDS—"Speaking to one another in psalms and hymns and spiritual songs . . . making melody with your heart to the Lord" (v. 19).

As you have noticed, the first letters of *truthful, uplifting, forgiving, thankful,* and *scriptural* spell *TUFTS.* You may be thinking you already have enough acronyms to keep track of: C-O-U-P-L-E if you're a husband and C-H-A-I-R-S if you're a wife. As we have seen, C-O-U-P-L-E and C-H-A-I-R-S are at the heart of the Energizing Cycle because they provide a veritable toolbox of things a husband or a wife can do to be loving or respectful and thereby energize his or her spouse. So, why add

T-U-F-T-S? Because these five kinds of words—the Jesus Way of Speaking—are foundational to communicating with Love and Respect.

A word picture can assist you in remembering this word *TUFTS*. A tuft is a cluster of something, like grapes. In this case, think of *TUFTS* as a cluster of five types of words which together create the Jesus Way of Talking. Why did I choose these five terms to describe the Jesus Way of Speaking? For two reasons. First, these five traits come straight from what Paul wrote to teach Christians how to communicate with the mouth. Second, Paul knew that if anything can lead a believer back into the "old self" kind of life, it is how he or she talks.

These five traits of speech are part of how Paul spells out what Christians should do as they put on the new self (see Ephesians 4:25–5:21). Then he applies this teaching to different groups, and in his first application he lays down his matchless treatise on marriage in Ephesians 5:22–33. It is as if he is saying, "Husbands and wives, *this* is how to put on the new self; *this* is how God wants you to live; *this* is how He wants you to talk to each other; *this* is how He guides your words of Love or Respect with little reason for second-guessing on your part. "T-U-F-T-S is the foundation on which you build loving and respectful communication.

> *"We speak as Christ would have us speak in the presence of God"* (1 Corinthians 12:19 GNB).

- Here is why: words of Love or Respect must be Truthful because lies and half-truths will undermine your relationship.
- Words of Love or Respect must Uplift your spouse, edifying—and never manipulating—him or her.
- Words of Love or Respect must include Forgiveness because your spouse is bound to fail you.
- Words of Love or Respect must include Thankfulness spoken to or about your spouse; don't fixate on weaknesses and faults.

- Words of Love or Respect must be based and focused on Scripture; avoid ideas that are contrary to the heart of Christ.

Why It Is Hard to Speak T-U-F-T-S Consistently

One of the major reasons we fail to speak T-U-F-T-S consistently to each other is our very human tendency to become more upset about our spouse's poor communication efforts than our own. A wife hears her husband's unloving words, and naturally she is hurt and angry. He has no excuse for talking to her this way! So she uses some disrespectful words herself, but she doesn't hear these words the way she heard her husband's words. Besides, he should understand why she spoke as she did. After all, he made her upset.

Of course, the reverse situation is also true. A husband hears his wife's disrespectful words, and he becomes angry and defensive. She has no excuse for talking to him this way! So he responds with angry, unloving words, or perhaps he stonewalls her and speaks no words at all, the unkindest "reply" he could possibly offer his Pinkie wife. Whatever he does, he thinks that surely she should understand and realize she was at fault first.

Dispositional versus Situational Thinking Is a Trap

Why do husbands and wives tend to favor themselves when someone's air hose gets pinched? One psychological explanation is rooted in the dispositional versus the situational perspective on conversations. If your spouse speaks in a hurtful way, it is natural to conclude that the hurtful words were caused by your spouse's lousy disposition; your spouse (more's the pity) has some real character flaws. But, of course, when you say something that is hurtful, it is natural for you to conclude it was not your fault; it was simply caused by the situation at hand. You were a victim of circumstances. Here's how this happens.

It has been a long, hard day for a wife at home with two preschool children plus an infant. She has tried to get dinner ready on time, but her husband arrives home late from work because the freeways were worse than usual. As he walks in the door, the baby is shrieking his little lungs out, one of her preschoolers is hanging on her leg, the roast is drying out in the oven, and the soup is boiling over. She boils over, too, and lets her husband know he is *always* late for dinner—and how can he be so inconsiderate?

The wife's barrage catches her husband totally off guard. After another chaotic commute, he has been expecting a little peace, some quiet, and maybe a tall, cool one before sitting down to a wonderful meal. So he yells back at her that it was more peaceful out on the freeways than it is in this house. Then he stomps off to the living room and flips on the news, leaving her to assess what happened—which is not hard at all. In her opinion she may have spoken disrespectfully to him because of stressful circumstances. Couldn't he see what kind of day she had been having? No wonder she boiled over along with the soup. As for him, however, she just knows he practically shouted unloving nasty things because he is an insensitive, uncaring clod!

Now let's take a look at this situation from the husband's point of view. He is out there on the freeway where traffic is more stop than go, his engine is overheating, and he can't get through to his wife on his cell phone to remind her he needs a fresh shirt ironed for the church board meeting he has to attend later that evening. When she finally hears the phone ringing over the clamor of the kids and answers his call, she hears a string of angry remarks coming in bits and pieces from his barely-in-range cell phone. Where has she been? He's been trying to reach her for over half an hour. What does

> *"Don't bad-mouth each other, friends. It's God's Word, his Message, his Royal Rule, that takes a beating in that kind of talk. You're supposed to be honoring the Message, not writing graffiti all over it"* (James 4:11 MSG).

she do all day anyway? The freeway is a mess, and his car is overheating—and be sure to get his blue shirt ironed! He wants to wear it to the board meeting tonight.

Taken totally aback by his angry demands, she yells right back. She has been working harder all day than he has. If she took time to tell him everywhere she had been, he would get tired just hearing about it. And as for what she does all day, it seems that lots of days she is just his slave—and he can iron his own shirt! She slams down the phone, leaving our noble freeway-fighter assessing the conversation from his viewpoint. Yes, he had spoken a bit impatiently, but surely she should have been able to tell he was in a frustrating situation, in bumper-to-bumper traffic with his car's temperature gauge approaching 212°. As for his wife, she had no right to reply so disrespectfully. Obviously she has to do something about her belligerent disposition.

If you and your spouse have frequent encounters anything like those described above, one or both of you will in time begin to feel, "I am really the better person in this marriage." At this juncture you need to consider the Word of God: "Do you, my friend, pass judgment on others? You have no excuse at all, whoever you are. For when you judge others and then do the same things which they do, you condemn yourself" (Romans 2:1 GNB). In other words, before the Lord you are equally guilty. And when you are equally guilty, Paul as well as Jesus (Matthew 7:1–5) teach that you must never be one-sided in your judgment; instead you must be totally honest about what you are also doing. According to Paul, it is not a good idea "to do those very things for which you pass judgment on others!" (Romans 2:3 GNB).

Perhaps you do not intend to be biased in your own favor, but I have seen it happen in too many marriages. Instead of speaking T-U-F-T-S to your mate, you start muttering things like these to yourself:

- "It may be true that I am sometimes wrong in what I say, but I am not going to admit it. *He* never admits he is wrong. He is arrogant."
- "Why should I build her up? All she does is tear me down, and I'm

just not interested in being Mr. Nice Guy in response to her toxic personality."

- "I am not going to just take it when he says harsh, cruel things even though he says he's just joking. He's basically mean and on a mission to hurt me. I won't forgive him."

- "Why should I tell her I appreciate everything she does for the family? Yes, she works hard with the children, but when was the last time I heard a word of thanks from her

> *"Stupid people always think they are right. Wise people listen to advice" (Proverbs 12:15 GNB).*

about how I bust my tail every day to make us a living? Always, it's all about her!"

"But You Don't Know My Spouse the Way I Do!"

It's easy to see why dispositional versus situational thinking can lead you to make judgments and draw conclusions that will cause you to stop loving or respecting. Not only that, but this kind of attitude will also keep you on the Crazy Cycle. After all, what hope is there if your spouse is "damaged goods"? From too many people I hear, "If my situation were different and my spouse were willing to change, maybe Love and Respect would work for us, but I feel my marriage is an exception to your teaching. To be honest, my spouse has personal problems. Others may think my spouse is such a wonderful person, but I know otherwise. You don't know my spouse the way I do."

There is much less hope for healing a marriage when one spouse holds this kind of attitude. If you have been making comments at all like those just stated, I ask you to step back and ask yourself, "Do I let myself off the hook for my reactions and comments, which are just as negative and damaging as anything my spouse might do or say? Do I give myself grace and my spouse judgment?" I urge you to give the same grace to your spouse that you give yourself. If you don't, you will judge your spouse in ways that will make both of you want to give up. Stop passing judgment and start extending mercy! Stop psychologically profiling your spouse in a way that God does not. I can point to many couples who have trusted my counsel, and although they have struggled and suffered for a period of time, eventually they have experienced a turnaround in their marriage.

So I encourage every husband and wife to commit to the Jesus Way of Talking. Instead of allowing the stress of the situation to control you, you can say to yourself, "Because I love the Lord and I know that He rewards every good word, I am going to be truthful even if my spouse is not. I will also be uplifting, forgiving, thankful, and scriptural in my speech because my ultimate goal is to please the Lord. Whatever my spouse's weaknesses or bad habits might be, I will not let them cause me to sin with my lips."

The Old Testament hero Job and his wife are a graphic illustration of the impact of our perspective on the circumstances of life. They suffered the tragic loss of their family through terrible calamities. Notice his wife's words and Job's reply: "Then his wife said to him, 'Do you still hold fast your integrity? Curse God and die!' But Job responded: 'You speak as one of the foolish women speaks. Shall we accept good from God and not accept adversity?' In all this Job did not sin with his lips" (Job 2:9–10).

Your spouse may chide you, criticize you, or even abuse you verbally, but your spouse cannot *make* you sin with your lips. That is your decision. Your reactions to your spouse will reveal to God your commitment to speak in a way that blesses Him and results in an eternal reward for you. The way to bless God and your mate with your words is to practice T-U-F-T-S, which is really foundational to practicing Love and Respect. But how does this "blessing" get done? In the next two chapters, as we look more closely at each of the five guidelines in the Jesus Way of Talking, I will give you specific ways you can bless your spouse.

---·······ᴄᴍᴍᴧᴘᴍᴍᴘ·······---

The Jesus Way of Talking— Part II

To Love and Respect, Use Truthful, Uplifting, and Forgiving Words

In chapter 14 you were introduced to the Jesus Way of Talking with Truthful Words, Uplifting Words, Forgiving Words, Thankful Words, and Scriptural Words (T-U-F-T-S), words that provide a foundation for speaking with Love and Respect. You also noted the triangle illustration, which shows how whatever you say to your mate you also say to God. He is an audience of One who listens to all your conversations. But whenever you use T-U-F-T-S, you know you are speaking as God intends.

This chapter will focus on the first three principles in T-U-F-T-S— how to speak truthfully, upliftingly, and forgivingly. Chapter 16 will cover speaking thankfully and scripturally. As you read this chapter and the next, I invite you to make a commitment to be more like Jesus by talking the Jesus Way. Even if your spouse does not respond, Jesus is listening—and He always responds to hearts open to Him.

TRUTHFUL WORDS:
Always speak the truth, since the smallest of lies
discredits your words of Love or Respect.

As Paul begins his short course on how to "put on the new self" (Ephesians 4:24), the first thing he mentions is being truthful (i.e., honest): "Therefore, laying aside falsehood, speak truth each one of you, with his neighbor, for we are members of one another" (v. 25). This is the first step in the Jesus Way of Talking, which God wanted the Ephesians (and us) to learn. Because Jesus did not lie, the Ephesians were not to lie. Because Jesus never sinned and always spoke the truth (John 8:45–46), the Ephesians were to speak the truth. A few verses later, when Paul addresses marriage (Ephesians 5:22–33), he expects married couples to remember the Jesus Way of saying things: to be a loving husband or a respectful wife, truthful words are to roll from our lips.

Sadly enough, even in Christian marriages, this is not always the case. Lying does go on, and nothing can be more destructive to any relationship, particularly a marriage. The habitual liar is on dangerous ground and easy prey for Satan's attack. Jesus had strong words for the Pharisees when He told them they were like their father, the devil, because they wanted to do what he desired. "The devil," said Jesus, "does not stand in the truth because there is no truth in him. Whenever he speaks a lie, he speaks from his own nature, for he is a liar and the father of lies" (John 8:44).

Jesus has more unsettling words for the Pharisees in Matthew's Gospel when He tells them:

> Make a tree good and its fruit will be good, or make a tree bad
> and its fruit will be bad, for a tree is recognized by its fruit. You
> brood of vipers, how can you who are evil say anything good? For
> out of the overflow of the heart the mouth speaks. The good man

brings good things out of the good stored up in him, and the evil man brings evil things out of the evil stored up in him. (Matthew 12:33–35 NIV)

Lying or evil words come from the heart. For example, what do you get when a lying, alcoholic used-car salesman stops drinking? A lying, sober used-car salesman. This is not to say a liar cannot stop lying, but it does mean that such a person must confess that lying is deep in the DNA of his or her being. Lying is not caused by one's surroundings.

Note that truthful or good words also come from the heart. Listen in as a man courts a widow. Her first husband was a habitual liar, and naturally she is prompted to ask, "If I marry you, will you always speak truthfully to me?" He replies, "Whether you marry me or not, I will speak truthfully." It would do this widow well to give this man strong consideration as a possible husband. He is telling her that he will always speak truthfully because he has chosen to be a truthful person. Good fruit comes from a good root.

I hear from goodwilled spouses who mistakenly think they have married someone equally goodwilled. In one case a wife heard a rumor that her husband was having an affair. She relates: "He told me, 'I just wanted to let you know there is a rumor going around that I cheated on you, and it is not true. I would never do anything to jeopardize our marriage or hurt you and the kids.'" Being a loving, trusting wife, she put thoughts of the rumor aside—until she saw the cell phone bill. He had sent 518 text messages to his mistress, and she had sent 516 text messages to him. In addition they had spent 918 minutes talking together. Her letter concludes: "I was furious and so hurt. But instead of apologizing, he got angry at me because he got caught."

My e-mail reveals that this husband's mind-set is all too prevalent in marriages

> *True or false?*
> *When you lie, "you*
> *have not lied to*
> *men but to God"*
> *(Acts 5:4).*

today. But I wonder what he would have said had the roles been reversed and his wife had the affair. Whatever the case, liars cannot be lovers or respecters of their mate. Something else I hear from betrayed spouses, especially women, is that they could forgive their straying mate for the adultery, but what gets to them is the lying. This is much harder to forgive.

The text-message adulterer is an example of a blatant liar, but there are other ways a spouse can be sucked into being deceptive even though he or she is basically goodwilled. Being goodwilled does not make you impervious to temptation to sin. An all-too-typical scenario that I hear about in my mail is the couple who attends a Love and Respect Conference and decides to "try this Love and Respect thing" for six weeks or possibly six months, but his wife is not as interested as he is. (Usually it is the other way around, but not always.) The husband does his best to be loving toward his wife, but he gets little or no respect in return. After a month or two, he begins to wonder if this effort is worth it. Then one day he spends a little more time than necessary talking to a very attractive coworker who is separated from her husband. She is easy to talk to, and soon he is sharing his problems (in a very casual way, of course) about what is happening at home.

Soon he finds he is going to lunch now and then with this attractive woman who is so understanding. He starts being less than honest when his wife asks what is going on at work. Because she has shown him so little respect (while his new friend shows him a *lot* of respect), he does not feel guilty about shaving the truth so his wife will never know about this other woman. By now he has drifted into an emotional affair that is headed for something full blown. While he still tries to practice Love at home, being truthful with his wife is no longer his priority (see Ephesians 4:25). T-U-F-T-S, which is foundational to Love and Respect, has a big crack in it, and the inevitable often happens.

In this instance, the husband's shading of the truth renders his words of love for his wife hollow, particularly in God's eyes. And when his lie is exposed, it undermines not only his love for his wife but her trust as well.

Could this same kind of scenario happen with the wife becoming the one who starts to shade the truth? Of course it could, but the more important question is whether this could happen to you. Could you grow weary if your spouse did not respond to your need for Love or Respect, especially if you were trying to hold up your end of the bargain?

Perhaps the idea of slipping into an emotional affair sounds a bit farfetched to you, but there are many other ways to start cutting corners off the truth. No matter how or why this dishonesty happens, you turn from being a person committed to the truth and able to always speak the truth; instead you slip over to the dark side of deception.

> *Pray when enticed to lie: "I hate lying; I am disgusted with it. I love your teachings" (Psalm 119:163 GW).*

There Are Many Ways to Lie

For many husbands and wives reading this book, the above stories may not seem to apply. They do not cheat on or blatantly lie to each other, so perhaps this Truthful Words section is of little use to them. Most of us instinctively know otherwise. There are many ways to be untruthful and dishonest. For example, some spouses go on for years never being truthful or honest with themselves about how they are contributing to the problems in their marriage.

One wife wrote to tell me she and her husband had attended a Love and Respect Conference, which she preferred to call my "log-removal seminar"—for obvious reasons. For over twenty years she had been trying to remove her husband's "speck" (see Matthew 7:3–5). On the way home her husband was choked with emotion. What he had heard about his need for respect had finally made him feel understood instead of condemned. The wife realized that she had been the one who had made him feel condemned, and this truth hit her like a Mack truck: "After the Love and Respect Conference, I had a deep period of confession to the Lord, to my husband, and to my family for my lack of respect. For a week the Lord gently brought many things to my attention that I needed to confess in this area."

I love this woman's heart. For twenty years she hadn't intended to be disrespectful, but she was so fixed on what she saw as a lack of love from her husband that she had not seen her disrespect for him. The conference made her aware of the log in her own eye, and she got truthful with herself, confessed her faults, and made some changes.

But truthful words must be handled with care: a husband or wife is not to speak truth in an unloving or disrespectful way. To say things that just lay your spouse out and then explain, "I was only trying to be honest" can be cruel and deceptive. I know of one husband who finally realized he would use the truth in such a way that he was clubbing people with it, including his wife. He cut way back on his "I'm just being honest" remarks because he realized how unloving he sounded.

Much more could be said about how to handle the truth (for example, withholding the truth because you fear your spouse will react in an angry or contemptuous way). At times you must tell the truth and be willing to take the hit. Perhaps the best way to sum it up is this: In most situations, it is good to err on the side of truth, but I would add that, as you speak the truth, it is crucial to speak that truth with Love and Respect.

> *"Giving an honest answer is a sign of true friendship"* (Proverbs 24:26 CEV).

As you try to always use Truthful Words, you'll encounter many pitfalls along the way. To avoid these pitfalls, make a commitment with words like these:

Ultimately, lies are incompatible with the Jesus Way of Talking. Lying is not the way I learned Christ.[1] Jesus always speaks what is true, and so will I.

UPLIFTING WORDS
Always speak in an uplifting way for your spouse's sake, and do not use Love or Respect as a manipulative ploy to meet your own need for Love or Respect.

As he continues teaching the Ephesian Christians how to walk and talk as unto Christ, Paul introduces Uplifting Words: "Let no unwholesome word proceed from your mouth, but only such a word as is good for edification, according to the need of the moment, so that it will give grace to those who hear" (Ephesians 4:29). The NIV translation uses a simpler term for "edification," saying "only what is helpful for *building others up*." In a marriage that is functioning with any Love and Respect at all, both spouses speak upliftingly, with gracious words for each other. In so doing they emulate another way that Jesus talked. As Luke points out, "all were speaking well of Him, and wondering at the gracious words which were falling from His lips" (Luke 4:22).

How One Husband Builds Up His Wife

While I was working on this book, a great example of how a husband can use gracious, uplifting words seemed to drop into my lap when I visited some good friends, Gary and Carla. While I was there, Gary and I spent some time

> *"Encourage one another and build one another up, just as you are doing"* (1 Thessalonians 5:11 ESV).

together, and I shared a bit about what I was trying to write that could help married couples communicate better. As I was talking about the importance of being uplifting, it occurred to me to ask, "What kinds of words do you use to build up Carla?"

As if on cue, Gary said, "It's interesting you would ask because I was thinking about that just this morning. Carla has been especially joyful recently, and she tells me that one of the reasons for her joy is how I have been doing more to affirm her—both who she is and what she does.

"In recent years Carla has developed a great career by pursuing things in keeping with her giftedness as a writer and editor. She now works full-time for a firm that specializes in marketing to secular high schools curriculum that focuses on how the Bible affected the people who founded and built our country.

"Earlier in our marriage, when the children were young, Carla had no time for a career outside the home, and she had to put her interests and talents on hold. As she has gone to work doing something she loves and that serves the Lord, it has finally dawned on me that she made a lot of sacrifices for our family, so I have been making it a point to do some things I think you could call 'building up your wife.'"

"Like what?" I wanted to know, hoping for one or two good ideas. Gary had a lot more than that, however, and I hastily scribbled notes as he rattled off an impressive list of ways he was edifying his wife.

"I praise Carla in front of others at every opportunity," he explained. "For example, when we have dinner guests, sometime during the meal I make it a point to mention Carla's talents, which include her musical abilities. Recently, I told our guests that she was singing a solo at our church that coming Sunday and we would love to have them attend. And of course I love to talk about the impact she is making on thousands of school kids throughout the country as she helps market books that talk about the Bible's role in American history. And I mustn't forget the tremendous impact Carla has had on our own children by praying faithfully for them as they grew up. Our youngest daughter is headed for Africa this summer on a short-term missions trip, and there is no question in my mind that Lisa has a heart for missions because of Carla's prayers."

"Great ideas, Gary," I said, expecting him to say that was it, but he was just getting started. He continued:

We have lived in this town over twenty-five years, and my own work gives me occasion to get around and talk to people who know both of us. I make it a point to relay to Carla anything complimentary someone says about her that day. Even if it's just a small comment in passing, I don't keep it to myself. For instance, someone told me recently that Carla had edited some materials he was developing to promote a concert, and he had been very impressed by her work. I made it a point to share this with her, something I might have forgotten to mention a few years ago.

"Anything else?" I asked, aware I was developing a mild case of writer's cramp.

"Well, over the years Carla prepared all the meals for the family or for guests, and she is an excellent cook. But now that she is working full-time, many times I do the grocery shopping and fix the meals."

As I recalled what Gary had been like in younger days, I commented that this didn't sound too macho for someone who used to get in fights at the slightest provocation and who once took on an entire police department after an officer had taken issue with how he was driving. Gary just smiled and explained, "I kind of enjoy cooking, and it's easy for me to arrange my schedule to do this. So, if we decide not to eat out, I will fix the evening meal. This is no problem for me, but the best part is seeing how it energizes Carla when she comes through the door, and I have dinner ready."

Gary paused for a few seconds and then added, "Oh yes, there is one other thing. I have male friends or colleagues over to our home on a regular basis, and I make it a point to invite Carla to join us if she wishes. I tell her I enjoy involving her like this because of the impact she makes on our conversations."

Perhaps Gary's list of "Carla builders" sounds too good to be true, and a lot of husbands might say, "Impressive, but I know I can't do all that stuff." That might be so, but the point is, almost every husband can do a lot more to build up his wife. Gary's list contains ideas that anyone can adapt. In fact, I got a couple of tips myself on how to say more to build up Sarah.

Can a Wife Ever Be Too Friendly?

Uplifting words are powerful. I came across a striking example of a wife whose friendly and affirming words had tremendous impact on her husband, who plays in the National Football League. This wife attended a women's Bible study where the teacher challenged each wife present to build up her husband with words of affirmation and admiration. About that same time her husband started complaining about not feeling well. He scheduled a physical, which included several lab tests.

As the NFL player and his wife waited to see the test results, she continued to be friendly and affirming, so much so that he began to wonder what was going on. Finally, thinking she had gotten a call from the doctor loaded with bad news, he anxiously blurted out, "Okay, give it to me straight. You talked to the doctor, and he told you I have a terminal illness. That's why you've been so nice to me. You're just trying to make me feel good before I die."

This true story is amusing, but it underlines a basic truth: uplifting words should be used often, especially by wives who could be a bit friendlier to their husbands. As I have said elsewhere, my advice to wives who want their husbands to be more loving is: 1. Be his friend. 2. Be friendly. 3. Be his friendly friend. P.S. In case I forgot to tell you, be his friend!

I have just shared two great examples of how a husband or a wife can be more affirming in a marriage, but I hear from all too many who experience the opposite. Perhaps your spouse does not use uplifting words, but chooses to do nothing or, worse, to criticize and tear down. If you choose to live on the Rewarded Cycle, you face a challenge: "Will I seek to meet my spouse's need with uplifting words of Love or Respect because this is what Jesus wills for me, or will I shut down because my needs are not met?"

At such a moment, that spouse has a powerful helper: the Holy Spirit of Christ comes alongside. Obviously, husbands and wives both need His help. At Love and Respect Conferences, I challenge men again and again to be more loving and to act on the six qualities reflected in C-O-U-P-L-E (see especially chapters 8 and 10). But I know from many years of trying to help wives that the power often lies with them and how willing they are to respect their husbands unconditionally. I cannot repeat too often that, in a typical marriage, if a wife wants her husband to be more loving, she must consciously and purposefully practice unconditional respect, and a major part of that is cutting back on criticism even though he may "deserve" it.

Valuable advice for any wife is found in Proverbs 14:1—"The wise woman builds her house, but the foolish tears it down with her own hands." And, I might add, the foolish woman can tear down her home with her *mouth*. Because of the hundreds of e-mails I get, I am persuaded that women tend to fixate on the negative. Furthermore, they are not aware of their natural bent for seeing what is wrong with their husbands and trying to help and correct them, much as they do with their children.

Why Wives Tend to Mother Their Husbands

No doubt the typical wife is often right in seeing her husband's mistakes or wrongdoings. But by concentrating on her husband's lacks—what *isn't* there—she utterly fails to see what *is* there. Her man is created in the image of God. Though he is still in process, he is still God's handiwork. Yet, like most wives, she scrutinizes

> *Tempted to be negative? Pray: "Set a guard, O LORD, over my mouth; keep watch over the door of my lips"* (Psalm 141:3).

the incomplete part. She forms lists of negatives in her mind and goes over these lists daily. Women seem naturally equipped to worry—about their marriage, the children, even their best friend's upcoming baby shower. There is something within the nature of a woman that needs to be burdened about something or someone. And often it is her husband. She needs to help him be better—especially better at making her feel loved.

Early in our marriage, years before I discovered the Love and Respect Connection, Sarah and I would have conflicts over who knows what. Every month it seemed she was complaining to me about something. One day I turned to her and spoke not with a Bible verse, but with a comment based on Scripture. She remembers that I lovingly said, "Sarah, you want life to be perfect. Life cannot be perfect because of sin." I wasn't trying to let myself and my faults off the hook; I said it because she was pushing for a conflict-free marriage. She wanted our marriage to be perfect, but her unrealistic expectations were frustrating her—and me.

Sarah says my comment changed her life *and* her approach to our marriage. From then on she tried hard to have a more positive outlook on life. She also worked to adjust and control her womanly propensities to be a mother. We didn't have children at the time, but like all women, Sarah was designed to be a mother, created with the inherent desires to correct and make better. This is what mothers do, and in her efforts to make our marriage perfect, Sarah had been trying to mother me. But wives are not to be mothers to their husbands. As one husband said, "I have a mother. I don't need another one, thank you."

When you combine the mothering perfectionism of wives with an imperfect world and an imperfect spouse, you have the ingredients for a complaining wife and a stubborn husband. Sarah recognized this fact and sought to curb her perfectionism, particularly in regard to me. And it made a huge difference. I started hearing fewer complaining words and more uplifting words, and the pattern has continued (although she still wonders why I leave wet towels lying about). At the same time, I know Sarah's motives are pure. She is a godly woman, and her mothering is rooted in her longing to serve and help me. I tell men not to impugn their wives' motives when they act like mothers. For heaven's sake, most of them *are* mothers! Even if a woman has no children, she is born to care and nurture, and we men should not forget that.

But back to the female tendency to critique, if not criticize. Because wives tend to be the more critical spouse, I often ask women to step back and ask, "Would I want my husband to criticize me the way I am criticizing him?" Fortunately, the typical wife is a goodwilled woman who longs to improve her marriage. She is critical not because she is mean-spirited, but to help her husband better understand her frustrations and how to enhance the relationship. My question about being critical causes most women to see themselves and their husbands in a different light, and many of these goodwilled women try to change. Everywhere I go, I am extremely impressed by the teachability of women.

One wife wrote to say she has begun focusing on the good things in her relationship with her husband (Philippians 4:8–9) because she doesn't want to tear down her marriage. She states: "Lately I have thought about my husband's sensitivity in apologizing, etc., and realize he is trying to do better and how I would be tearing down his efforts if I were to complain about what he is not doing." Bingo! This wife "gets it." You see, respect works; attacking does not.

Having held up a mirror for wives, I now want to share with husbands a mistake I made early in life. I learned that uplifting words and truthful words are often connected, but not necessarily in a positive way. As a college student I was permitted to speak in chapel, and afterward I asked the campus chaplain for feedback. His comment was "Don't beat the sheep." That was painful to hear, but I never forgot it. Even when we husbands are well intentioned, our words can bash and thrash. Speaking truthful words that are not uplifting can only discourage and defeat your wife. So, if you must speak truth that may be hard for her to hear, do it gently, like a gentleman. What you say may not lift up your wife to extraordinary heights, but there is no need to beat her down.

Never Seek Quid Pro Quo with Uplifting Words

Please realize that you can try to sound loving or respectful but fail to be truly uplifting as God intends. *Always check your motives for being loving or respectful.* For example, it never works to use Uplifting Words to manipulate your spouse. Never speak Uplifting Words while, in the back of your mind, you are hoping for returns of some kind, sort of a quid pro quo arrangement.

I heard from one wife who had used the Respect Test, an exercise for wives to do in order to discover the impact respect can have on a husband. I ask wives to test this respect idea by approaching their husband and saying to him, "I was thinking of you today and all the things about you I respect, and I want you to know that I respect you." Then the wife exits the room![2]

> "You may think everything you do is right, but the Lord judges your motives" (Proverbs 16:2 GNB).

In typical male fashion, her husband followed her to find out more. He also began to serve and love her without nagging or prompting. A month later, however, she wrote to me complaining, "He isn't loving me the way he did right after the Respect Test."

When I inquired further, she admitted she had been telling her husband positive things to motivate him to change, not really to meet his need for respect! For example, she had been telling him he was a good dad in order to motivate him to become a better father to the children. Her words were more manipulation than motivation, and when he caught on (which was inevitable), he shut down on her completely.

When spouses use Love or Respect words for selfish purposes, their efforts almost always backfire. It is appalling when a husband says to his wife, "Okay, I have been loving all day, so why can't we have sex tonight?" When a man's motivation is self-serving, he crushes the spirit of his wife. She quickly sees he wasn't trying to meet her need for Love as an end in itself, but as a means to an end—to satisfy his need for sex.

The wise husband is aware that his wife needs a lot of uplifting; she needs assurance and encouragement pretty much on a continual basis. Following is something I share in conferences, something I call:

Emerson's Fundamental Observation

Women are uplifted by talking. If we husbands talk about the problems and needs our wives feel deep in their souls and seek to build them up by reassuring them, they will feel healed—at least for today.

A wife wrote to say of her husband: "He is a source of encouragement. When I err and apologize, he reminds me not to get discouraged and points out that, a few short months ago, I would not have even seen a need for an apology."

And another wife's e-mail said: "My husband is a real blessing. He has done and said all the right things for me this year as I have gone through breast cancer, including chemo and a double mastectomy. How beautifully Christ's love and acceptance have been mirrored in my husband's commitment to me—no matter what!"

It's always good when husband and wife can lift up each other, as one husband explained when he wrote to me: "We have had many conversations where we applied the techniques of decoding and responding with Love or Respect without even knowing it! Then later we would say to each other, 'Hey, we did a good job understanding and responding.'"

Husband and wife responding to each other with Love and Respect—this wholesome speech truly edifies and builds up. Married couples that succeed with good verbal communication affirm the positive. And research confirms that there needs to be a five to one ratio: five positive comments for every negative one. This is why T-U-F-T-S is so important and why every husband or wife should make this commitment:

> Tearing down my spouse is not the Jesus Way of Talking. Building up my spouse is the way I learned Christ. Jesus gave grace to those who heard Him, using Uplifting Words to meet their needs, and so will I.

FORGIVING WORDS:
Knowing my spouse will not be able to love or respect me perfectly, I commit to having a forgiving spirit so that I may never speak hatefully or contemptuously.

Paul saw the Ephesian Christians as very typical people with very typical issues. So, as he moves on, he tells them to get rid of bitterness, rage, anger, harsh words, slander, and all other malicious conduct (see Ephesians 4:31). Instead of all this crazy behavior, he advises them to "be kind to one another, tender-hearted, forgiving each other, just as God in Christ also has forgiven you" (Ephesians 4:32). If Paul wanted the Ephesians to remember anything of the way they had learned Christ (see Ephesians 4:20), it was forgiveness. Forgiving words are at the center of the Jesus Way of Talking because forgiveness was central to Christ's very nature, being, and purpose on this earth.

As He hung on the cross in terrible agony, dying in order to gain forgiveness for our sins, Jesus said, "Father, forgive them for they do not know what they are doing" (Luke 23:34). And when He walked this earth, He taught His followers to forgive others (Matthew 18:23–35), and warned about consequences if we do not forgive our brother as God forgave us (Matthew 6:14–15).[3]

> *"Hate stirs up trouble, but love forgives all offenses" (Proverbs 10:12 GNB).*

We have already had a good look at forgiveness in chapter 7, but we need to revisit this most difficult of actions to see why it is so vital to the Jesus Way of Talking. Sometimes your spouse will fail to speak lovingly or respectfully to you even though you have just tried to speak words of Love or Respect to your spouse—and few things can make us so angry! We all know we should use Forgiving Words without hesitation, but sometimes they stick in our throats. At this kind of moment, we must decide whether to respond with hateful or contemptuous words or stay the course of unconditional

Love and Respect. In some situations you may need to confront your spouse's sinful behavior, but again you must choose: Will I confront my mate from a spirit of forgiveness or a spirit of angry bitterness? It is certain that you cannot speak words of Love or Respect when you are embittered and longing to tell people how awful your mate is. (For help with confronting a spouse who is being cruel or destructive, see Appendix B, "Forgiving—But Also Confronting—the Three A's: Adultery, Abuse, Addiction," p. 338.)

True Forgiveness Can't Coexist with Resentment

Many couples stop the Crazy Cycle, get on the Energizing Cycle, and see the need for unconditional Rewarded-Cycle thinking as well. But it is all too easy to slip back into the old critical mode without realizing it. This is especially true for wives who, as I have already noted, have natural tendencies to correct and confront. And—let's face it, husbands—a wife may have good reason to be critical. A husband may sincerely want to be on the Energizing Cycle, but he seldom gets rid of bad habits overnight. He could easily be pinching his wife's air hose without realizing it, and she may run out of patience and forgiveness.

For example, a wife reads *Love & Respect* and sincerely tries to be respectful, but her husband shows little interest in trying to be loving. This goes on for several months, and she begins to grow weary of being the one making all the effort. She resolves to keep at it, but while she appears to speak respectfully to her husband at home, she has begun keeping a list of the negative things he is doing that feel unloving.

Before she realizes it, she starts feeling real resentment toward her husband. She tells herself, "What's the use of trying to be respectful anymore?" and becomes more and more critical and judgmental. Paul's instructions regarding forgiveness in Ephesians 4:31–32 go unheeded, as does most of his teaching in T-U-F-T-S, particularly on the call to be uplifting and thankful. These are hard moments, and the wife faces a major decision: stop trying to respect her husband altogether or determine that, by the grace of God, she will unconditionally respect this man who is being such a jerk. If she chooses the latter, the typical wife, who is naturally gifted with incredible verbal skills, must pray for still more patience because once words are used to tear down her husband, it will be difficult to build him back up again.

In an e-mail I received, one wife admitted that she finally recognized how disrespected her husband feels when she is moody, sharp, short, or sarcastic with him. She has been working hard at being forgiving and says, "I have been able to refrain from saying all the very hurtful berating things that are coursing through my brain. I understand that once any of

> *"Let no one become like a bitter plant that grows up and causes many troubles with its poison" (Hebrews 12:15 GNB).*

it is spoken, there is no remedy for another's soul. So, I am thankful for at least that much self-control."

I understand this wife's frustration, and she is making good progress. Biting her tongue when critical words well up is the first important step. Now she needs to pray for the ability to extend the complete kind of forgiveness that comes from her heart. This may take time, but I have seen it happen with many wives.

The reason I emphasize a wife's need to curb her criticism and truly forgive her husband is that being critical can easily cause her to talk to him in disrespectful ways that no man would ever talk to him. I have counseled many husbands who say, "Everybody respects me but my wife." It is no wonder, then, that a wife might hear her husband say, "Honey, with you I can never be good enough." When a wife hears remarks like this, her husband is crying out for respect (and maybe some forgiveness). These cries are not rooted in arrogance, nor are they of marginal concern. In response to this deep need for friendly respect that God put in her husband, a wife can try criticizing him less. And, if he still isn't understanding her needs for love, she should respectfully let him know the ways he is stepping on her air hose.

Forgiveness Can Be Manipulative Too

Another pitfall when using Forgiving Words is to speak forgivingly with the hidden agenda of getting your spouse to seek forgiveness. A crass example would be a husband who announces, "I forgive you. Now tell me you won't do that again." This seldom works, especially if your wife doesn't feel she did anything bad, or she just isn't in a repentant mood and doesn't want your forgiveness. To go up to a wife who is in an unrepentant frame of mind and say "I forgive you!" is offensive (and not very wise) because it sounds condescending. All you accomplish is shutting your wife down and making it even harder for her to feel repentant and to want to change. If you ever do this, you yourself need to seek forgiveness!

Granting forgiveness to your spouse should always be an end in itself because the Lord commands you to forgive. However, if you are continually feeling that you need to forgive your spouse, it could mean one of two things: your spouse is continually wronging you because of serious personal problems, or you may just be too easily offended.

For instance, I have heard from numerous wives who have gotten upset when their husbands walk on ahead of them from church to the parking lot. They tell their husbands they are unloving and say, "We need to talk about this. What will people think when they see you walking ahead of me like that?" These reports leave me with mixed emotions. Too often a wife will determine "truth" according to how she feels. If she feels offended, she automatically concludes that her husband is offensive and unloving. She has escalated his carelessness or preoccupation into a Love and Respect issue when the occasion didn't merit it.

Certainly walking together to the car would be more appropriate and attentive on the husband's part. Sarah has tactfully pointed this out to me when I get preoccupied with my thoughts and walk on ahead. However, she doesn't escalate the incident by accusing me of being offensive and unloving. She simply says, "Please wait for me. I enjoy walking with you." That snaps me out of my preoccupied trance, I apologize, and we go on from there. To take offense at something like this is like straining out a gnat and "swallowing a camel" (Matthew 23:24). Becoming so easily offended can plant bad seeds that could sprout into real trouble down the line if this kind of judgmentalism continues.

So, husbands and wives, beware. If you are forever struggling with having to forgive your spouse, you may be consumed with hostility or contempt. I saw that in my father. After he came to Christ, my father confessed that he had often been resentful toward my mother over little things. Dad had taken offense at decisions Mom made that he felt were done solely to upset him. He had not trusted her good motives and had often been angry and hostile because he had simply not understood Mom's heart.

When he began to follow Christ, Dad began to realize that much of his rage was rooted in his mistaken beliefs about what Mom was doing and why. He was feeling provoked over matters that were mostly in his mind. As he grew in his Christian walk, he recognized that Mom's actions were not causing his anger, but only revealing that he was sitting on a ton of negative emotions, which quickly turned to raging anger when he felt offended. For the most part, he tamed his volcanic reactions by learning to see conflict as a normal part of life with his wife, rather than interpreting disagreements as evidence that she intended to disregard and disrespect him.

When we are angry and unforgiving, our feelings usually go much deeper than the infractions that prompt them. You need to evaluate why you have these feelings. What is really bugging you? If nothing immoral, dangerous, or abusive has happened, you may be making a big deal out of petty issues.

And all of us are capable of holding petty resentments because we tend to focus on what we are doing well and what our spouse is doing poorly. This is a subtle thing because it is hard to detect our own weaknesses. Remember the difference between the dispositional and the situational discussed in chapter 14? If your wife is especially biting or critical, you tend to think it is her poor *disposition* (a character flaw). But if you mess up and "lose it" for a minute, you credit the *situation,* which "caused" you to get angry. Psychological terms are interesting, but the bottom line is that we are talking about our inability to see our own sin for what it is.

One more comment about forgiveness. During our conferences I caution everyone by saying, "Please understand something. Many of you will leave this conference intending to talk to each other in a loving and respectful way, but when one of you blows it, the other will be tempted to harbor just a bit of resentment. And as one or the other makes mistakes (because none of us is perfect), the resentment can build. Soon your Love and Respect marriage is on shaky ground because you cannot be genuinely loving or respectful *and* be nursing an unforgiving spirit at the same time."

How Unforgiveness Can Lead to Slander

I hear of it all the time in my e-mails. I truly wish I could say the following is not the case, but unfortunately it happens too often. A wife will slander her husband without realizing it. Slander is a false and malicious report about someone. The typical wife would never deliberately slander her husband, but because she is so hurt and resentful about some particular conflict, she vents. Further, because she can see only pink while he sees blue, her report makes him out to be the villain. Because she feels so vulnerable to her husband, who is typically strong and stubborn and quite possibly insensitive and unloving at times, she may color the facts a bit pink to solicit and gain sympathy. If her husband hears of this, he can become infuriated by the one-sidedness of it all, and his anger can easily turn to bitterness, drawing away, and stonewalling.

It is striking to note that Paul's only comment to husbands in his letter to Colossae is "Husbands, love your wives and do not be embittered against them" (Colossians 3:19). Was Paul thinking about the female propensity to slide into slander and the male propensity to get angry and harsh? It's hard to say, but a wife may do well to consider Proverbs 25:23—"The north wind brings forth rain, and a backbiting tongue, an angry countenance."

> *"Whoever goes about slandering reveals secrets, but he who is trustworthy in spirit keeps a thing covered" (Proverbs 11:13 ESV).*

It is the wise wife who is careful not to risk slandering her husband by talking behind his back to family, including children, friends, or coworkers. He knows he is not perfect, but when he also knows his wife doesn't criticize him in front of others, he rises up to call her blessed (see Proverbs 31:26–31, especially v. 28). Following is an example from a husband who wrote to express appreciation for his wife's early commitment never to talk poorly about him to other women:

Very shortly after we were married, my wife went to a bachelorette party for one of her best friends. Many of the women there were married, and my wife was shocked at the amount of criticism they were leveling at their absent husbands. Even then my wife had a pretty thorough understanding of a lot of my shortcomings, but she refused to join in on the complaint session. It was—and continues to be—her perspective that she should never be critical of me in front of other people.

Wife, the best motive for staying away from slander and concentrating on forgiving your husband is to remember God forgave you (see Ephesians 4:32; Colossians 3:13). Husband, if your wife does say something you consider slanderous, you should forgive her for the very same reason. Realize, too, that she tends to turn to others for support. Yes, she can cross a line that you would not cross, but if you were a woman, you'd seek support, too, if your husband did not welcome you humbly and gently. Do not judge your wife as intending to embarrass you in front of others. That is not her goal. If you had been more tender with her, she would have come to you and not turned to others. She would have released her negative feelings as you empathized with her, listened to her burdens, and prayed with her. Remember, she is a goodwilled woman. Her aim is not to slander you but to connect with you! Forgive her!

When you possess a forgiving spirit, words of Love or Respect will flow authentically from your lips—and realize that the Lord Himself is listening to you at moments like these. He knows you are not powerless, but actually full of power that He has granted you. He knows you are not weak, foolish, or afraid, wanting peace at any price. Instead He sees you as godly and wise, committed to imitating Him, and longing to hear His "Well done!"

As with your commitment to be truthful and uplifting, make a commitment to be forgiving:

An unforgiving spirit is not compatible with the Jesus Way of Talking. Forgiving my mate is the way I learned Christ. Jesus forgave me therefore I will forgive my spouse.

We have looked at Truthful Words, Uplifting Words, Forgiving Words—the first three parts of T-U-F-T-S—but two important principles remain. Does your spouse hear many Thankful Words coming from your lips? Do you use Scriptural Words in your home? These and other important questions will be asked and answered as we complete our discussion of the Rewarded Cycle in chapter 16.

CHAPTER SIXTEEN

—————◆◆◆—————

The Jesus Way of Talking— Part III

To Love or Respect: Be Thankful, Scriptural—and Faithful

We have two more strands of T-U-F-T-S to examine. Thankful Words and Scriptural Words also originate with God. When you and your mate can use them unconditionally to bless each other, they will bless God in a special way. He is pleased with people who are thankful and scriptural.

THANKFUL WORDS:
Since it is easy to be negative, focus on your mate's good qualities and express thanks with positive words of Love or Respect.

How often do you thank your spouse for what he or she does for you every day? Do you sometimes withhold words of thanks because you feel your spouse doesn't deserve them or won't receive them? As Paul moves on in his letter to the Ephesians, he warns them against such obvious pitfalls as immorality, impurity, and greed (see 5:3) and then adds "there must be no filthiness and silly talk, or coarse jesting, which are not fitting, but rather giving of thanks" (v. 4).

It is not surprising that Thankful Words are part of the Jesus Way of Talking that Paul describes for the Ephesians and for us. Jesus Himself put a high priority on thankfulness, and He gave thanks whenever the occasion warranted it (for example, before He fed the five thousand [John 6:11]). The way of Jesus is to give thanks, and He expects His followers to give thanks to God and to others. When He healed ten lepers, He noted that only one of them—and a Samaritan at that!—returned to thank Him (Luke 17:11–19).

But why, we may wonder, *does Paul contrast the giving of thanks with negative things like filthiness, silly talk, and coarse jesting?* I believe Paul wanted those who received his letter to think about the huge difference between the thankful person and one who is into obscenities, talking foolish trash, or telling dirty jokes. Paul believed strongly that if believers of his time would give thanks, it would be a strong deterrent to slipping back into the old immoral ways from which many of them had been freed by the gospel. Paul's words are just as true for us today. From what the couples I counsel tell me, there is more than a little coarse speech happening in too many marriages.

To cite a couple of examples, it is coarse and degrading for a husband to relentlessly tease his wife about putting on weight—and doing so in front of others—and it is equally degrading for a wife to continually sigh, roll her eyes, and say to her husband, especially when others are around, "You just don't get it." The Jesus Way of Talking calls us to focus on the positive and not get caught up in those things about our spouse that we do not like and that we try to change through such rude comments.

Does this mean spouses can never tease each other in a spirit of good fun? Of course not, but the trick is to be sure it is good fun that does not devalue the other person. It is easy to step over a fine line into territory where you are cynically or sarcastically saying to your spouse, "I don't value or appreciate you."

But back to the point of being thankful. I'm guessing that husbands or wives reading this chapter will have different answers to the question "How thankful are you for your spouse?" You may be one of those who has to admit you are being silly, coarse, degrading, or even obscene toward your spouse. Perhaps it is all rather subtle, and you claim you are just joking around, but the truth may be that you have fixated on the negative and are overlooking the positive and the good. You may have a problem with the way God designed your spouse. You didn't bargain on getting someone who is so different from you. (If this is the case for you, it might be a good idea to go back and reread chapter 3 and rethink why God made one of you pink and one of you blue.) To remain unthankful for your spouse because you two are "so different" is a sure way to get on the Crazy Cycle, and this lack of gratitude for your spouse will not be any help in getting off.

Or you may be one of those husbands or wives who believes you have good reason to *not* be thankful for your spouse—at least right now—because your spouse is doing or saying extremely unlovable or disrespectful things. I could fill a book with letters from husbands and wives whose spouses are committing adultery, taking drugs, drowning in alcohol, taking no interest in the family, investing nothing in the marriage, etc. If you can see little in your spouse to thank God for, you can at least express thanks for the trials God is allowing in your marriage because they can deepen your faith in Him. Remember, thankful people find things for which they give God thanks. They are not thankful

> *"Whatever happens, give thanks, because it is God's will in Christ Jesus that you do this"* (1 Thessalonians 5:18 GW).

only for the good; they can be thankful in the midst of the bad as well.

Or perhaps you and your spouse are doing pretty well at staying on the Energizing Cycle a good deal of the time. As you try to practice C-O-U-P-L-E and C-H-A-I-R-S, do you ever thank God for your mate? As a wife you may want to ask yourself, "Am I thankful about what my husband is saying and doing to be Close, Open, Understanding, Peacemaking, Loyal, and Esteeming? Or do I sometimes slip into being negative and critical, cracking sarcastic jokes now and then about what he isn't saying or doing?" And as a husband you can ask yourself, "Am I thankful to God for my wife and what she is saying or doing to practice C-H-A-I-R-S—appreciating my desire to work and achieve, to protect and provide, to serve and lead, to analyze and counsel, to have shoulder-to-shoulder friendship, and to be sexually intimate? Or am I sometimes guilty of teasing her in coarse ways and of feeling negative and even bitter about what she isn't doing or saying?"

Obviously, a husband who wants to speak lovingly to his wife cannot also be ungrateful for her. And a wife who wants to speak respectfully cannot also be complaining about her husband. If you attempt to use Thankful Words but have not made a conscious commitment to be loving or respectful, your words will sound phony, gruff, or sarcastic. To be respectful toward your husband, you must speak Thankful Words respectfully. You do not want to sound like this: "Thank you for putting gas in my car—after the third time I asked you." And to be loving toward your wife, you must speak thankful words lovingly and sincerely instead of getting in a sly dig: "Thanks for cleaning the house—for the first time this month!"

Also keep in mind that thankfulness in marriage is to be a very reciprocal kind of thing. If you want your husband to express appreciation for your attempts to be respectful, you must speak thankfully when he tries to be loving. And if you want your wife to express appreciation for your attempts to be loving, you must use Thankful Words when she tries to speak or act respectfully.

Is Giving Thanks Really about Your Spouse?

Perhaps all of this sounds awfully basic and simple. Of course you know you should be thankful to God for your spouse and for a lot of other things as well. But just like everything else we talk about in the Rewarded Cycle, you don't try to be thankful in your own power. If you believe in the Jesus Way of Talking, you use Thankful Words in your marriage because doing so really isn't about your spouse and how well he or she is performing. Instead you pray, "Lord, because I love You, I am asking You to make me a thankful person because my ultimate goal is to please You and to hear Your 'Well done' and maybe Your 'Well said.'"

Look back for a moment at Ephesians 5:1–2 where Paul says, "Therefore be imitators of God . . . and walk in love, just as Christ also loved you, and gave Himself up for us." When you seek to imitate God and walk in love, it is a lot easier to look at your spouse more positively than negatively. A wife wants her marriage to be more positive, yet she can fixate on the negatives in her husband, which feeds her negativity. A husband wants his marriage to be less negative, yet he does little to make it more positive, which can only sustain the negative. To give the positive a chance to flourish, turn to God first, seek to imitate Him, and it will be easier to give thanks for each other and to make your marriage more positive.

> *"With my mouth I will give thanks abundantly to the LORD; and in the midst of many I will praise Him"* (Psalm 109:30).

My own wife is a person who has chosen to be thankful as unto Christ. I have watched God empower Sarah to see the positive in almost any situation. In the past few years, for instance, we have had to make some crossroad decisions, a few of which have not been her first choice. But it makes no difference which path we take. Once a decision is made, Sarah will say, "Going this way is good," and then gives several reasons why this is so.

This is not to say that sometimes Sarah wouldn't prefer to go in a different direction. She can and will be strong in stating her opinions. But if circumstances do not allow us to go the way she prefers, she does not sulk. Choosing to be thankful and positive, Sarah looks for the good things God is bringing her way. She truly reminds me of what Paul told the Philippians: "I have learned the secret of being content in any and every situation" (Philippians 4:12 NIV).

Opportunities to Be Thankful Are Always There

I get frequent e-mails from Love and Respect spouses who are finding opportunities to give thanks or be appreciative because of what God has done in their lives and their marriage. Here is just a sampling.

One husband wrote:

> Part of my plan is to remind myself to be appreciative to the Lord for my wife. She has stuck by me for many years and has been a wonderful mother to our three children. Ten years ago this month I had a major heart attack, nearly died, had open-heart surgery, followed by the loss of my executive career. We lost our home and all our savings. She went out and got a realtor's license and has been the major wage earner ever since. I have never again found a management position, but work by the hour. Every time my wife seems to be critical, sarcastic, or disrespectful, I remind myself how lucky I am that she is still with me. I'm determined to work on my relationship to Christ, more prayer in particular, so that I will be prepared when conflict comes. My desire is to be more receptive to the leading of the Holy Spirit in those moments, to react slowly, kindly, and patiently.

A wife reported: "Every day I am writing one thing I am thankful for about my husband and then most days sharing it with him as an encouragement. I want to set my mind on my husband's good points and am praying that God will restore desire and love and trust for him once again."

Another wife creatively expressed her thanks by sending her husband a message through the local radio station, which had a policy to broadcast whatever people want to say to friends or loved ones every hour for a twenty-four-hour period. Kim sponsored Valentine's Day for her husband, and this was the message that he and dozens of friends and associates heard on the air:

> Kim is dedicating this programming to her husband, Kary, on Valentine's Day. Ephesians 5:33 says, "To sum up, each one of you is to love his wife as himself, and the wife is to respect her husband." Kim says, "Kary, thank you for being a husband who loves me and our kids as Christ loves us—sacrificially and unconditionally. Thank you for working hard for our family to make life easier and more fun. I know that you would lay down your life for us if necessary. I am proud to be your wife. My love for you has grown through the years, but my respect for you as a husband and man has grown even more. With all my respect, Kim.

Her letter continues: "You wouldn't believe the feedback we've gotten from people who heard it! All the men are envious! The women think it's sweet, but don't get it."

When Kary heard Kim's words over the radio, he wept with gratitude. Not only had his wife thanked him for being the husband and the man he is, but she had uplifted him as well.

Be Thankful Even If It Doesn't Seem Natural

Saying Thankful Words and praising one's spouse are such simple things, but for various reasons some people struggle to do so. One husband who admits he has "a fabulous wife" with traits he "could not find in any other woman" confesses this: "Because of my upbringing . . . I find it hard to praise her without feeling strange about it. It's easier for me to criticize. . . . It's tough for her to handle."

By contrast, a wife who had been married forty years began reading

Love & Respect, but her husband would not read it with her. She began feeling negative about him and asked the Lord for help. That night, lying awake, she felt God saying to her: "I want you to imagine you are a giant highlighter, and I want you to highlight all those things that are honorable and true about your husband. See your husband through My eyes." She got up and started writing, filling pages with why she respected her husband and was thankful for him. She decided she didn't mind that he refused to read the book. She would just be blessed and thankful for him and show him the respect he was needing. She writes:

> God filled me with His love for my husband and shone His light into our relationship. The rest of the week was like a second honeymoon—in fact, it was better than our first honeymoon! My husband is sharing more and loving more and I feel so blessed, so fulfilled as his wife. It's a beautiful story of what God wants to do in our marriages if we will just open our hearts and allow Him to change the way we think.

The way you think is all-important when you are being thankful for whatever God sends. What I admire in Sarah is that she is thankful for me and the rest of the family because she can look beyond us and thank God. In fact, one of Sarah's favorite verses is Psalm 50:23—"He who offers a sacrifice of thanksgiving honors Me." She writes in her journal:

> I remember when our son David had broken his leg quite severely, while playing baseball in the eighth grade. As I saw his heart breaking over the loss of a dream to play in the major league someday, I realized I could not fix his leg or his dream. Now my heart was breaking also. How would I get through this? Then God showed me this wasn't a crisis with my son, but a crisis of faith for me. I knew it was God's will that I give thanks in all things, but this didn't feel like something for which to be thankful. And that is when I learned about a "sacrifice of thanksgiving" in Psalm 50:23.

When I came upon this verse while David was recuperating, at first it didn't sound like a natural thing to do. But then I thought of Abraham, who was asked to sacrifice his only son on the altar. That wasn't a very natural thing to do either. I realized that sometimes we have to offer a sacrifice of thanksgiving even when things are not going well.

> *"Through Him then, let us continually offer up a sacrifice of praise to God, that is, the fruit of lips that give thanks to His name" (Hebrews 13:15).*

That was the first of many more times in my life when I would offer a sacrifice of praise and thanksgiving. It was like a pre-game warm-up with many practices in between. Little did I know I was practicing for the big game yet to come—the day I would hear the words *breast cancer.* Throughout the ten years between my son's disappointment and then cancer for me, I had been finding joy in giving thanks. Each time I offered thanksgiving as a sacrifice, I knew I was honoring God. Even though my circumstances did not always change, something was happening in the heavens *and* something was happening in my soul!

Sarah went on to have a double mastectomy and did not need further treatments of any kind. Today she is cancer free. Through it all she kept giving sacrifices of praise and thanksgiving because she looks beyond her circumstances to God—and that is what being thankful is all about. Whatever your relationship to your spouse may be right now—something for which to be very thankful, somewhat thankful, or not very thankful at all—I urge you to use Sarah's approach to your circumstances. To avoid or climb out of the pit of unthankfulness, make a commitment like the following:

With God's help I will counter negative thoughts about my spouse by giving thanks for all his or her good qualities. I know Jesus does not let my weaknesses or faults control His view of me. He does not view me as worthless or make me the butt of silly jokes. I will treat my spouse as Jesus treats me. This is the way I learned Christ!

SCRIPTURAL WORDS:
To stay the course in speaking words of Love or Respect, keep your heart in Scripture, trusting in and talking about His promises to help you.

The last strand of T-U-F-T-S is Scriptural Words, to which Paul refers as he completes his comparison of how the Christian is to walk and talk to the way the ungodly walk and talk (Ephesians 4:17–5:21). Paul has touched on using Truthful, Uplifting, Forgiving, and Thankful Words. Now, in Ephesians 5:18–21, he makes what seems to be an odd comparison between the old self and the new self: the Ephesians are to "not get drunk with wine" but instead "be filled with the Spirit" (v. 18). Then he goes on to say they should speak "to one another in psalms and hymns and spiritual songs, singing and making melody with your heart to the Lord" (v. 19).

At first glance you might think Paul is waxing eloquent about how believers should conduct a worship service, and some commentators do think that is what Paul means. But I believe a closer look at the context shows that he is also referring to how we are to talk to one another on a daily basis.

First, though, why does Paul contrast drunkenness with speaking psalms and hymns? We find the answer when Paul says believers should not get drunk to excess but "be filled with the Spirit." To be drunk to the point of debauchery is to be controlled by an excess of wine and therefore self-absorbed. In contrast to the drunk, who is focused only on his own wants, disappointments, or guilt, believers are to be focused on the words and Spirit of Christ, allowing Him to take control and influence how they communicate—by using psalms, hymns, and spiritual songs.

Instead of indulging in "It's all about me" self-absorption, Paul says the believer should become Spirit-absorbed, that is, filled with the Spirit, which means you allow the Spirit to reign in your life. You are focused on God's desires, His intentions, and His grace.

Paul gives us a huge clue about the best way to be filled with the Spirit in the parallel passage Colossians 3:16: "Let the word of Christ richly dwell within you." We are to let the words of Christ fill our hearts because when His words flood our soul, the Spirit can work more freely in our life.

As Paul continues his letter to the Ephesians, I do not think it is a coincidence that he soon talks directly to husbands and wives in Ephesians 5:22–33, the most profound passage on marriage in the Bible. If any relationship should be marked by the use of Scriptural Words, it is marriage.

As with the other four kinds of words, Jesus is a model of how to use Scriptural Words. He constantly talked about the Scriptures, often asking His listeners, "Have you not read?" In Matthew 19:4–5 the Pharisees are trying to trap Jesus with questions about when divorce is permissible. Jesus said, "Have you not read that He who created them from the beginning made them male and female . . . and the two shall become one flesh?" (For other examples of "Have you not read?" see Mark 2:25; 12:10; 12:26.) If the Ephesians had "learned Christ" at all (see Ephesians 4:20), they understood how much importance He placed on the Scriptures.

> *Jesus responded three times to the devil with "it is written" (Matthew 4:4, 7, 10). To Jesus, what Scripture said, God said, and what God said, Scripture said.*

Again, we must understand that the scriptural way of talking is not primarily about your spouse, but about your relationship to God in Christ. If you are serious about the Jesus Way of Talking, you will avoid saying anything that contradicts His words. You will avoid being self-absorbed, as a drunken person might be, and instead you will be absorbed in pleasing the Lord with scriptural thoughts, words, and actions. To speak scripturally, you must make a decision to be biblical in your outlook. You may remember the WWJD?—(What Would Jesus Do?)—wristbands. Wearing this simple little band was a powerful reminder to think the thoughts of Jesus and Scripture.

In a very real sense, the WWJD wristband is like my suggestion to imagine seeing Jesus just past your spouse's shoulder, especially in any conversation that is at all tense. In fact, you could ask yourself the following question as you look past your spouse to Jesus: "What would Jesus *say* (WWJS) right now to be loving or respectful?"

Scriptural Words Can Stop the Crazy Cycle

Speaking Scriptural Words does not mean that you must quote the Bible every time you open your mouth, but it does mean that you are thinking about God's promises and trusting Him. Speaking Scriptural Words is living and talking according to God's principles and values. For example, you purpose to seek first God's kingdom and righteousness, and you try not to let worry or the "cares of this world" (like paying the bills) dominate your speech and thinking. If the cares of the world are your focus rather than God and His truth, it is likely the Crazy Cycle will start up. Scriptural thinking and talking can keep it at bay.

At the same time, Scripture in and of itself is no silver bullet. You can memorize a lot of verses but miss their correct application. For example, a wife wrote to say she had ordered a lot of our materials and "the Lord is retraining me. Prior to that I had memorized large passages of 1 Peter on respect, but did not know why my deeds and words had no effect. I did not understand what respect was—that it is a choice."

This wife is on the Rewarded Cycle, not the Crazy Cycle. She says, "Even if I see no change in the marriage, I know I am doing what pleases God, and this alone gives me peace and takes the edge off the hurt and pain. The emotions are less and less significant, and there is hope. When I fail, I just thank God for His mercy and patience."

Another wife's e-mail told of how she borrowed a copy of *Love & Respect* from a friend and was soon in tears as she saw how her marriage was "defined by the Crazy Cycle." They were married nine years ago, have gone to counseling since year three, would find themselves doing better for a while, and then hit "THE WALL" and wonder if their marriage was a mistake. But they couldn't ever really believe that "because we are both believers and know that God works all things together for good . . . but we just didn't understand why we argued so much."

Again, I must emphasize that the Scriptures are not magical, nor are they like a prescription ("Read so many verses or chapters a day, and all will be well"). Commitment, discipline, and trust in God must be present. When life's problems close in, it is easy to turn away from Scriptural Words because they don't seem to be working for you. Perhaps someone loses a job, money is short, sickness hits, and on and on. To top it off, your Love or Respect for your spouse is not being reciprocated. At times like these, you are tempted to get angry with God. You thought if you acted according to His commands, life would be much better, but it hasn't worked as well as you hoped. I understand because Sarah and I have been there. And we have learned that when things go bad, *those* are the times we need to turn to Scripture and to God more than ever.

Following is a letter from a wife whose family faced a serious financial crisis. Even though her husband was not really responsible for their situation, he took all the blame and was depressed for days. Because God was doing a work in her soul and she

> *"How sweet are Your words to my taste! . . . From Your precepts I get understanding . . . Your word is a lamp to my feet and a light to my path . . . I am exceedingly afflicted; revive me, O LORD, according to Your word"* (Psalm 119:103–107).

desired to trust His promises, she decided to respond differently to her husband than she would have in the past, when she usually had been negative and critical.

She writes: "I determined in my heart I was not going to lash out at him. I kept telling him that we were going to be okay . . . that God would work it out on our behalf. I refused to let the enemy get hold of my heart and tongue and put us on the Crazy Cycle." Their financial circumstances suddenly took a turn for the better, and she credits God with doing it all: "I believe God provided us with a miracle because I chose to control my tongue and my attitude, and I showed my husband support and respect during a very scary financial problem."

I hear from many spouses who deal with difficulties by staying faithful to Scripture. In fact, the reason a simple analogy like the Crazy Cycle turns on the light for them is because it is based on Scripture (see Ephesians 5:33). I cannot emphasize too strongly that stopping the Crazy Cycle and keeping it stopped will work for the long haul only if you and your spouse use Scriptural Words, stand on God's promises, and trust Him. It gladdens my heart when people write and sign their e-mails with a verse like Proverbs 3:5–6: "Trust in the Lord with all your heart, and lean not on your own understanding; in all your ways acknowledge Him, and He shall direct your paths" (NKJV).

Over the years Sarah and I have focused on key scriptures to encourage and guide us, including Proverbs 3:5–6. I longed to be used of God, but I experienced times of real discouragement. I would wonder, *Does God really want to use me?* In those moments of doubt, Sarah and I both found refreshment in Psalm 37:3–5:

> Trust in the LORD and do good;
>> Dwell in the land and cultivate faithfulness.
> Delight yourself in the LORD;
>> And He will give you the desires of your heart.
> Commit your way to the LORD,
>> Trust also in Him, and He will do it.

And when Sarah went through breast cancer, God gave us Psalm 112:7—
"They do not fear bad news; they confidently trust the Lord to care for
them" (NLT). When I learned I had melanoma, this same verse also ministered to my heart.[1]

Scripture Can Draw You Closer to Each Other

An extra benefit that Sarah and I enjoy as we concentrate on God's promises in Scripture is that it draws us closer together and makes our marriage stronger. I hear from other couples who experience this same thing.
One young husband writes:

> Our relationship is improving because we're trying to follow
> Christ's example. We're trying to lay down our lives for one
> another and regard each other as the more important one.
> Within the last year we have grown spiritually beyond anything
> we ever expected. God is doing this work in our lives and we are
> truly amazed. The ability of God to change our hearts and to
> change habits that we've established over five years of marriage
> (and even twenty-seven years of life) is more amazing to me than
> any sign or wonder I've ever seen or heard of.

*"But if we walk in
the light, as he is
in the light, we
have fellowship
with one another"
(1 John 1:7 ESV).*

There are some obvious reasons why
this young couple's marriage is improving.
First, this man and his wife sought to trust
God's Word (notice that he echoes 1 John
3:16 and Philippians 2:3). As they trusted
God, they also spoke His Word to each
other and acted on it. Doing this introduced healthy attitudes and actions, and
God honored them by changing their
hearts and even their long-held habits.
When you look to God and His Word as your ultimate source of signif-
icance and security, you don't demand that your spouse take that role in

your life. And as you draw strength from the Lord individually, He draws you closer together as a couple.

Unfortunately, my e-mail and conversations with husbands and wives tell me many couples tend not to pray together. If you and your spouse are not taking time to pray together, I urge you to do so. This can be a tremendous opportunity for the husband in particular as he invites his wife to talk to the Lord about whatever is concerning them. One thing is for sure: there is power when two people pray. For example, God may be allowing the two of you to have a problem because His deepest purpose is that the two of you come together and find wisdom and strength in Him. You need only spend a few minutes expressing to God the concerns of your heart. Yet I know some men feel praying with their wives is unmanly. On the contrary, if your wife is typical, she will see you as *more* of a man because she wants you to be the family's spiritual leader. She feels more secure when you take an active role in guiding Bible reading and praying together.

Husbands, please understand that you do not need a seminary degree to lead your family in focusing on God's Word. One wife told me, "Although we have prayer, it isn't the regular devotional type. But what I see is that God's Word is constantly intertwined in our family. Every discussion comes back to what God's truth is . . . as we deal with everyday situations. . . . The more I see [my husband] grow in strength before God, the more secure I feel."

In another letter a husband shared what he wrote to his wife during a time of great stress and conflict concerning a child in the family. As he tried to offer hope to his wife from a biblical perspective, he said: "I'm troubled about everything that's happening. I wish there were some fast and easy answers, but there haven't been any. I know somewhere in the Bible it says that when you marry there will be troubles—wish I could find that passage and quote it correctly. Anyway, we are to hang in there and work through this."

Many wives respond very positively when their husband in effect says: "Let's hang in there and trust God and His promises." An old hymn sums up the absolute necessity to apply Scripture to your marriage. While the following is not the exact quoting of a psalm, it is a "spiritual song" that beautifully describes why we must "stand on God's promises":

> Standing on the promises that cannot fail,
> When the howling storms of doubt and fear assail.
> By the living Word of God I shall prevail,
> Standing on the promises of God.[2]

What some husbands and wives do not understand is that trying to unconditionally Love and Respect each other is, at its deepest level, a test of one's faith in Christ and the Scriptures. Those who do grasp this truth stay the course and are certain to hear God's "Well done!" To avoid the pitfall of neglecting Scripture, make the following commitment your personal prayer:

> Lord, keep my heart focused on the Scriptures and trusting Your promises to help me always speak words of unconditional Love or Respect.

An Unconditional Love Story

Throughout this book I have tried to teach many concepts that can help you move toward mutual understanding and better communication as husband and wife. Together we have looked at everything from why the mouth matters to how pink and blue communicate differently, from goodwill to forgiveness, and from decoding to clarifying. In our discussion of the Rewarded Cycle, we have studied the Jesus Way of Speaking with words that are Truthful, Uplifting, Forgiving, Thankful, and Scriptural. In these final chapters, as is true throughout this book, the key is in one word—*unconditional*. In a very real sense, speaking the Jesus Way is what *The Language of Love & Respect* is all about.

At the end of the day, when a lot has usually been said, you can measure how well you have lived according to Love and Respect by looking back and evaluating your words. Were they always unconditional? This is a high standard, too high to do in human strength alone. That is why the Rewarded Cycle stresses the need to do everything in your marriage as unto God. He comes first, and your spouse follows. Whatever happens, Abba Father is listening, providing, and sustaining.

To close this chapter and the Rewarded Cycle section, I want you to read one more letter. It is from a husband who tells how he and his wife were on the Crazy Cycle for years and how, through it all, he applied the principles of the Rewarded Cycle without really knowing about the Love and Respect Connection. Here is Jack's story:

> My wife and I married full of hope and love like every other couple. But my wife had scars from growing up with parents who didn't unconditionally love her and with boyfriends who were only looking for one thing. Deep down in her soul, she wasn't sure if I would be different, and during our first year of marriage, she put me to the test. Was I the man she thought she married? She never verbalized this, but years later it came out in counseling.
>
> She tried to manipulate and control the relationship so she could protect herself, but also to see if I would stand up to her and what that would look like. Would I react violently, would I give up, or would I stand by my word and stick it out? Hurtful words were her most lethal weapon, which she used with deadly precision. I came into the marriage with too high expectations for our sexual relationship, but she felt sex made her feel "used," and the less the better. This was an area where Lisa tested me a lot (more subconsciously than on purpose). We'd have a great evening together, talking and having fun, and even fooling around, but when we got to the bedroom, it would end, and I was expected to not be disappointed, or else I only wanted one thing.

This was really emotionally painful for me because making love to Lisa was a part of my love for her, but she used it as a weapon against me. Obviously, our physical relationship was a big source of friction. As my wife says, "It was a year of hell." As for me, I had never been hurt to the core of my being like that before.

But I had given my word, and divorce was too easy. I was also a Christian, and I knew that God's Word commanded me to love my wife no matter what. I'm no saint, and I made my share of mistakes in our relationship, but one thing I did do right was to love my wife even when she didn't deserve it. Some men may say, "I just can't do that," and to be honest there were times when I was so empty and hurting inside that I really didn't have any love left to give my wife. It was at those times that I would approach God and pray something like this: "Father, I hurt so bad. You know what's going on in my relationship to Lisa. You heard all the hurtful things she just said to me. I didn't deserve that. You know my heart, and I know Lisa is hurting too. She NEEDS my love, but it just isn't there in my heart right now. So, Father, I'm asking for Your help. I need You to fill my heart with Your love, so that I can go back in there and love her as You've asked me to."

You must "ask God from the wealth of his glory to give you power through his Spirit to be strong in your inner selves" (Ephesians 3:16 GNB).

I didn't pray this prayer very often, but every time I did, God supernaturally put that love in my heart. I could actually sense it inside my being. Mostly, I would feel His love for me, and then it was just natural to give some of that same love to my wife.

Jack remembers that during that first year there were some turning points. One that stands out is the night they had a "really big fight," and Lisa said she wanted to leave "for good." By then Jack had learned to recognize when she was manipulating him, and he had started standing up to her. He stood in the doorway of the only entrance to their apartment and wouldn't let her go by. He wasn't physical; he just wouldn't move despite her repeated blows of frustration. In about a minute she started crying, and he held her and told her he loved her. Lisa says that if Jack hadn't stopped her then, she would have left never to come back.

Jack believes this was a key turning point because Lisa had already known that he would not leave no matter how she treated him, and she learned that even when she didn't have the strength to keep going and wanted to leave him, he would still be there to hold the relationship together. His letter continues:

> I think she finally knew that it was impossible for the relationship to dissolve and she was safe. I wish I could say it got better immediately. It didn't. We were on and off the Crazy Cycle for the first several years of our marriage. For the most part our marriage was unfulfilling for both of us. But slowly and surely, the love that God gave me began to heal the wounds in my wife and our relationship. As the Bible rightly says, "Love covers a multitude of sins."[3]

Jack goes on:

> I can recall another turning point that occurred about ten years into our marriage. From the beginning, Lisa had made me responsible for her happiness, and of course no human can possibly fulfill that. As Lisa began to heal from her past, she also began to trust God more—that He was good and loving and could be trusted. She began to find joy and happiness in her relationship with God instead of only from me.

Lisa and Jack have been married nineteen years now, and for the last several years their relationship "has been fantastic." In fact, it's everything that he had dreamed of as a young, newly married man—and more. Now there are no more nights when they have a good time with each other, but when they get to the bedroom, he is told he "only wants one thing."

Now Lisa knows deep down that part of Jack's love for her is making love to her, but that he doesn't love her "just for sex." His letter concludes:

> "These things I have spoken to you so that My joy may be in you, and that your joy may be made full" (John 15:11).

Now Lisa looks me in the eye and says, "You're the most honorable man I've ever known.'" And she means it. I can't describe to you how much love I have for her. Emerson, as you have said, it may take weeks, months, and even years before a relationship is healed. Lisa and I are living proof that through God's grace it can happen. And out of the sweet fragrance of our relationship, God is drawing others to Himself.

This husband's commitment to unconditionally love his wife "no matter what" is a model for all husbands—and wives for that matter. It makes no difference: you may be struggling as Jack did, or you may have a few problems but nothing that bad, or you may be blessed with an energizing Love and Respect marriage. In every case, your Love and Respect for each other must be *unconditional*, and the only way you can offer this to your spouse is by being faithful—to God, to His Word, and to your spouse. No matter how many times you may slip up, fail, or just plain blow it with your mate, your faithfulness to Jesus Christ will bring you through.

In the conclusion to this book, I will share my own heart about marriage, unconditional Love and Respect, and the importance of deep faith in Christ with my son Jonathan and his wife, Sarah, who have been married only a short time. I invite you to listen in.

CONCLUSION

In God Always Trust

To conclude The Language of Love & Respect, *I have written a letter of counsel to my son Jonathan and his wife, Sarah. (Yes, we now have two Sarahs in the family.) Jonathan and Sarah have just started their life together, and I want to share my heart with them—and also with you—to point to the only sure pathway to mutual trust and understanding and a satisfying marriage. As you can tell by the title above, marriage is not about us; it's about Him.*

Dear Jonathan and Sarah,

You will have been married for eighteen months by the time this book is published, but it seems like only a few days ago that I performed your marriage ceremony on beautiful Mackinac Island, Michigan. The day of your wedding was a picture fit for a postcard with its gorgeous blue sky, bright warm sun, and gentle waves from Lake Huron lapping at the shore not far from where the two of you, our family, and some friends gathered to celebrate the exchanging of your vows. My charge to you that day was to fill your marriage with unconditional Love and Respect, and after the "I do's" what a joy it was for Mom and me to watch you ride through the streets in horse-and-buggy style, waving to the crowds as the "Just Married" couple.

Storybook stuff. Surely there should have been a sign on the back of the buggy: "And they lived happily ever after." If anyone wants you to be happily ever after, it's us—Mom and Dad—but we know that real life is not continual bliss. As I have tried to make clear in this book, real life brings Monday mornings, stress, pressure, problems, and—because you are both wonderful but still human—conflict. As Paul warned the Corinthians, "Those who marry will face many troubles in this life."[1]

Trust in the Lord

So, you are probably not at all surprised that Dad wants to give you some advice and counsel because Mom and I know from personal experience that misunderstandings are sure to happen. Sarah, you will get upset with Jonathan and send him coded messages about your hurts, messages that you feel are as plain as the nose on his face. Jonathan, you will get frustrated with Sarah and expect her to know what is going on inside you. After all, it is crystal clear what is wrong—crystal clear to you!

You will discover (in fact, in eighteen months you already have learned) that decoding one another is not always simple. This book has been written to help you—and countless other couples—understand how to decode the messages that every husband and wife send each other. It is chock-full of principles, ideas, tips, strategies, and practical advice on how to practice unconditional Love and Respect. All of that is helpful, but this book has one more vital ingredient: every idea, every principle, is based on God's Word. I do not base everything on Scripture in order to be "spiritually correct"; I do so because I firmly believe that in the Bible we all can learn God's deepest intent for marriage—that husband and wife should always trust Him.

You see, two atheists can have a great marriage. I know some who do.

And two atheists could practice many of the principles in this book to their benefit, but their marriage would not gladden God's heart because, as the writer to the Hebrews put it, "without faith, it is impossible to please Him."[2] I do not say this to belittle atheists or agnostics, but only to point out that, for the believer in Christ, the call is clear: "Trust in the LORD with all your heart, and do not lean on your own understanding. In all your ways, acknowledge Him, and He will make your paths straight."[3]

I could stop right here, and you would have the main piece of advice I want to give. But you know your dad. I have a few more points—actually, a few stories—I want to share about how different people have trusted God in different circumstances and how God honored their trust. I will keep them brief, but Mom and I hope these accounts will inspire both of you to make the decision to always trust in God in the big stuff and the small stuff. May "In God We Trust" be the theme of your hearts as you go forward in your God-ordained marriage. Remember, God is for you; He is behind your marriage every step of your way. As Jesus said, "What therefore God has joined together, let no man separate."[4]

Jonathan and Sarah, because God has joined you together, He wants you to trust Him completely. Especially in the tough times, He does not want you to "throw away your confidence [in Him], which has a great reward."[5] God intends to use your problems and life's painful, frustrating circumstances (including communication glitches and misunderstandings) to accomplish His purposes in you and through you.

As I said, I have some stories to share, and each one focuses on the needs and challenges that can come to us all. Each one, however, is an example of what Mom and I have learned—and are still learning—about how God calls us to trust Him. My first bit of advice, then, is this:

When one of you makes a mistake, control any anger you may feel and trust God completely no matter what happens.

Sarah, Jonathan will make mistakes, but your faith can compensate. Jonathan, Sarah will make mistakes, but your faith can help provide a solution. I'm sure you remember the story of how Mom drank one of my contacts. This was back when contact lenses were very expensive. She made a big mistake, but I compounded it by yelling at her in front of my parents. This happened well before I learned about the Love and Respect Connection, but we were definitely on the Crazy Cycle for a few minutes. After calming down, however, we asked forgiveness of each other and prayed together. My prayer was short: "Lord, You know about the contact. Your will be done. Please direct our paths. Thank You."

As soon as possible I went to see the optometrist who had fitted me with contacts, and I told him what had happened. He examined my eyes, which had always needed contacts of different strengths. Then he told me the bad news: the contact I still had was no longer powerful enough for that eye. My heart sank because it looked like I would have to buy two new contacts, something we could not afford at that time. But then he said: "The good news is that you only need one contact, since the one you have is what your other eye needs now. The one you lost needed to be replaced anyway since it wasn't strong enough."

I went home and told Mom the news, and we thanked God, reassured that He does cause all things to work together for the good of those who love Him.[6] In the Great Scheme of Things, the swallowed contact was hardly a blip on God's radar screen, but for us it was one of many small miracles we have seen Him perform over the years.

We have also seen that a good marriage is not about being great communicators who never raise their voices. It's about talking to God and listening for His answers. Sometimes He allows contacts to be swallowed so we can truly see. And a good marriage is about not staying angry at each other for days over a mistake; it's about swallowing your pride, stopping to pray, and seeking Christ's guidance.

Paul and Marilyn offer another great example of controlling your anger when your spouse blows it. (Jonathan, you might remember this couple because they often spent a day with our family while we were vacationing on the shores of Lake Michigan.) They wound up owing the bank

$1,500 because Paul made an incorrect deposit in their checking account. Instead of ranting at Paul for his slipup, Marilyn decided to pray about their need, and she urged Paul and the children to do the same. Paul replied, "What are you going to pray? I suppose you're going to ask the Lord to send a check for $1,500." A pastor with a good-sized congregation, Paul agreed to pray, but he had to admit he was a bit skeptical, especially since he was responsible for the mistake.

As the days went by, Paul would call Marilyn from the church to playfully bait her a bit, wanting to know if the check had come in the mail yet. When she had to say no, he would tease her and say, "Marilyn, you really need to pray about that." And then he would laugh at his little joke. Marilyn never got angry about his phone calls, and she always showed her husband unconditional respect even though, with his sarcasm, he might not have deserved it. But—as I have always emphasized—none of us deserve unconditional Love or Respect. With God's help, however, we can extend it to each other.

Marilyn continued to pray with quiet faith, and ten days after they learned of the overdraft, a big envelope arrived by Express Mail, sent by a couple who had been in their church before they moved to the West Coast. Inside were two smaller envelopes, one containing a check for $1,500 and the other a note: "Please accept this gift, not from us, but from the Lord." When Paul got home that evening and Marilyn showed him the check and the note, he fell backward into his chair in disbelief. And then, a bit chastened and perhaps wiser in the ways of prayer, he led the whole family in getting down on their knees and thanking the Lord for His answer.

Later, a phone call to the couple who had sent the money revealed that they had been praying together and suddenly became convinced that Paul and Marilyn had a need. Not only that, but both of them independently arrived at the same amount to send—$1,500!

There are different morals to these two stories, but for a young couple like yourselves who are in the early years of marriage, perhaps the best lesson is this: When a mistake is made, don't blame and argue and stay angry for days on end, as many couples I have counseled have done. When Mom and I start to argue over something (yes, it still happens), one of us will stop and say, "What's the point if we can't trust God with this?" At these moments we recall James' admonition to believers who were quarreling and arguing: "You do not have because you do not ask."[7] James is telling everyone to pray to God and ask God to help. In fact, James is saying that the reason many do not receive from God is that they do not ask! Jonathan and Sarah, *always ask God to meet whatever need is causing the stress.* Especially ask when one of you may be failing to show proper Love and Respect, which brings us to my next point . . .

Depend on the Lord

It's an interesting fact: your mate cannot possibly meet all your needs. A lot of couples spend years on the Crazy Cycle because she thinks he should meet all her needs for Love and he thinks she should meet all his needs for Respect. Mom and I did this for a while until we both realized that thinking your spouse can meet all your needs is a dead end. So we settled the "meet all my needs" issue quite awhile ago. We both know we are called to Love and Respect each other, and God wants us to meet many of each other's needs. But meet them *all?* It will never happen, because we are human, not God. So . . .

Depend on God, not your mate, to meet all your needs.

As you know, I get hundreds of e-mails every month. One wife wrote to tell about her eye-opening experience. It was as though the Lord spoke to her and said, "If your husband could fulfill all of your desires, you would never come to Me." There it is! This is why He never did require us to meet all of each other's needs. The woman's letter continues:

> It hit me like a ton of bricks. All of a sudden it was as if my eyes were opened for the first time to see what I had been doing. All this time I had been trying to change my husband into someone I needed him to be. In essence, I was saying, "I need to fix you,

so that you can turn around and fix *me*, because . . . deep down inside, I have an unfulfilled desire, and you need to meet it." But you know what? He'll *never* meet it. He can't because he's not perfect. But the deep, unfulfilled desire in my heart is for perfection, and that can only be met in Christ and Christ alone.

This gal gets it! Ultimately, no human being can meet all of our deepest needs. Some, yes, but not all, and part of the journey is figuring out which needs to let go of and which to hang on to.

Another wife wrote and related that, since the day of her wedding, there had been conflict between her and her husband. This went on for some twenty years as she felt God wouldn't forgive her. Finally, however, she decided to quit trying to make things change by herself and seek the Lord, His help, and His forgiveness. An unexplainable feeling of peace and contentment replaced her feelings of panic and worry. As a result, she was able to communicate with her husband in a totally different way.

Her letter continues:

I was shocked over the way I was just able to express the hurt I felt and not attack him or get angry . . . The peace I felt and desire to please God amazed me. Usually I just want to prove my point and know he is wrong . . . Also, after watching the Love and Respect videos, I am beginning to understand more of how he communicates . . . He is not a woman, so he doesn't communicate like a woman. That helps me not to get so upset. At times I still hurt—a lot—but there is an incredible sense of trusting God and letting Him deal with situations.

Jonathan and Sarah, two thoughts: First, this lady is right on. One of you is pink and the other is blue, and you communicate differently. The trick is exchanging sunglasses and hearing aids now and then—and see and hear as the other sees and hears. Second, as the two of you launch your marriage, there will be times of discontent and anxiety. Stop and ask the Lord if these times are wake-up calls asking you to find your deepest contentment and peace in Him, not in each other. Oh yes, one more thing. When your spouse starts demanding that you meet some need, never say, "Quit making me your god. I cannot meet your needs." That would be an excellent way to be right but to use the truth in entirely the wrong way.

Trust God with the Whys

My letter is winding down, but one other bit of advice is crucial:

Above all, trust God when the whys of life threaten to overwhelm you.

Of course everybody asks, "Why?" Even Jesus, as He hung on the cross, cried, "My God, my God, why have You forsaken Me?"[8]

We know God doesn't answer all our questions, particularly those that begin with "Why?" During those moments, will we close off to God or continue to trust Him? Jesus trusted His heavenly Father even when the cross seemed to render the Almighty loveless and powerless. We, too, may have moments when something very painful is beyond our understanding. It is natural to ask "Why?"—but what then? Where do we go from there?

Years ago I married a godly couple, he with a genetic defect that confined him to a wheelchair, she with horrible scars all over her body from burns that had also left her maimed. Nonetheless, Mark and Kim envisioned a wonderful life together, one that would include having children. They consulted specialists who assured them they could have a healthy child.

They prayed and prayed for God's guidance. Finally, feeling the advice from genetics experts was part of His leading, they went ahead and had a baby girl, Elizabeth—who was born with the same genetic defects as her father.

Shock turned to deep disillusionment. Mark and Kim both felt bushwhacked by God. They asked the inevitable question: "Why?" When He did not answer, they pulled back from God and away from each other. Their anger and disenchantment grew, and even though our elders prayed with them, their home remained full of negative tension, and their hearts remained cold toward God.

Two years later Kim came to my office to tell me about something extraordinary that had happened. Although numb toward God, she had continued having a devotional time. A Christian friend had encouraged her to keep reading the Bible, and because she respected this friend so much, she did so even though she didn't feel like it. One morning during her devotional time, Kim sensed Christ's presence on the other side of the room. Then she heard an inaudible voice: "Kim, are you ready to open your heart to Me?"

"No!" she said firmly, and the Presence was gone. Christ had stood at the door of Kim's heart and knocked, and she did not invite Him in for sweet communion that she enjoyed in the past.[9] But she could not remain hardened after her Encounter, and she had come to me, her pastor, for help. We prayed and Kim opened the door of her heart, saying, "Lord, not my will, but Your will be done." His presence filled her soul, and we rejoiced together. Not long after Kim regained fellowship with God, Mark turned the corner as well, yet to this day their heavenly Father has been silent about the "Why?"

The point of this story is simple, but not always easy to accept: God won't answer all of our prayers our way. His thoughts are not our thoughts, and His ways are not ours either.[10] There will be those "Why?" situations that we cannot understand, but God calls us to trust Him in light of what we *do* understand. As Mark, who—despite his handicap—became a successful insurance agent and a nine-time qualifying member of the Million Dollar Round Table, puts it, "We cannot affect the winds, but we can adjust the sails."

Jonathan and Sarah, I cannot close without talking just a bit about the ultimate "Why?"—the "why?" we ask when someone dies, particularly if the death is premature or totally unexpected. I don't want to be morbid, especially around vibrant young people like yourselves who have a full life to live. But God sometimes takes early those with everything to live for, including Clyde McDowell, one of my closest friends from college. He had several fruitful pastorates and eventually became a seminary president. Then one day he phoned: "Pray for me, Emerson. I have a brain tumor."

The news hit everyone hard, but Clyde did not spend much time asking "Why?" During his illness, with the help of his lovely wife, Lee, he wrote a pamphlet called "Reflections on an Unexpected Journey." He told how he and his family had reflected together on their lives and their blessings, but at the same time they had acknowledged there would be hard days ahead according to God's sovereign plan. They weren't doubting God's goodness, only admitting that becoming like Jesus could mean painful suffering as well as joyful blessings.[11]

And then Clyde wrote: "In light of the current events in our lives as a couple, we willingly accept whatever God has for us . . . so, while this is the hardest in our twenty-five years of marriage, we're closer to God than ever, closer to each other, and our kids are more bonded to us than any other time."

Within the year Clyde was with the Lord, but his testimony lives in many hearts, including Mom's and mine. The reason I bring up something as sad as this is not to be depressing, but honest. The reality of death helps Mom and me not to sweat the small stuff. We have our tiffs, but because of our experiences in life, we see many problems as inconsequential. So, my final bit of advice is to *never stop unconditionally Loving and Respecting each other because of Mickey Mouse concerns.* This doesn't mean you can't argue over mundane issues, of which there will be many. Have your arguments and tiffs, but drop them quickly. Don't spend your lives as some couples do, arguing and quarreling over where to go on vacation or what color carpet to buy.

Sometimes as I have listened to couples duel over all kinds of small stuff, I have thought, "You should walk through a graveyard for an hour or so and read the tombstones. Remind yourself that life is too short to fuss and fret over trivial irritations."

I love the song you requested be sung at your wedding. "When It's All Been Said and Done" sums up the Rewarded Cycle as well as this entire book. Life is not first about the two of you and your marriage. It's first about your commitment to Jesus Christ and doing everything you do for Him. Do *that* and then unconditional Love and Respect will be yours. As the song says:

> When it's all been said and done, there is just one thing that matters.
> Did I do my best to live for truth? Did I live my life for You?
> When it's all been said and done, all my treasures will mean nothing.
> Only what I've done for love's Reward will stand the test of time.
> For You've shown me Heaven's my true home . . .
> When it's all been said and done, You're my life when life is gone.[12]

That's it. That's our advice and counsel to you as you continue along on the greatest adventure two people could ever have—living together to glorify the Lord. We know you will do it well, as in God you always trust.

With Love and Respect,
Dad and Mom

ENDNOTES

Introduction

1. Focus on the Family, Ministry Analysis Department, "2005 Love and Respect Survey," p. 12. Focus on the Family is a sponsor of many Love and Respect marriage conferences, and at our request its Ministry Analysis Department conducted research to learn what is happening long-term with married couples who are familiar with the Love and Respect message. The survey included over eight hundred respondents who had either read *Love & Respect*, attended a Love and Respect Conference, watched a Love and Respect video, or learned about Love and Respect from our website. Results of the survey are very encouraging:

* 49% of respondents were extremely or very much helped to have a stronger marriage.
* 88% of respondents were still applying Love and Respect principles in their marriage.
* 72% of those who had been contemplating separation were no longer doing so after learning about Love and Respect.
* 54% of those who had been separated had reconciled after learning about and applying the principles of Love and Respect.
* 72% of those who had been contemplating divorce were no longer doing so after learning about the Love and Respect principles.
* 64% of those who had been taking active steps toward a divorce were no longer doing so after being exposed to Love and Respect materials.

Research also showed that men and women strongly agreed that the clear teaching of Ephesians 5:33—wives must unconditionally respect their husbands—was a new concept for them and should continue to be stressed as a key difference between the Love and Respect message and other marriage materials and programs.

Chapter 3

1. Anytime we address male and female differences, we obviously generalize to some degree. Generalizations are dangerous if they are not generally true, but if a generalization *is* generally true, it gives us a glimpse into another person's soul. I realize that there are males and females who are exceptions to my general observations, but these exceptions do not negate the truth of the generalizations, which are based on my observation of thousands of married couples. Whenever I make a generalization, my intent is not to negatively stereotype anyone, but to create greater understanding.

2. In Part III, "Communicate to Stop the Crazy Cycle," I devote an entire chapter to a tool all couples must learn to use well—forgiveness.

3. Emerson Eggerichs, *Love & Respect* (Nashville: Integrity, 2004), 145–146.

4. Judges 4:6–15 is the account of how Deborah accompanies Barak, general of the Israelite forces, into battle and then draws out Sisera and his Canaanite army in order to give them into Barak's hand.

5. For those struggling with pornographic addiction, contact http://www.pureintimacy.org, a ministry under Focus on the Family. Or call 1-800-A-FAMILY (232-6459), talk with a counselor, and rest assured of strict confidentiality.

6. When using the phrase *not wrong, just different*, we are referring to the normal differences between male and female that exist as a result of God's creation. We are not suggesting that a husband or wife is never wrong. When a husband or wife sins, he or she is wrong!

Chapter 4

1. Paul was wrestling with the civil war between the human spirit and the carnal flesh. On the one hand, Paul experienced the law of God in his inner person. He was created in the image of God, and part of that image included the law of God within him. Yet he battled the law of sin which resides in the carnal flesh. Paul talked about this battle in Romans 7:25—"So then, on the one hand I myself with my mind am serving the law of God, but on the other, with my flesh the law of sin." Which side wins? Sin wins by keeping us out of heaven apart from faith in Jesus Christ's substitutionary atonement for us, yet we can still have goodwill while living on earth.

But because the law of sin exists, some argue that no person can intend or do good. Some have interpreted the theological term *total depravity* to mean that humans are absolutely incapable of doing one ounce of good or having one pure motive. But *total* doesn't mean absolute. An analogy is dye in a vase of water. When we put a drop of black dye into a vase of pure water, the dye *totally* colors the vase, yet H_2O is still in the vase. In the same way, sin colors the totality of a person's being, yet the law of God within still remains. Sin does not absolutely or totally obliterate the image of God or the law of God in us.

And both saved and unsaved people can serve that law of God at a certain level. Each can act on the residual image of God within. For instance, people can do good and even have goodwill. An unsaved mother has goodwill toward her children and does good for her children, and an unsaved spouse can hold goodwill toward his or her mate and do much good. But proper motives and benevolent deeds cannot save people, that is, earn them entrance into heaven. A person cannot serve the law of God sufficiently to merit eternal life. Only faith in what Jesus Christ did on the cross saves an individual.

Further, every believer struggles with overcoming the carnal flesh. The good news is that the Holy Spirit—the Helper—is now in the believer and can be depended upon to help overcome the carnal flesh. If you are a believer, the more you trust in and depend on the Holy Spirit, the more you can show goodwill toward your mate and act more consistently with those intentions.

2. In Ephesians 6:5–9 Paul is addressing slaves and masters, but his teaching about "serving with good will" applies to all believers. Slaves are to render service with goodwill (v. 7), and masters are to "do the same things to them" because there is no partiality with God (v. 9). Bottom line, if slaves can serve with goodwill, married people can!

3. In 1 Corinthians 7:25–35, Paul is saying that celibacy is desirable because it is easier to concentrate on serving the Lord, but marriage is permissible. Paul had the gift of celibacy, but he realized "it is better to marry than to burn with passion" (1 Corinthians 7:9 NIV). Here Paul echoes the teaching of Jesus in Matthew 19 where He closes the door on all divorce except in cases of immorality. When His disciples hear Him state that marriage is such a binding agreement, they respond, "It is better not to marry" (v. 10 NIV). Jesus tells them that not everyone can accept His teaching and then goes on to say: "For example, some men are celibate because they were born that way. Others are celibate because they were castrated. Still others have decided to be celibate because of the kingdom of heaven. If anyone can do what you've suggested, then he should do it" (Matthew 19:12 GW). In other words, Jesus was saying that everyone, except those who are celibate, must get married and remain married. Paul was also well aware that marriage demanded maturity and commitment. In 1 Corinthians 7:28, he says: "But if you do get married, it is not a sin. . . . However, I am trying to spare you the extra problems that come with marriage" (NLT). In 1 Corinthians 7 Paul does not dwell on the negative; he wants the church at Corinth to know there is an upside to marriage, but that a good marriage will take work and growing together. Paul explains that husband and wife are concerned with pleasing each other, that this is a good thing, and that both spouses must trust in that foundational fact. In other words, with all the pressures and challenges of marriage, spouses must believe that their mates have goodwill toward them.

Chapter 6

1. Some scholars speculate that Michal was so upset with David's behavior because his linen ephod didn't cover him properly, especially in front of servant girls who were part of the cheering crowd welcoming back the ark of the covenant (see, for example, 2 Samuel 6:20 in the Contemporary English Version). But my own research leaves no question in my mind that, in addition to the ephod, David wore linen breeches that reached "from the loins even to the thighs" (see Exodus 28:42). In my view David would not have taken only the partial garb of a Levite priest on this very holy occasion and then risk "exposing himself" inappropriately. Doing so would have been totally contrary to God's commands to the Levites. In Exodus 20:26, for example, God spoke to the people through Moses: "And you may not approach my altar by steps. If you do, someone might look up under the skirts of your clothing and see your nakedness" (NLT). Exposing one's nakedness in any measure was a horrible violation of God's law. In light of this

historical background, it is hard to say what Michal really had on her mind. Perhaps she did think David was dressed "shamelessly," and perhaps from her distant vantage point he looked as if he were exposing himself. It is also possible that Michal simply felt—and this would have been totally *her* problem—that David was not acting and dressing like a proper king, which brought disgrace not only on him but on her, his wife, as well. Because of her contempt, I am convinced that she exaggerates what David did in order to embarrass him in the same way that she felt he had embarrassed her. The fact that she called David's actions "shameless," however, does not make them so. Interestingly, David does not believe that the servant girls who watched him dance before the Lord were ashamed of him; in fact he is persuaded that they would feel nothing but honor for him (2 Samuel 6:22). Finally, due to the fact that Michal remained barren for the rest of her life, I believe God judged her for her contemptuous attitude and bitter, untruthful words.

2. See "To Communicate Feelings or Start Discussion," "Taboos," and "Things to Say to Lighten Up the Relationship" in Emerson Eggerichs, *Love & Respect* (Nashville: Integrity, 2004), 306–307.

3. Our thanks and appreciation to Roy Bronkema, who attended one of our Love and Respect Conferences and then wrote to tell us how it helped his marriage. Roy contributed many of the ideas for the John and Mary discussion.

Chapter 7

1. God commands us to forgive, but He never asks us to be foolish. For ideas on what to do about a spouse who is committing serious offenses that put you and your children in danger, see Appendix B, "Forgiving—But Also Confronting—the Three A's: Adultery, Abuse, Addiction," p. 338.

Chapter 9

1. See Ephesians 4:26.

2. For a complete discussion of Conquest—appreciating a husband's desire to work and achieve—see chapter 16 in *Love & Respect* (Nashville: Integrity, 2004).

3. For an explanation of biblical hierarchy and how both male chauvinism and radical feminism misinterpret Scripture, see chapter 17, "Hierarchy—Appreciate His Desire to Protect and Provide," *Love & Respect*, especially pp. 205–209.

4. For a complete explanation of the "51 percent rule" and other aspects of Authority—appreciating a husband's desire to serve and to lead—see chapter 18 of *Love & Respect*, especially pp. 221–222.

5. See chapter 19, "Insight—Appreciate His Desire to Analyze and Counsel," in *Love & Respect*, especially pp. 229–230.

6. For a fuller explanation, with illustrations of how shoulder-to-shoulder activities work, see chapter 20, "Relationship—Appreciate His Desire for Shoulder-to-Shoulder Friendship" in *Love & Respect*.

7. For a more complete discussion, see chapter 21, "Sexuality—Appreciate His Desire for Sexual Intimacy" in *Love & Respect*, pp. 249.

8. See Patrick Kampert, "Whetting Your Appetite for Sex," Chicago Tribune, © 2003.

Mr. Kampert's insightful article on Michelle Weiner-Davis's approach to counseling married couples on sex can be accessed on the Smart Marriages website—http://smartmarriages. com/. To learn more about Weiner-Davis, a licensed clinical social worker with a master's degree in social work from the University of Kansas, see her two books: *The Sex-Starved Marriage: A Couple's Guide to Boosting Their Marriage Libido* (New York: Simon & Schuster, 2003) and *Divorce Busting* (New York: Simon & Schuster, 1993).

Chapter 10

1. Just because a wife feels unloved does not mean that her husband is in fact unloving. Regardless, he must still deal with her negativity in a positive way that will help keep the Energizing Cycle going.

Chapter 12

1. John Gottman, arguably the most respected marriage researcher around, writes: "In the research literature on marital interaction that has used observational methods, women's marital interaction . . . has been consistently described as more confronting, demanding, coercive, and highly emotional . . . than the interaction of their husbands." See John M. Gottman, *What Predicts Divorce? The Relationship between Marital Processes and Marital Outcomes* (Hillsdale, NJ: Lawrence Erlbaum, 1994), iii.

2. The phrase *weaker vessel* should not be interpreted to mean that a woman is inferior to a man. Peter is speaking of how God made the wife to be like a delicate porcelain bowl, not a copper or cast-iron pot. For more on this, see *Love & Respect* (Integrity, 2004), 146–147.

Chapter 13

1. In 1 Peter 2, Peter teaches Christians who are under persecution to live as God's chosen people, honoring Him in all circumstances, no matter how they are treated. After setting this standard for all believers, slave or free, the apostle goes on to address wives and then husbands about living in this same way to honor God. The wife who unconditionally respects her husband with a gentle and quiet spirit when he has been unloving and doesn't deserve it finds favor with God (see 1 Peter 3:1–6). Likewise, a husband who seeks to be understanding of his wife when he finds it hard to understand her, especially when she has been disrespectful, finds favor with God (see 1 Peter 3:7). Treating a spouse with unconditional love and respect earns God's blessing and rewards.

2. When Peter says that "the Spirit of glory and of God rests on you," he uses the present middle indicative. This grammatical term simply means that the subject (the Holy Spirit, who is "the Spirit of glory and of God") is acting so as to participate in some way in the results of the action. In other words, the Holy Spirit rests upon the believer and, by implication, gives the believer rest and refreshment. (The idea is similar to what Jesus promised in Matthew 11:28.) I have worked with many husbands or wives who can sense the Holy Spirit resting upon them in the midst of their suffering in a troubled marriage.

3. What is a Respect card? From *Love & Respect* (Integrity, 2004), we read:

Suppose you are a wife who trusts her husband. He may not be perfect as the head of the family, but you are quite willing to allow him to live that role as you submit to his leadership. How can you apply what I've been saying? Can you show him respect in his role as the head and the leader? One of the simplest methods that I suggest for wives is to send their husbands what I call a "respect card." According to my research, men seldom keep love cards their wives send them with all the little hearts, Xs, and Os. But I will guarantee you he will keep a card you send him that says, "I was thinking about you the other day, that you would die for me. That is an overwhelming thought to me." Sign it, "With all my respect, the one who still admires you." Remember, do not sign it, "With all my love." He knows you love him. Sign it, "With all my respect." Your husband will keep that card forever. You will walk in on him years from now and find him re-reading that card. Why? Because you said it his way—in his mother tongue. To speak in a husband's mother tongue of respect is very powerful, indeed (p. 212).

4. See Emerson Eggerichs, *Love & Respect* (Integrity, 2004), 274–275. This "Cha Ching!" word picture is from my own imagination. No one knows exactly how the Lord is keeping a record of what we do and say in order to reward us.

5. As you have been reading this chapter, perhaps you have felt the need to stop and talk to God about your situation, particularly if you are currently facing extremely difficult trials in your marriage. For encouragement in asking something of God right now, see Appendix F, "My Prayer in This Time of Trial," p. 354.

6. Statistics from "Marriage Friendly Therapy," a paper presented at the Smart Marriages Conference in Atlanta, Georgia, June 2006, by Dr. William Doherty, member of the Department of Family Social Service, University of Minnesota. Dr. Doherty has become increasingly burdened about therapists who are not friendly toward the institution of marriage. His article "How Therapists Harm Marriages and What We Can Do about It" is available on his website http://www.marriagefriendlytherapists.com/. Go to his website for assistance in asking the right questions of your therapist.

7. Here John warns Christians about the teaching of the Gnostics, a heretical movement very prominent in the culture of his day. This teaching had infiltrated the church and was spreading such heresy as the incarnation and Jesus' resurrection did not happen. What John writes can, however, also be taken as a warning to believers today because our culture bombards us with ideas that are anti-Christian and anti-marriage.

Chapter 15

1. This is an allusion to Ephesians 4:20–21 where Paul says emphatically, "That is not the way you learned Christ!—assuming that you have heard about him and were taught in him, as the truth is in Jesus" (ESV).

2. A discussion of "How to Use the Respect Test with Your Husband" is found on pages 185–186 of *Love & Respect*.

3. Matthew 6:14–15 should not be interpreted to mean that a believer in Christ forfeits salvation for not forgiving someone. Instead, the believer's fellowship with God is disrupted. See chapter 7, p. 118.

Chapter 16

1. While writing this book, I noticed a dark spot on my forearm. I knew that something like that should be examined by a doctor, so I went in for a checkup. My doctor diagnosed it as melanoma and said I needed a biopsy to determine how serious it was. For several days I wondered if my melanoma was the deadly type (6,500 out of 32,000 people diagnosed with melanoma die each year). In the midst of my uncertainties, I also realized that I was ready to go home because I am in God's hands. Sarah and I rejoiced when the tests came back showing my melanoma was superficial. A few days later a surgeon removed it, and I was pronounced 100 percent cured. I am encouraged and thankful that once again God showed me I do not have to fear bad news; all I have to do is trust in His care for me (see Psalm 112:7).

2. "Standing on the Promises of God," R. Kelso Carter, 1886.

3. See 1 Peter 4:8.

Conclusion

1. 1 Corinthians 7:28 NIV.

2. Hebrews 11:6.

3. Proverbs 3:5–6.

4. Matthew 19:6.

5. Hebrews 10:35.

6. See Romans 8:28 NLT.

7. James 4:2.

8. Matthew 27:46 NIV.

9. See Revelation 3:20, a verse often used incorrectly concerning salvation. It is actually a verse for believers who are out of fellowship with Jesus.

10. See Isaiah 55:8–9.

11. See Philippians 3:10–11.

12. "When It's All Been Said and Done"

Appendix A

1. For how to deal with a spouse who has committed or is still committing serious moral offenses, see Appendix B, p. 338. It explains how to confront as well as forgive the offender. Forgiveness may well include consequences that need to be lovingly communicated and firmly enforced.

How to Get Off a Chronic Crazy Cycle Caused by Low-Grade Resentment

I hear from couples all across America and around the world who are on what I call "a chronic Crazy Cycle." They have been spinning on this cycle for months or even years, but they don't understand why. In most of these cases, there is no adultery, abuse, or addiction. Both spouses have basic goodwill and are faithful. But they still manage to treat each other in ways that leave her feeling unloved and him feeling disrespected. As a result of the craziness, she feels offended and he feels offended. Both hold a grudge and feel low-grade resentment toward the other.

Sadly, adultery, abuse, and addiction often arise in such an atmosphere. When both feel offended and hold a grudge, one or both are more vulnerable to temptations and pressures to commit one of the 3 A's. How can a couple break out of their chronic Crazy Cycle before something devastating happens?

First, realize that since you have been on the Crazy Cycle for months or even years, both of you are contributing to the craziness. Wife, though you feel unloved, you have been feeding the Crazy Cycle by appearing disrespectful. Husband, though you feel disrespected, you have been feeding the Crazy Cycle by appearing unloving.

Negative feelings toward a spouse can subside when we see ourselves as equally sinful. A wife's challenge is to realize her disrespect is as wrong as her husband's lack of love. She, too, is disobeying God's command to respect. A husband's challenge is to realize his lack of love is as wrong as his wife's disrespect. He, too, is disobeying God's command to love. What Jesus taught can motivate us to look at ourselves. "He who is without sin among you, let him be the first to throw a stone" (John 8:7).

If both of you are willing to admit that it takes two to keep a Crazy Cycle going, then there is hope. Both of you must admit that nursing grudges and a low-grade resentment has been doing no good. Something needs to change, and together you can make it happen by following the same three steps of forgiveness described in chapter 7. Here is what you can do:

First, sympathize with each other.

Husband, sympathize with your wife. Assume that, generally speaking, she feels you have been as unloving to her as you feel she has been disrespectful to you. Feel her pain as you expect her to feel yours. Trust that, just as you did not intend to be unloving, she did not intend to be disrespectful. And just as you defensively reacted in a way that offended her, so she defensively reacted in a way that offended you. Be aware that she reacted disrespectfully because she felt you were overlooking or neglecting her deepest need—love.

Don't judge her for this; sympathize with her. Look beyond the offense (her disrespect) to see other factors that explain why she offended you (something was making her feel unloved). Try to look more deeply into the heart of your wife. When you do, you will be able to pray, "Father, forgive her, for she did not know what she was doing." I receive countless e-mails from wives who admit they didn't know they were being so disrespectful. As one wife put it:

> I disrespected and dishonored my husband out of my own pain, never even realizing that it was equivalent to his not showing me the love I needed in the way that I needed it. I am ashamed and remorseful, especially after reading how much I've hurt him by my lack of respect. I just didn't know . . .

Wife, sympathize with your husband. Assume that, generally speaking, he feels you have been as disrespectful to him as you feel he has been unloving to you. Feel his pain as you expect him to feel yours. Trust that, just as you did not intend to be disrespectful, he did not intend to be unloving. Just as you defensively reacted in a way that offended him, so he defensively reacted in a way that offended you. Realize that he reacted unlovingly because he felt you were overlooking or neglecting his deepest need—respect.

Don't judge him for this; sympathize with him. Look beyond the offense (his failure to love) to see other factors that explain why he offended you (something was making him feel disrespected). When you look more deeply into his heart, you will be able to pray, "Father, forgive him, for he did not know what he was doing." In their e-mails, husbands tell me:

> I didn't realize what was going on inside me, nor how I was coming across to my wife. In reading your book I realized that my need for respect was not being met, but I had not been able to put my finger on this. All I knew was that I was frustrated and angry. I did what you say the typical guy does. I shut her out. I wasn't going to let her treat me this way. In doing this I crushed her. She wanted to be close to me, but I pushed her away.

Second, relinquish your will to God's will.

Husband, when you feel disrespected, do you get angry and decide to be unloving in order to teach your wife a lesson? Do you say to yourself, "I'm not going to be lovey-dovey until she starts showing me more respect"? Perhaps you engage in stonewalling (withdrawing and saying nothing). When you act this way, does your wife react even more disrespectfully and accuse you of being unloving? Do you, in turn, react by pulling away from her even more? I understand your feelings because I have been there and done the same thing.

Acting like this, however, only feeds the Crazy Cycle. Suppose your wife starts something by getting red hot toward you for no real reason. If you react defensively, you simply toss gasoline on the fire. You inflame things with your unloving reactions. You act not like a firefighter but an arsonist. In effect, you are saying to God, "Not Your will but my will be done!" But, of course, your will and your way will not work. Though you cannot control your wife's will, you can surrender your will to God's will, and God's will is for you to love your wife. When you do this, several things happen. You stop feeding the craziness by your willful lack of love. When you obey God's will to love your wife, she tends to soften, and, amazingly, your low-grade resentment evaporates along with the grudge you were holding against your wife. Here is what husbands continue to tell me:

> Whenever we argued, I felt she was attacking me. To defend myself, I would fire back with verbal assaults. I thought that this way I could get her to back off, but she didn't, and over time I just resented her. So, next I tried stonewalling her, just refusing to say anything, which only made it worse. After hearing about Love and Respect, it hit me hard that my attitude was not achieving anything in my wife's heart but hurt and disillusionment. Teaching her a lesson made me feel good for a few minutes, but it didn't change anything. It was then I knew I had to do things differently.

Wife, when you feel unloved, do you get angry and decide to be disrespectful in order to teach your husband a lesson? Do you say, "I don't feel much respect toward you when you are so unloving"? If you say anything like this, all he hears is disrespectful criticism. He may or may not accuse you of being disrespectful because he is probably not accustomed to using the term, but he *feels* disrespected nonetheless. Then he probably reacts even more unlovingly, and you, in turn, try to sting your husband with more belittling words. My wife, Sarah, understands your feelings because she has done the same thing.

Acting like this, however, only feeds the Crazy Cycle. Though your husband may have started things by getting red hot toward you, when you react defensively, you simply throw gasoline on the conflict. You inflame the situation with your disrespectful reactions. You act not like a firefighter but an arsonist. In effect, you are saying to God, "Not your will but my will be done!" But, of course, your will and your way will not work. Though you cannot control your husband's will, you can surrender your will to God's will, and God's will is for you to respect your husband. When you do this, several things happen. You stop feeding the craziness your willful lack of respect is causing. When you obey God's will to respect your husband, he tends to soften, and, amazingly, your low-grade resentment evaporates along with the grudge you were holding against your husband. A wife who realized she had to let go and try God's way wrote:

> Before I became familiar with the message of Love and Respect, I treated my husband poorly. I would nag him, remind him to do stuff over and over, roll my eyes, make sarcastic remarks, and, when those methods failed me (which they almost always did), I would either throw a temper tantrum and threaten divorce or get depressed and stop talking completely. My husband has not read *Love & Respect* and is only vaguely familiar with the message, but by my making changes [in] myself, I think our marriage is a lot stronger. I try to soften my tone, show him respect in what I say and do, and treat him as I would someone I am trying to impress! I am trying to do what God commands in His Word, and it

works! We get along better, my husband takes his role as leader of the family more seriously, and he treats me better. Once I became convinced that I was never going to change my husband and I could only change myself, I became willing to try a different way. Now my way and God's way are one.

Third, anticipate God helping you on His terms.

Husband, when you surrender your will to God's will, you are coming to God on His terms. He is pleased, and you can anticipate His help at some level. You will know you have surrendered to His will when you can be loving in the face of your wife's disrespect. The very things she has been doing to "cause" you to be unforgiving and unloving will now trigger a loving response in you. Paradoxical? Yes. Unfair? Yes, but this response of unconditional love is what God favors. Your attitude of unconditional love for your wife can precipitate the working of God's Spirit in your lives. This does not mean you endorse her sinful ways, but that you forgive her and then confront her with an attitude of love that is unconditional.

Is showing *unconditional* love difficult? Indeed it is, but if you are to confidently anticipate that God will work in your marriage, that attitude is crucial. So, like Jesus, will you believe that—as you entrust yourself to your heavenly Father—He will judge the situation righteously? Do you believe that He will fulfill His will when you say, "Thy will be done"? Then *unconditionally* forgive and love your wife and leave the rest in God's hands.

A husband e-mailed me to say he was walking and praying one evening, complaining to God about his marriage: "Dear Father in heaven, You know I love You and want to serve You in this marriage, but I am dying. I can stay married, but I have no love for my wife. I don't even like her. If we weren't married, we wouldn't even be friends."

At that moment God spoke to him, not in an audible voice, but Kevin still heard God say, "Kevin, when you prayed and asked Me for a wife, you said the most important reason for getting married is to love someone other than yourself and to lead any children you have closer to Me. Well, I have given you a woman who needs a LOT of love. Now go and love her."

Right then Kevin realized that God helped him by speaking to him very clearly. It wasn't necessarily the kind of help Kevin was looking for, but he knew God was helping him in the way he needed to be helped. He decided to listen to what God had said and trust Him to work. He went home, wept before his wife, and told her he would stop trying to change her. Kevin experienced what the psalmist describes: "In my distress . . . I cried to my God for help. From his temple he heard my voice" (Psalm 18:6 NIV).

Wife, when you surrender your will to God's will, you are coming to God on His terms. He is pleased, and you can anticipate His help at some level.

You will know you have surrendered to His will when you can be respectful in the face of your husband's lack of love. The very things he has been doing to "cause" you to be unforgiving and disrespectful should trigger a respectful response in you. Paradoxical? Yes. Unfair? Yes, but this response of unconditional respect is what God favors. Your act of unconditional respect for your husband can precipitate the working of God's Spirit in your lives.

Is showing *unconditional* respect difficult? Indeed it is, but if you are to confidently anticipate that God will work in your marriage, that attitude is crucial. So, like Jesus, will you believe that—as you entrust yourself to your heavenly Father—He will judge the situation righteously? Do you believe that He will fulfill His will when you say, "Your will be done"? Then *unconditionally* forgive and respect your husband and leave the rest in God's hands.

A wife writes:

We do still struggle at times. Mostly the struggle is within me, when I feel frustrated that I have to do all the work. But I keep reminding myself that the old way didn't work out, so my only choice is to take responsibility for my part—my actions, words, and thoughts. I pray for God's help not to slip into my old ways (which were selfish and usually involved thinking of ways to manipulate my husband or divorce him). Things are not perfect, and we have a lot of stress in our lives (two small children, financial struggles, and a cross-country move), but I am hopeful that things will continue to get better.

Things are "getting better" as this wife anticipates that God is at work. When Jesus said, "I will ask the Father, and He will give you another Helper, that He may be with you forever" (John 14:16), He intended for us to believe the Helper truly does help!

What to Say When Forgiving Less Serious Offenses

Suppose your spouse has committed no serious moral transgression, such as adultery, abuse, or addiction.[1] The offense has been something everyday, such as stepping on your air hose in any one of a dozen ways. Bottom line, your spouse has been frustrating you by acting in ways that feel unloving (if you're a wife) or disrespectful (if you're a husband). Though you have successfully taken the three important steps of sympathizing with your spouse, relinquishing your will to God's will, and anticipating God's help (the problem at hand isn't major so these three steps are easy enough to take), something seems to be missing. It may be that you need to extend forgiveness and seek forgiveness. To turn that corner and get off the Crazy Cycle related to matters that don't come close to the three A's, here is something you might say or possibly write in a note. You may want to use the following verbatim or adapt it to your own way of saying things:

I was angry at myself for not understanding earlier what you were feeling and then reacting to you so negatively. But I was also angry with your reaction to me. We seem to get on this

Crazy Cycle all too quickly over the smallest of issues. You hurt me, and I hurt you over little things. But I think you'll agree that God has revealed to us that you have goodwill toward me and I have goodwill toward you. I am sure God wants us to stop this petty craziness. We have both acted defensively, but it's time to try to understand each other and forgive each other. I forgive you for [whatever the little offense might have been], and I ask you to forgive me for my words or actions that helped cause the problem.

If you are writing a note based on the above, sign it "With all my love" if you're writing to your wife or "With all my respect" if you are writing to your husband.

How One Wife Lost Her Resentment and Saved Her Marriage

If you are still unconvinced that the three steps to forgiveness can really help you get rid of low-grade resentment toward your spouse, please read the following story. Often what it takes is *a change in perspective*, as one wife discovered. She wrote to tell of how her husband, a music director, had to take a job in a church eighty miles from their home. She did not want him to take the position but agreed that it appeared to be the best place for him to serve despite the 160-mile drive each day. Her husband commuted for two years, but then newly diagnosed health problems, along with the long drive, took their toll. They decided to sell their home and move to the town where he worked, but it meant moving from a 2,800-square-foot home they had custom built to a 1,500-square-foot older home that cost more than the larger home due to a difference in property values.

While their children adjusted quite well, being moved out of her comfort zone made this wife subtly resentful. She began putting her husband down with angry comments that were more covert than overt, all the while assuming the stance of "Look what I did for my husband." As a result he slowly withdrew from her, and when she tried to get him to talk, he withdrew even more. For months they were on the Crazy Cycle, the wife feeling her husband was the one who needed to change. Then she began reading *Love & Respect* and listening to our CD. Absorbing the Love and Respect message was like taking blinders off her eyes. Her resentment and bitterness melted away, and she wrote her husband a letter listing reasons why she respected him. Her letter to me continues:

> I apologized for hurting him and for wounding the spirit that God gave him as a man. I also told him that, when decisions needed to be made and we could not reach a compromise, his word would stand. I also tried to explain to him that, if he can learn to move toward me when I seem upset, this will defuse the "upset" very much. It was strange, but the more I focused on the things that I respected about my husband, the more love I began to feel toward him once again. I absolutely feel like a weight has been lifted from us. I know I still have a long way to go to get this respect concept to come more naturally, but for the first time in a long time, I am excited to be with my husband, and he seems equally excited to be in my presence. Thank you for bringing this biblical truth to light for me. I have wasted so much time simply because I did not understand how to connect with my husband. I can hardly wait to practice this more and more because I know that we are now going to create a win-win partnership instead of a lose-lose relationship, and I know our children will really be the benefactors as they see our relationship strengthened and they see God reflected through our marriage.

What If Your Spouse Does Not Respond to Your Forgiveness?

If you have been on a chronic Crazy Cycle for months or quite possibly years, these three steps provide the way out. But after you relinquish your bitterness and resentment to God and move toward forgiveness, can you be sure your spouse will respond positively? Not necessarily. One wife wrote to tell me she let go of her hurt and anger and told her husband she forgave him and that she was "the luckiest woman in the world to be married to him." His reaction? He got angry, threatened divorce, and made accusations against her that "totally came out of the blue."

These things happen. Keep in mind that Jesus also surrendered His will to the Father and nothing about His circumstances changed. His refusal to retaliate did not stop people from reviling and eventually torturing Him to death. Remember, you relinquish your bitterness because of what that bitterness is doing to your soul. You don't relinquish your bitterness primarily to produce change in your spouse. I cannot promise your spouse will change. What I can say is that you will be more like Christ and your resentment will not be there. (For more on how to deal with less than perfect endings, see Part V, "The Rewarded Cycle: The Unconditional Dimension of Communication.")

-----••••-----

Forgiving—but Also Confronting—the Three A's: Adultery, Abuse, Addiction

When I urge you to have a forgiving spirit by sympathizing with your spouse, relinquishing your will to God's will, and anticipating God's help, I don't mean that you are to protect him or her from all consequences of the serious moral transgressions. If there has been adultery, abuse, or addiction, you are not required to just forgive and forget. Yes, you are to have a forgiving spirit because God in Christ has forgiven you for your sins, but He would not want you to allow your spouse to continue having an affair, to beat you and the children, or to snort cocaine while you say nothing. This would be ludicrous!

If your spouse does not repent and make real changes, you would be naive to assume that forgiving means forgetting and moving on as though nothing has happened. Jesus would not want you to be so foolish or uncaring. He intends that you care enough to confront your spouse, but to do so in a loving and respectful way.

If you are currently at a point where you need to tell your spouse that you have a forgiving spirit, but that definite changes must be made, you may want to use or adapt the following suggestions for a loving and respectful confrontation.

Please note that the comments below are to be stated tenderly and truthfully. The goal is for you to speak in ways that will soften rather than harden the spirit of your spouse so he or she will open up and honestly deal with the sin affecting your marriage. I recognize that you are in pain and being treated unjustly. Your spouse may deserve wrath, but your aim is to bring about a positive change, and this is more likely if you speak with an empathetic and forgiving tone. This won't be easy, so prepare yourself emotionally and spiritually. Know, too, that a compassionate tone will be more convicting and effective than your hostile, contemptuous, and bitter remarks or your ignoring the situation all together. Approach your spouse in the way you would want your spouse to approach you if the situation were reversed.

If there has been adultery: "I am in pain beyond what I can describe, but I am also angry with myself for not understanding better what you had been going through. I am trusting that God is going to reveal to us how to deal with this and to help us through it. Although I have been badly hurt, I do forgive you, and I hope you forgive me for where I have failed you. But you must close the door on this other relationship. And we need to meet with somebody who can counsel us on how to get our marriage back on track."

If there has been abuse: "What you have done is unacceptable. There is no excuse. While I am hurt and fearful, I do forgive you, but this can't happen again. You must learn how to manage your anger toward me and the rest of the family. We need to meet with professionals who can help both of us take steps to bring healing to our marriage and family. I have several phone numbers of people in our area to call for help. Who do you prefer among these selections? I prefer [your choice].". (Note: if you are in harm's way, get out of harm's way and turn to a professional or an authority figure for help.)

If there is addiction (drugs, alcohol, pornography, anorexia, etc.): "We all have temptations and issues, so I am not throwing stones. But your addiction is controlling you big-time, contrary to what you know is best for you and us. I know God intends for us to face this. I believe He will get us through this. Although I am hurt and disappointed, I do forgive you, and I hope you will forgive me for where I have failed you. We need to contact someone who deals with this kind of addiction and get the help we need to fight this thing and beat it. Here are some phone numbers of professionals in our area who can serve us."

All of the above suggestions are just that—suggestions. Use them as an outline to put what you want to say into your own words. Your goal is to firmly, lovingly, and respectfully confront your spouse. Along with speaking face-to-face or writing a note, I recommend that you turn to a pastor, a Christian counselor, or some other authority who is a believer and capable in the area where you need help. *Do not put this off.* Plan a way to confront the adultery, abuse, or addiction. There are many groups ready to serve you. If you know of none in your community, contact Focus on the Family at http://www.family.org or call them at 1-800-A-FAMILY (1-800-232-6459).

‑‑‑‑‑‑⟫⟪‑‑‑‑‑‑

How to Write a Love Note or Make a Good "I Love You" Speech to Your Wife

I often get letters from wives who complain their husbands don't express their love to them enough, if at all. It seems that the typically nontalkative Blue is at a loss for words in the "I love you" department.

For example, I got an e-mail from Frank, a man of thirty-nine who attended one of our Love and Respect Conferences with his fiancée Emily. They enjoyed the sessions and later decided to "put what they learned into practice." Being a classic Pinkie, Emily quickly and eloquently reeled off all the reasons why she respected Frank, and it moved him deeply. Her words made him feel wonderful, and he told her so.

Then it was Frank's turn to say why he loved Emily, but he couldn't come up with much. And what he had heard in one of the sessions—that men have difficulty with this sort of thing—didn't help him at that moment. Neither did being an engineer with an introvert type of personality. Frank stumbled badly with his words, and Emily was left with the impression he "had to think awhile" to figure out why he loved her. In a way that is exactly what he needed. His e-mail continues:

> The truth is that I love Emily deeply and would do anything for her. Her character, her sense of fun, her positive attitude, her charming personality, the way she builds me up, the way she makes me feel when she writes a kind note in a card or leaves a beautiful voice message, how she lives out her Christian faith, how she shows interest in the things I'm interested in, how beautiful she is, and how I get so excited at seeing her sparkling eyes and sharing hugs and kisses . . . and just the whole lovely person she is to me are among the reasons I cherish her.

All of THAT Frank wrote to me, but he couldn't get any of it out to his fiancée! He admits that his slowness to respond was partially due to his wanting to say something as wonderful as what she had said to him. But he had always experienced difficulty talking to women, his conversations with them plagued by long pauses. Emily, who had never been married before either, was the first woman Frank had ever had a significant relationship with, so here he was, at a Love and Respect Conference, trying to think of something eloquent he could say to this woman he loved very much. But when the words didn't start coming out the way he wanted them to, he fumbled even more, and she was left feeling hurt and upset. His e-mail concludes:

> I apologized and said I would work on getting better in this area, and I want to. I am not good at making speeches or spontaneously putting together polished words in verbal form. I can think of things and write them, but verbally and on the spot, I stumble. By the end of the evening, we kissed and made up, and I accepted her forgiveness and said I wouldn't bring this episode up again. To honor her, though, I need to meet her needs as I ful-

fill my duty to love her as commanded. I need to make myself better in this area. Where should I begin?

My suggestion to Frank was to study what he said about his fiancée in his e-mail to me—as eloquent a statement of love for a woman as I have ever read. Then he must try to work on expressing these words of admiration, affection, and esteem in notes directly to her. As he gains confidence, he can try expressing these thoughts and feelings aloud. What he has in his heart *can* come out of his mouth if he trusts God for the courage to say them!

That being said, I have a word for Frank's wife-to-be—and to all wives for that matter. Many of you have husbands who love you deeply, but they are not designed to express their feelings as easily as you do. This is a simple truth that many women just don't seem to grasp.

Frank, for instance, is an introvert and an engineer. I can guess that, in the first grade, he sat in the back, afraid to say much of anything. As he got older, he developed his own approach to conversation: he was not impulsive in his speech, and he needed a pen in hand and plenty of time to capture what was going on inside. And look at what he wrote about his fiancée!

To give Emily the benefit of the doubt, she didn't realize what was going on inside of Frank when he couldn't spontaneously speak glowing words of love. She became so hurt that she started the Crazy Cycle turning. Had they not been able to make up—due in great part to his asking forgiveness—the situation could have escalated, and she might possibly have closed the door on her relationship to a man who loved her deeply.

At the same time, there are things the nonexpressive male can do to improve in this area. For all men who struggle with expressing their love for their wives, I have two ideas. First, do not be bashful about adapting some of the phrases from the e-mail that Frank wrote to me, which is a model of how to express your fondness and devotion to the woman you love. Second, while I cannot tell you precisely what you should say to your wife, I can give you starter thoughts that come straight out of C-O-U-P-L-E, which we refer to in *Love & Respect* as "How to Spell Love to Your Wife."

Remember, gentlemen, wives want *connection,* which means much more than connecting sexually. Here are some sample ideas from one of the principles in C-O-U-P-L-E on how to let your wife know you want to connect with her

CLOSENESS — Review "Your Wife Feels Close to You When. . . ," p. 133, *Love & Respect* (Integrity, 2004) and think of ways to respond to the suggestions with words, spoken or written. For example:

- Hug her and say, "I love to hold you. You mean everything to me."
- Write her a note that says, "I'm sorry I've been too busy to tell you how much I love you. Let's grab some take-out when I get home from work and drive out to the lake for a picnic."
- Grab her hand and say, "Let's go for a walk. I have a list of things to say about why I love you so much." (Be sure you have your list in mind or even written down to get you started.)

These are just a few possibilities. Adapt them or think of other things that work better for you. The point is, you can let her know you want to connect and be close *if you want to.* Your words don't have to be perfectly phrased, eloquent, or orchestrated. All you need to be is sincere. Here are a few additional ideas from one more principle in C-O-U-P-L-E:

OPENNESS — Review "Your Wife Feels You Are Open to Her When. . . ," (*Love & Respect,* p. 144) and think of ways—spoken or written—you can apply the suggestions. For example:

- Say, "I would enjoy talking to you tonight. It's been tough lately at work, and I need your opinion on some things."
- Write her a note that says, "I have been noticing what a great job you do with getting the kids to do their homework. How can I help?"

- Say, "Let's go for a walk or a drive. I want to tell you why I fell in love with you."

For more ideas on how to craft words to write or tell to your wife, see the "Your Wife Will Feel . . ." sections at the end of chapters 11–14 in *Love & Respect* (Integrity, 2004).

The above suggestions can help you tell your wife you want to connect with her. The real problem is not what to say; it's wanting to take the time and make the effort to say it. And when you do, your wife will melt.

Using Feedback to Clarify Your Conversations

Following are additional ideas and insights concerning how to use feedback to meet the Everyday Challenge (see chapter 11).

• ***Always see your mate as an ally.*** Feedback is of little use if you see your spouse as an enemy. Giving and receiving constructive feedback is based on feelings of goodwill in both partners. Both of you need to remember that, even if you don't always agree and even if you become irritated or angry, you are friends, and neither of you means to hurt the other.

• ***Whose problem is it, really?*** When a husband or wife says, "We have communication problems!" what does that remark mean? Generally, the person who says this means that the *other* spouse is speaking carelessly or isn't listening carefully enough. People seldom think that a problem is with them because they tend to assume the best about themselves. But in our Love and Respect offices, we continue to get letters from husbands and wives who formerly blamed their spouses for their marital difficulties, but now they realize they are the real culprits or at least equally to blame for the problem.

For example, one wife didn't understand why her marriage wasn't working until she attended a Love and Respect Conference. She writes:

> I have always disrespected [my husband] in so many ways. The way I speak to him, the way I undermine his authority in front of our son, how I name call, etc. I never saw how *I* was coming across. I always thought I was great, and he was the flawed one. I finally realized I'm just as much to blame for all our problems. Coming from a home where my mother made it a recreational activity to ridicule, disrespect, and belittle my dad, I didn't know how much that had affected me. But God can break those chains, and with His help, I know it will happen. I'm constantly checking myself to make sure I'm not disrespecting [my husband].

• *Never assume you understand.* Giving and receiving feedback often involves emotions. When my conversations with Sarah start to get at all emotional, I have two rules:

1. I never assume I understand what Sarah said until she tells me that I did understand correctly.
2. I never assume Sarah understood what I said until she tells me what she thought she heard me say and I can verify it.

When our conversations get emotional, Sarah doesn't say things as well as she normally would, and I don't listen as well as I normally would. If we allow a misunderstanding to go unclarified, we will experience an undercurrent of negativity that will drain our energy. Giving and receiving feedback can be tedious at times, but it prevents both of us from making wrong assumptions about what we said or heard; it also enables us to get on the same page.

• *You can skillfully make the first move.* If Sarah and I have even a small glitch in communication, we both like to make the first move and take responsibility. We know we have goodwill toward each other so, if we have a misunderstanding, we assume that one of us probably didn't speak clearly enough or listen carefully enough. We stop the conversation, revisit what was said, and straighten out the misunderstanding. Taking this kind of initiative makes both of us feel we have the power to do something about our problems, not feel like helpless victims. Sometimes I take the initiative and sometimes she does. We don't like it when we cross our wires, but when it happens, we don't let it shock us. We have developed the skills and confidence to clarify things—mainly because we've had a ton of practice!

• *Get the bee out of your glove.* It's foolish to think you don't have the time or energy to give and receive feedback. In the best of marriages, there are always possibilities for the sting of negativity and possible conflict of some kind. To think you can ignore these negative emotions is to be like a gardener who ignores a bee that has flown into the cuff of her glove while she was transplanting some flowers. She needs to remove the glove before the bee stings her. In marriage, giving feedback is like removing the glove to get rid of the bee. There is no guarantee that feedback will prevent the potential sting, but failing to give or receive feedback is like keeping the glove on, and you are far more likely to get stung.

Sarah and I wish we never had to experience the potential sting of misunderstandings and the negative emotions they can create. But instead of resigning ourselves to their inevitability, we prefer to adjust and say, "I'm sorry. I heard you say such and such. Is that correct?" or "I'm sorry. I was trying to say such and such. What did you hear?" Here is an example:

Dinner guests are due to arrive soon. Sarah is setting the table, and she asks: "Could you get the water glasses for me?" I say I will be happy to and, in my inimitable male fashion, go find something that will hold water and ice—namely, the regular drinking glasses we use every day.

"No, not those," says Sarah when she sees what I have placed at every setting. "Why would you get those?"

I am puzzled, but then she explains, "I meant the goblets. Something nice for our guests."

Again, we have a simple, almost mundane, scene similar to that encounter on the patio on a fine June morning. And, again, the point is that there could have been friction or even heated words because Sarah was not totally clear about what she wanted, and I was not tuned in on how to set the table properly for dinner guests. I could have felt inadequate and disrespected by her question "Why would you bring those?" It would have been easy enough for me to unlovingly reply, "Water glasses are water glasses. Why are you always so fussy?" And the conversation could have escalated from there. Another possible result is that I could have let it go, nursed my bruised and seemingly disrespected feelings all evening, and made Sarah wonder why I was so cool and distant.

Instead, we both chose to get the bee out of the glove. I said, "Sorry about that. This kind of thing with water glasses is not something I naturally would figure out. It will take me just a minute to switch them."

"That's okay," Sarah replied. "It seemed like common sense to use the goblets, but I'm sorry I wasn't as clear as I could have been."

It does baffle Sarah when I don't understand things that are common sense to her, but she tries to be patient. Good help is hard to find—especially right before dinner. At any rate, I didn't drop a single goblet, and we had a great time with our friends!

• **Use "I hear you saying" sparingly.** Feedback is not something new on the marital communication scene. It was been around for years, often referred to as "active listening." A favorite suggestion made to active listeners is to respond with "I hear you saying . . ." followed by whatever feedback is appropriate. Be aware, however, that you can overdo giving feedback and the "I hear you saying . . ." line.

I recall talking to a mother who was trying to learn how to actively listen to her teenage daughter. One day the girl came home from school, and the mother asked, "How was your day?" In typical teenage style, the daughter answered, "It was fine." The mother responded, "I hear you saying it was fine. So what was fine about it?" Her teenager said, "Well, I got an A on my English paper." Mom replied, "So, I hear you saying you got an A on your English paper. How do you feel about that?" Her daughter could stand it no longer and she screamed, "MOTHER, HAVE YOU BEEN READING ANOTHER BOOK ON PARENTING? STOP THIS!"

Obviously, the mother had gone way over the top with her active listening/giving feedback approach, and you can do the same with your spouse. Like any technique, giving and receiving feedback needs to be used wisely. Whatever you do, use the "I hear you saying . . ." phrase sparingly. Repeating it several times in one conversation may get you a reaction like: "HAVE YOU BEEN READING ANOTHER BOOK ON MARRIAGE? STOP THIS!" To echo the writer of Ecclesiastes, there is a time for feedback, and there is a time when it's not needed. As you live with your mate, you will learn which is which.

APPENDIX E

———⊱≻∘≺⊰———

Unconditional Love and Respect Do Not Operate on a Scale of 1–10

What would you think if your husband said something like the following?

"On a scale of 1–10, you have to be at least a 7 according to my standards before I will speak to you with a loving tone of voice. If you are a 6 or below, I will talk to you any way I like. If I sound a little rough or crude, get used to it."

What would you think if your wife said something like the following? "On a scale of 1–10, you have to be at least a 7 according to my standards before I will speak to you respectfully. If you are a 6 or below, I will say what I like, usually with some contempt."

Judging each other on a scale of 1–10 is no way to have a good marriage, but I have counseled many couples who appeared to approach each other from just this perspective. The mentality seems to be "You have to earn my loving or respectful speech because I am placing conditions on just how much I will love or respect you."

But if you want to try to live out the unconditional love and respect we teach in our conferences, there is no place for demanding—either openly or subtly—that your spouse perform at a certain level. Using words of unconditional love and respect simply means:

- You determine *beforehand* that you will speak lovingly or respectfully *regardless* of how your spouse acts or speaks.
- You commit yourself to never using words of hostility or contempt, even though in certain situations your spouse's words or actions may come up a zero on a ten-point scale.
- You determine to speak lovingly or respectfully because you want to reverence and obey God.
- As a follower of Christ, you govern your speech and actions by what you believe He wants from you. Your spouse's speech or actions are irrelevant.
- Always remember that your speech or actions are your choice and your responsibility. Your spouse cannot *make* you say or do anything unloving or disrespectful.
- When you fail to speak words of unconditional love or respect perfectly, you ask for forgiveness—first from God and then from your spouse—and you *keep trying*.

I am often asked if committing to unconditionally love or respect means that you must turn a blind eye to definite wrongdoing on your spouse's part. This is a point that trips up a lot of people, especially wives who learn that God calls them to speak to their husband with unconditional respect (see Ephesians 5:33). These wives conclude that if she must speak with unconditional respect, she must agree with, and acquiesce to, everything her husband is doing or saying. If not, she would be disrespectful. I comment that, according to that kind of reasoning, a wife should be quite willing to tell her husband, "I say this respectfully. I love the fact that you are into pornography on the Internet." That would be comparable to a husband telling his wife, "I say this lovingly. I think it is wonderful that you are emotionally out of control a great deal of the time and that you are terrorizing the children."

Such absurd comments serve to make my point. Words that approve viewing pornography or abusing the children are not words of unconditional love or respect; they are simply pathetic endorsements of corrupt behavior. To use words of unconditional love or respect means you lovingly or respectfully confront your spouse's wrongdoing.

When your spouse is doing or saying something that is obviously wrong, immoral, or dangerous, you must confront that behavior. As you challenge your spouse, however, you are never justified in speaking words that are hostile or contemptuous. Common sense tells us that no one is persuaded by hateful or despising speech. Before the Lord, you are responsible to confront your spouse with words that come across as loving or respectful. The unconditional way of speaking is the only approach that motivates a spouse to deal long-term with the hurtful behavior. There is no guarantee a spouse will respond, but this manner is more likely to work than any other attitude.

If your spouse's words or behavior are in the gray zone—what your spouse is doing or saying does not suit your personal taste—you are to remain loving or respectful. Always do or say what you do or say knowing your speech or actions reflect who *you* are, not who your spouse is.

Wives also often tell me, "My husband doesn't receive my words of respect because he doesn't respect himself. So what's the point of being respectful of him?" I reply, "Are you saying that if you are struggling with loving yourself, your husband should stop speaking lovingly to you because you might reject his words?" These wives see the point. You speak lovingly or respectfully no matter *how* your spouse may speak to you in return. Your spouse is not the reason—good or bad—why you speak unconditional words of love or respect. God is the reason, and as you depend on Him, you will become increasingly able to speak lovingly and respectfully to your spouse.

APPENDIX F

My Prayer in
This Time of Trial

*T**he following prayer is for anyone going through deep waters in his or her marriage and needing God's sustaining love and help.*

Lord, whether or not my marriage turns around, I know You are using this struggle to reveal more of Yourself to me. I thank You for that because I need You in so many ways right now.

Father, I desire first of all Your presence. Suppose I had a "perfect" marriage. If I didn't feel Your presence, what good would my life be? My trials give me new opportunities to encounter You. And Your Word promises me that You will draw near to me if I draw near to You. So by faith I draw near to You right now, trusting that You draw near to me so that I might feel Your very presence.

Lord, I know that You say in Your Word, "My peace I give unto you." Right now, right here, I ask You to grant me Your peace. I confess that if

I were at total peace with my spouse, I would be tempted to live in a bubble of superficial contentment, thinking I do not need Your peace. But now, Lord, I am driven to seek You, the only Place where real Peace can be found. I open my heart to You, Lord. Grant to me Your peace—this day, this very hour.

Lord, Your Word also says that Your grace is sufficient for me and that Your power is made perfect in my weakness. Right now, Lord, I am very weak. My marriage is a mess, and I now know that—apart from You—I can do nothing. I thank You and praise You for bringing me to this place where I must depend entirely on You. I cannot straighten out my marriage in my own strength, which is a lesson You want me to learn. I praise Your name for the opportunity to walk by faith, trusting only You for each day. Now I know that when I am weak, then I am strong because Your power rests on me.

Father, forgive me for thinking in the midst of this pain and struggle that my life has no purpose. I know You have a purpose for me and for our marriage, and I ask You to reveal that purpose more clearly. Lord, I confess that I wanted fulfillment through my marriage when I should have been seeking Your will for my life. Thank You for making me go deeper to discover Your call on my life. I see that, without this trial, I would not have looked carefully to see what You want to do in and through me.

I am grateful to You for showing me Your marvelous ways, for using me in little ways throughout the day even when I was in pain from my marriage, and for always assuring me that I do matter to You. I am overwhelmed by the simple truth that You have not forsaken me and You never will. I know Your purpose for me is that I might bear fruit for You. Keep me close to You, Lord, and allow me to bear much fruit for You. In Jesus' name. Amen.